School-Age Education Programs
for Children with Autism

School-Age Education Programs for Children with Autism

Edited by

Jan S. Handleman
Sandra L. Harris

pro·ed
An International Publisher

8700 Shoal Creek Boulevard
Austin, Texas 78757-6897
800/897-3202   Fax 800/397-7633
www.proedinc.com

© 2006 by PRO-ED, Inc.
8700 Shoal Creek Boulevard
Austin, Texas 78757-6897
800/897-3202   Fax 800/397-7633
www.proedinc.com

Library of Congress Cataloging-in-Publication Data

School-age education programs for children with autism/edited by Jan S. Handleman
& Sandra L. Harris.
    p. cm.
  Includes bibliographical references and index.
  ISBN 1-4164-0130-X (hardcover : alk. paper)
   1. Autistic children—Education (Elementary)—United States—Case studies.
2. Classroom management—United States—Case studies.   I. Handleman,
Jan S.   II. Harris, Sandra L.

LC4718.S34 2006
371.94—dc22

                                                                2005005834

Art Director: Jason Crosier
Designer: Nancy McKinney-Point
This book is designed in Fairfield LH and Italia.

Printed in the United States of America

1 2 3 4 5 6 7 8 9 10   09 08 07 06 05

To Lauren Handleman, loving daughter,
and to Emma, Molly, and Jake Zuckerman and
Caroline, Jackson, and Samuel Snyder,
who brighten Sandra's days

Contents

Preface   *ix*

Contributors   *xiii*

1 An Introduction to School-Age Education Programs for Children with Autism   1
Sandra L. Harris and Jan S. Handleman

2 Alpine Learning Group   19
Linda S. Meyer, Bridget A. Taylor, Kathryn E. Cerino,
Julia R. Fisher, Linda Moran, and Erin Richard

3 The Children's Unit for Treatment and Evaluation   49
Raymond G. Romanczyk, Stephanie B. Lockshin, Linda Matey,
and Jennifer M. Gillis

4 The Douglass Developmental Disabilities Center   89
Jan S. Handleman, Sandra L. Harris, Maria S. Arnold,
Marlene Cohen, and Rita Gordon

5 The Lancaster–Lebanon IU 13 Autistic Support Program   115
Carolyn T. Bruey and Natalie Vorhis

6 Behavior Analysis and Intervention for School-Age Children at the Princeton Child Development Institute   143
Lynn E. McClannahan and Patricia J. Krantz

7 Application of the Pyramid Approach to Education Model in a Public School Setting   163
Andy Bondy and Kris Battaglini

8 Summit Academy: Implementing a System-Wide Intervention   195
Stephen R. Anderson, Marcus L. Thomeer, and Douglas C. King

9 The TEACCH Approach to School-Age Education   *221*
Victoria Shea and Gary B. Mesibov

10 The Valley Program   *247*
John McKeon, Kathleen Vuoncino, Rebecca Brenkert, Karen Dinnell-LoPresti,
Ellen Doyle, Mark Lampert, Michele Madden-Perez, and Scott Rossig

11 Graduating from Preschool   *269*
Mary Jane Weiss

12 Negotiating the School Years and Preparing
for Adulthood   *305*
Marlene Cohen

About the Editors   *327*

Preface

A decade ago, we published the first edition of a book describing treatment programs for preschool-age children with autism (*Preschool Education Programs for Children with Autism,* PRO-ED, 1994). That book proved helpful for consumers, and a few years later, we revised and updated a second version with additional programs. Those books continue to fill an important function for parents and educators concerned with the treatment of very young children on the autism spectrum, but we have become increasingly aware of the need to extend the sequence of books developmentally and offer a parallel volume for older children and adolescents; hence, our decision to edit the current book.

The gains achieved by very young children in intensive treatment are often impressive, and during the past 15 years, the treatment outcome literature has focused primarily on the substantial gains that preschool-age children with autism can achieve when provided with early, intensive programming. However, with the passage of time, children served by preschool programs grow up, and as they do, they create a demand for the development of school-age programs. Although some youngsters benefit a great deal from their preschool experience and may move seamlessly into the public school classrooms in their communities, many others, while showing clear benefits from their early education, continue to have specialized needs. For some of them, this may entail extra support in a regular education classroom; for others, it may mean a special education class with some degree of social integration.

This book is focused on programs to serve those youngsters who continue to need special services of some kind, whether in the public schools or in a specialized program for children with autism. We operate from the assumptions that all children with autism, regardless of age or extent of autistic involvement, can derive benefit from a high-quality educational experience and that there is a variety of service delivery models with which to provide these services.

In creating *School-Age Education Programs for Children with Autism,* we invited nine contributors to describe their programs for school-age children with autism. These particular programs were chosen based on their reputation among professionals and parents—in some cases, on research that had been done in the setting; and in most instances, on visits we or others had paid to them in the past. We also wanted programs from a variety of settings, including public, private, and university-based schools. We offer a nonrandom sample of programs with which we were familiar; there are no doubt countless other programs nationwide that might have been included equally well. The programs we selected were the Alpine Learning Group in Paramus, New Jersey; the Children's Unit for Treatment and Evaluation at the State University of New York at Binghamton; the Douglass Developmental Disabilities Center, our own program at Rutgers; the Lancaster–Lebanon Intermediate Unit in Lancaster and Lebanon Counties in Pennsylvania; the Princeton Child Development Institute in Princeton, New Jersey; the Pyramid Model as practiced at the Sussex Consortium in Delaware; the Summit Academy in Amherst, New York; the TEACCH program based in Chapel Hill, North Carolina; and the Valley Program in Bergen County, New Jersey. These programs are urban, suburban, and rural; private, public, and university based; long-standing and relatively new. The array of models they have adopted for serving students with autism will give the reader an appreciation of how one may adapt services to the setting in which one functions.

We asked each set of authors to address a set of common elements: (a) diagnosis and assessment; (b) staffing and administration; (c) curriculum, instructional management, and skill acquisition; (d) integration; (e) range of methods; (f) family involvement; (g) transitions from preschool to elementary, middle, and high school; and (h) outcome. We hope you will find it interesting to identify both the common elements that exist across programs and the distinctive features of each of them.

Following the program descriptions, there are two additional chapters that discuss the issues faced by students, their families, and their schools as the youngsters mature and move from preschool to school-age programs, and from the school system to their adult years.

We wish to thank our colleagues at the Douglass Developmental Disabilities Center and the Graduate School of Applied and Professional Psychology at Rutgers, the State University of New Jersey, for their ongoing support. For more than three decades we have been blessed with help from scores of individuals. We especially appreciate the many years of support from Maria Arnold, Jean Burton, Marlene Cohen, Lew Gantwerk, Rita Gordon, Barbara Kristoff, Ruth Schulman, and Mary Jane Weiss. We also thank Nadine Byczkowski for her help in preparing this manuscript. Special thanks goes to the families of the children we serve, for their trust in sending their children to our center, and to the staff of the DDDC for their dedication. On a personal note, Jan thanks Elaine and Lauren Handleman for their daily love, support, and encouragement; and Sandra thanks Ilona Harris and Gary Zuckerman for being great family.

Jan S. Handleman and
Sandra L. Harris
New Brunswick, New Jersey
Winter 2005

Contributors

Stephen R. Anderson, PhD
Summit Educational Resources, Inc.
300 Fries Road
Tonawanda, NY 14150
Phone: 716-837-2441
Fax: 716-837-5738
E-mail: sra@summiteducational.org

Maria S. Arnold, MEd
Douglass Developmental
   Disabilities Center
25 Gibbons Circle
New Brunswick, NJ 08901
Phone: 732-932-9137
Fax: 732-932-8011
E-mail: arnoldm@rci.rutgers.edu

Kris Battaglini, EdD
Program Director,
   Sussex Consortium
520 DuPont Avenue
Lewes, DE 19958
Phone: 302-645-7210
Fax: 302-645-5439
E-mail: kbattaglini@cape.k12.de.us

Andy Bondy, PhD
Pyramid Educational Consultants, Inc.
226 W. Park Place, Suite 1
Newark, DE 19711
Phone: 302-368-2515
Fax: 302-368-2516
E-mail: abondy@pecs.com

Rebecca Brenkert, MEd
The Valley Program
191 Walnut Street
Northvale, NJ 07647
Phone: 201-767-7224
Fax: 201-750-1142
E-mail: brenkert@nvnet.org

Carolyn T. Bruey, PsyD
Developmental Disabilities
   Resources
215 S. Broad Street
Lititz, PA 17543
Phone: 717-625-3480
Fax: 717-625-3481
E-mail: drbruey@aol.com

Kathryn E. Cerino, MSEd
Alpine Learning Group, Inc.
777 Paramus Road
Paramus, NJ 07652
Phone: 201-612-7800 x304
Fax: 201-612-7710
E-mail:
   kcerino@alpinelearninggroup.org

Marlene Cohen, EdD
Douglass Developmental
   Disabilities Center
151 Ryders Lane
New Brunswick, NJ 08901
Phone: 732-932-2791
Fax: 732-932-0077
E-mail: mcohen@rci.rutgers.edu

Karen Dinnell-LoPresti,
MEd, LDTC
The Valley Program
191 Walnut Street
Northvale, NJ 07647
Phone: 201-767-7224
Fax: 201-750-1142
E-mail: dinnell@nvnet.org

Ellen Doyle, MEd
The Valley Program
191 Walnut Street
Northvale, NJ 07647
Phone: 201-750-1142
Fax: 201-767-7224
E-mail: doyle@nvnet.org

Julia R. Fisher, MSW
Alpine Learning Group, Inc.
777 Paramus Road
Paramus, NJ 07652
Phone: 201-612-7800 x305
Fax: 201-612-7710
E-mail: jfisher@alpinelearninggroup.org

Jennifer M. Gillis, MA
Institute for Child Development
SUNY at Binghamton
Binghamton, NY 13902-6000
Phone: 607-777-2829
Fax: 607-777-6981
E-mail: jgillis@binghamton.edu

Rita Gordon, MEd
Douglass Developmental
    Disabilities Center
151 Ryders Lane
New Brunswick, NJ 08901
Phone: 732-932-3902
Fax: 732-932-4469
E-mail: rfg20@aol.com

Jan S. Handleman, EdD
Douglass Developmental
    Disabilities Center
151 Ryders Lane
New Brunswick, NJ 08901
Phone: 732-932-4500
Fax: 732-932-8134
E-mail: jansheldon@aol.com

Sandra L. Harris, PhD
Douglass Developmental
    Disabilities Center
151 Ryders Lane
New Brunswick, NJ 08901
Phone: 732-932-3017
Fax: 732-932-4510
E-mail: sharris@rci.rutgers.edu

Douglas C. King, MEd
Summit Educational Resources, Inc.
300 Fries Road
Tonawanda, NY 14150
Phone: 716-837-2441
Fax: 716-837-5738
E-mail: dking@summiteducational.org

Patricia J. Krantz, PhD
Princeton Child Development Institute
300 Cold Soil Road
Princeton, NJ 08540
Phone: 609-924-6280
Fax: 609-924-4119
E-mail: info@pcdi.org

Mark Lampert, MA
The Valley Program
191 Walnut Street
Northvale, NJ 07647
Phone: 201-767-7224
Fax: 201-750-1142
E-mail: lampert@nvnet.org

Stephanie B. Lockshin, PhD
Institute for Child Development
SUNY at Binghamton
Binghamton, NY 13902-6000
Phone: 607-777-2829
Fax: 607-777-6981
E-mail: slockshin@binghamton.edu

Michele Madden-Perez,
   MSEd, PhD
The Valley Program
191 Walnut Street
Northvale, NJ 07647
Phone: 201-767-7224
Fax: 201-750-1142
E-mail: madden-perez@nvnet.org

Linda Matey, MEd
Institute for Child Development
SUNY at Binghamton
Binghamton, NY 13902-6000
Phone: 607-777-2829
Fax: 607-777-6981
E-mail: lmatey@binghamton.edu

Lynn E. McClannahan, PhD
Princeton Child Development Institute
300 Cold Soil Road
Princeton, NJ 08540
Phone: 609-924-6280
Fax: 609-924-4119
E-mail: info@pcdi.org

John McKeon, EdD
The Valley Program
162 Knickerbocker Road
Demarest, NJ 07627
Phone: 201-768-2200
Fax: 201-768-5481
E-mail: mckeon@nvnet.org

Gary B. Mesibov, PhD
University of North Carolina
Division TEACCH, CB #7180
Chapel Hill, NC 27599-7180
Phone: 919-966-8189
Fax: 919-966-4127
E-mail: gary_mesibov@unc.edu

Linda S. Meyer, EdD, MPA
Alpine Learning Group, Inc.
777 Paramus Road
Paramus, NJ 07652
Phone: 201-612-7800 x308
Fax: 201-612-7710
E-mail: lmeyer@alpinelearninggroup.org

Linda Moran, BA
Alpine Learning Group, Inc.
777 Paramus Road
Paramus, NJ 07652
Phone: 201-612-7800 x302
Fax: 201-612-7710
E-mail: lmoran@alpinelearninggroup.org

Erin Richard, BA
Alpine Learning Group, Inc.
777 Paramus Road
Paramus, NJ 07652
Phone: 201-612-7800 x325
Fax: 201-612-7710
E-mail:
    erichard@alpinelearninggroup.org

Raymond G. Romanczyk, PhD
Institute for Child Development
SUNY at Binghamton
Binghamton, NY 13902-6000
Phone: 607-777-2829
Fax: 607-777-6981
E-mail: rromanc@binghamton.edu

Scott Rossig, MEd
The Valley Program
191 Walnut Street
Northvale, NJ 07647
Phone: 201-767-7224
Fax: 201-750-1142
E-mail: rossig@nvnet.org

Victoria Shea, PhD
University of North Carolina
Division TEACCH, CB #7180
Chapel Hill, NC 27599-7180
Phone: 919-929-0533
Fax: 919-966-4127
E-mail: victoria.shea@mindspring.com

Bridget A. Taylor, PsyD
Alpine Learning Group, Inc.
777 Paramus Road
Paramus, NJ 07652
Phone: 201-612-7800 x303
Fax: 201-612-7710
E-mail: btaylor@alpinelearninggroup.org

Marcus L. Thomeer, PhD
Summit Educational Resources, Inc.
300 Fries Road
Tonawanda, NY 14150
Phone: 716-837-2441
Fax: 716-837-5738
E-mail:
    mthomeer@summiteducational.org

Natalie Vorhis, MEd
Lancaster–Lebanon IU 13 Autistic
    Support Program
1650 Enterprise Road
East Petersburg, PA 17560
Phone: 717-560-4117
Fax: n/a
E-mail: natalie_vorhis@iu13.org

Kathleen Vuoncino, MEd, LDTC
The Valley Program
191 Walnut Street
Northvale, NJ 07647
Phone: 201-767-7224
Fax: 201-750-1142
E-mail: vuoncino@nvnet.org

Mary Jane Weiss, PhD
Douglass Developmental
    Disabilities Center
151 Ryders Lane
New Brunswick, NJ 08901
Phone: 732-932-3017
Fax: 732-932-3018
E-mail: weissnj@rci.rutgers.edu

An Introduction to School-Age Education Programs for Children with Autism

1

Sandra L. Harris and Jan S. Handleman

Much of the focus in educational intervention for children with autism has been on preschool-age children and their need for early, intensive behavioral treatment. The progress achieved by some very young children with autism has been gratifying to professionals and parents alike, and parents are often insistent on receiving many hours a week of intensive treatment for their young child. The data suggest that approximately half of the young children who receive these services are able to enter general education classes when they reach kindergarten or first grade, and there they benefit from the regular instruction that is provided by the classroom teacher, although they may need some ongoing support from a classroom assistant or shadow to help them cope with the complex demands of the classroom.

This book is the second in a sequence. The first book, *Preschool Education Programs for Children with Autism* (Harris & Handleman, 1994), recognized the need among consumers for information about preschool programs. It described eight programs for very young children that were highly visible and well respected around the country and identified some common themes that tied these otherwise relatively diverse programs together, including training parents in the application of the educational methods used in the classroom, providing many hours each week of individualized instruction, offering the preschool-age child opportunities for systematic exposure to typical peers, and the careful planning of the transition process from preschool to kindergarten or first grade. Many but not all of the programs in the book used the methods of applied behavior analysis. Beyond these commonalities, the programs differed considerably: Some were university based, and others were private schools; some offered home-based services, and others were center based; and some were

1

set in public schools. Differences in staffing patterns, curricula, and underlying philosophies distinguished the programs.

Having the opportunity to compare on some consistent dimensions this array of high-quality programs was useful to parents and professionals. They told us that the book was helpful to them in evaluating current programs and planning new ones. We published a second edition in 2001 (Handleman & Harris) in response to the ongoing need for consumer help in developing new educational programs for preschool-age children. The preschool book filled an important niche, but it made us aware of the need for another book to pick up where the preschool book leaves off. There is a range of outcomes for children with autism who participate in preschool programs: Some of these young children eventually blend smoothly into the larger cohort of their typical peers, some are able to do well academically in a general education class while having problems with socialization, and some remain in need of ongoing, highly specialized instruction as they move into their elementary school years and beyond.

Just as there are different approaches to educating the preschool child, there are different approaches to the education of the school-age child with autism. The focus of this book is on educational programs for those children who continue to need specialized services as they grow beyond their preschool years.

We asked eight of our colleagues from around the country to describe the educational programs they offer school-age children with autism, and we added to that mix a description of our own program, to make a total of nine settings for school-age children. The programs range from segregated settings that serve only children with autism or children with autism and peers with other disabilities, to public schools where the child with autism is included in general education classes to varying degrees or spends much of his or her time in a special education class located in a public school building. Some of the programs have been around for many years; others were developed more recently in response to the demand for services that has grown steadily as more children are given a diagnosis on the autism spectrum.

The Format

To facilitate use of this book, we asked the authors to follow a standard format in the descriptions of their programs. Although different authors highlight different aspects of their programs, each has, to some degree, touched on our specific questions. Every author was asked to address the following common elements (see Table 1.1): (a) the setting in which they work and their model of service delivery; (b) the population served; (c) methods of diagnosis and assessment; (d) staffing and administration; (e) curriculum, instructional and behavior management, and skill acquisition; (f) range of teaching methods; (g) family involvement; (h) integration with peers; (i) transitions from preschool to middle and secondary schooling; and (j) outcome data concerning skill acquisition and placements.

In addition to the program descriptions in Chapters 2 through 10, two chapters provide the reader with a perspective on the dynamic educational planning necessary to meet the needs of students with autism. In Chapter 11, Mary Jane Weiss describes some of the issues involved in helping a child make the transition from preschool to kindergarten or first grade. Marlene Cohen writes in Chapter 12 about how to facilitate movement through the school years to adulthood.

The Setting

The nine programs described in this book represent a variety of settings. Three of them are private, not-for-profit schools. Two of these, the Alpine Learning Group (Chapter 2) and the Princeton Child Development

Table 1.1
Questions for Authors

Describe your setting.

Who are your students?

What diagnostic and assessment procedures do you use?

Describe your staffing patterns and administered structure.

Describe your curriculum, instructional management, and skill acquisition procedures.

Describe the range of teaching methods you employ.

What kind of family involvement does your program expect/support?

How do you address integration with typically developing peers?

How do you handle the transitions from preschool to elementary school to middle school and high school?

Describe what you know about outcome for the students in your program.

Institute (Chapter 6) educate only children on the autism spectrum. A third, the Summit Academy (Chapter 8) includes children with related disabilities. Two of the programs, the Children's Unit at Binghamton University (Chapter 3) and the Douglass Developmental Disabilities Center at Rutgers University (Chapter 4) are university-based programs. The TEACCH program (Chapter 9) was founded at the University of North Carolina in Chapel Hill but has classrooms scattered around the state as well as in a variety of national and international settings. Both the Children's Unit and the TEACCH program serve children in a large geographic area that includes urban and rural settings. The Sussex Consortium in Delaware is a statewide public school program based on the Pyramid Model (Chapter 7). Two other public school models are the Lancaster–Lebanon IU 13 program developed in Pennsylvania (Chapter 5) and the Valley Program in New Jersey (Chapter 10). Each of these programs, regardless of setting, show some similarities with the others in the book, but each has its own strengths and has been developed to meet the needs of the specific ecological niche it serves. The reader will find useful information from the broad range of perspectives represented.

Service Delivery Model

Several formats have evolved over the years for educating children with autism. Home-, center-, and school-based programs have been developed, providing children and families with a variety of educational opportunities. There are no comparative data regarding the efficacy of program types, and each format tends to offer different, although overlapping, experiences. For example, home-based programs are typically highly individualized and involve children in daily one-on-one specialized programming. Although home-based programs are more common for very young children, some families may elect to continue home-based instruction as their child grows up, perhaps using it to supplement a day program in a school or specialized center. Center-based programs are uniquely designed for students with autism and, when appropriate, can offer one-on-one instruction, along with a broader range of specialized teaching. The school-based option can provide children with a blended program that includes a range of specialized and integrated experiences. Our own program, the Douglass Developmental Disabilities Center, covers the spectrum of services: home based, center based, and school based.

Public school programs, like the Valley Program described by John McKeon and his colleagues, and the Lancaster–Lebanon IU 13 Autistic Support Program, offer several options, including a segregated class specifically for students with autism, a resource room, and an integrated classroom, as available resources. A university-based setting, such as Raymond Romanczyk and his colleagues from the Children's Unit at Binghamton University describe, might provide segregated classrooms with opportunities to go into the community for some social activities or to have children from a local school make periodic visits to the program. Linda Meyer and her co-authors at the Alpine Learning Group and Lynn McClannahan and Patricia Krantz at the Princeton Child Development Institute similarly seek opportunities to expose their children to typical peers. The Summit Academy provides opportunities for integration with peers who have other disabilities in school and in the broader community.

The Students

People with autism are found along a spectrum ranging from individuals with severe symptoms and mental retardation to those of average or higher intellectual ability whose symptoms of autism are relatively mild. What works for people at one point on the spectrum may be less effective for those at another. As a result, it is important for the reader to be aware of the extent to which the children being served in a given setting resemble those for whom he or she wishes to provide services.

A word about terminology. The diagnostic vocabulary of autism changes over time. Many people use the term *autism* for what the current *Diagnostic and Statistical Manual of Mental Disorders–Fourth Edition–Text Revision* (DSM–IV–TR; American Psychiatric Association, 2000) calls Autistic Disorder, and some may use it more broadly to refer to the range of disorders on the autism spectrum. Furthermore, the term *autism spectrum disorders,* although not an official part of the DSM–IV–TR nomenclature, is commonly used to refer to what are called Pervasive Developmental Disorders in the DSM–IV–TR. You may find those terms used interchangeably in different chapters, and that reflects the variation in common practice.

In the DSM–IV–TR, the Pervasive Developmental Disorders include Autistic Disorder, Pervasive Developmental Disorder–Not Otherwise Specified (PDD-NOS), Asperger syndrome, Childhood Disintegrative

Disorder, and Rett's Disorder. According to the DSM–IV–TR, these conditions differ with respect to the presence of specific characteristics in the areas of social development, communication, behavior and activity, and age of onset. Most discussions throughout the book reference DSM criteria. In most programs, DSM–IV–TR criteria are used for diagnosis and are confirmed by consulting psychologists and neurologists.

All of the autism spectrum disorders are present at a young age and alter fundamental behaviors such as social responsiveness, the ability to communicate, and the establishment of relationships with others. Repetitive, stereotypic behaviors are also common. Autistic disorder is usually present before age 2 years and must be present by age 3 years. The latest onset of symptoms is seen in childhood disintegrative disorder, in which symptoms appear after age 2 years and before age 10 years. Neurobiological factors, including genetic patterns, appear to contribute to the etiology of the disorders on the autism spectrum, although specific mechanisms have not yet been identified.

There is no known cure for the disorders on the autism spectrum, and specialized education is currently the most effective intervention available to promote personal independence and social responsibility by individuals on this spectrum. Inconclusive evidence indicates that certain medications may treat some of the troubling symptoms of autism spectrum disorders, such as aggression, self-injury, and sleep problems, but not the disorders themselves. In some cases, medication may make the child more accessible to education (Tsai, 2005).

Each of the nine programs represented in this book describe the population they serve as being on the spectrum of autism or as having autism. For purposes of service, they do not distinguish among the specific disorders that fall under this heading, relying on the student's behavior, learning strengths, and skill deficits as guides to placement and intervention rather than a specific diagnostic category beyond "autism." In the description of the Douglass Developmental Disabilities Center, however, the reader will find a discussion of a specialized program for students with Asperger syndrome.

The students described in this book are between 6 and 21 years of age. The transitional emphasis in the various chapters enables the reader to narrow this fairly long age span into the groupings of elementary, middle, and secondary schooling. For example, Stephen Anderson and his colleagues discuss the elementary and secondary school programs at the Summit Academy, a private school. Similarly, Carolyn Bruey and

Natalie Vorhis describe the broad age range of students served in a public school context by the Lancaster–Lebanon IU 13 Autistic Support Program. The lifelong nature of the disorder makes planning for the adult years a necessary focus of programming. At the Princeton Child Development Institute and the Douglass Developmental Disabilities Center, adult programming is available, and all of the programs help families plan for life beyond school.

Assessment Methods

The complex learning patterns of children on the autism spectrum pose a challenge to educational programming and make the assessment process particularly important. For example, diverse school, home, and community needs dictate an individualized and comprehensive assessment, planning, and monitoring process. The successful development and implementation of the educational plan, therefore, require information about the child's performance in all these settings and of the participation by parents and professionals.

Current assessment practices for people with autism typically include interdisciplinary planning; input from various professionals is viewed as a necessary component of programming. Educators, psychologists, physicians, social workers, and speech–language pathologists are among the professionals who contribute to educational decision making. The particular influence of psychology on the evaluation process has resulted in the united effort known as psychoeducational assessment. Psychoeducational evaluation practices with students with autism typically include both traditional testing and behavioral assessment techniques. Although the merits and weaknesses of each approach have been debated, current strategies reflect a blending of these two components. Use of this combined approach can produce a profile of a student's relative standing and individual performance.

As is shown in Table 1.2, programs vary considerably in the assessment procedures they use with students. It is common for children to receive an evaluation by their local school district, including a test of cognitive ability such as one of the Wechsler IQ tests (Wechsler, 1989, 1991) or the *Stanford–Binet Intelligence Scale–Fifth Edition* (Roid, 2003) and the *Vineland Adaptive Behavior Scales* (Sparrow, Balla, & Cicchetti, 1984), as

Table 1.2
Commonly Used Assessment and Diagnostic Tools

Program	ABLLS	ADI	ADOS	CARS	DSM	SB	Vine	Wechsler	Peabody
Alpine Learning Group	Yes					Yes	Yes		Yes
Children's Unit for Treatment and Evaluations				Yes	Yes				
Douglass Developmental Disabilities Center	Yes	Yes	Yes		Yes	Yes			Yes
Lancaster–Lebanon IU 13	Yes	Yes	Yes	Yes	Yes	Yes	Yes	Yes	
Princeton Child Development Institute					Yes				
Pyramid Approach			Yes	Yes	Yes				
Summit Academy		Yes	Yes		Yes				
TEACCH				Yes					
Valley Program									

Note. ABLLS = *Assessment of Basic Language and Learning Skills* (Partington & Sundberg, 1998); ADI = *Autism Diagnostic Interview–Revised* (Lord, Rutter, & LeCouteur, 1994); ADOS = *Autism Diagnostic Observation Schedule–Generic* (Lord et al., 2000); CARS = *Childhood Autism Rating Scale* (Schopler, Reichler, DeVellis, & Daly, 1988); DSM = *Diagnostic and Statistical Manual of Mental Disorders–Fourth Edition–Text Revision* (American Psychiatric Association, 2000); SB = *Stanford–Binet Intelligence Scale–Fifth Edition* (Roid, 2003); Vine = *Vineland Adaptive Behavior Scales* (Sparros, Balla, & Cicchetti, 1984); Wechsler = *Wechsler Intelligence Scale for Children–Third Edition* (Wechsler, 1992); Peabody = *Peabody Language Scale* (Zimmerman, Steiner, & Pond, 1992).

well as an instrument to detect the presence of autism, such as the *Childhood Autism Rating Scale* (CARS; Schopler, Reichler, DeVellis, & Daly, 1988), which was developed by investigators at the TEACCH program (Chapter 9); the *Autism Diagnostic Interview–Revised* (Lord, Rutter, & LeCouteur, 1994); or the *Autism Diagnostic Observation Schedule–Generic* (Lord et al., 2000). Most of the programs use some of these instruments as well in their own diagnostic and assessment process. All of the programs but three indicated that they use DSM criteria to confirm a diagnosis on the autism spectrum that was made by other professionals prior to the student's referral to their program.

Although traditional testing has its place in the evaluation of the child (e.g., Handleman & Delmolino, 2005), the most important aspect of the assessment process concerns evaluating the child's current skills, knowledge, and behavior in order to identify the right teaching context and appropriate instructional programs. For many programs, this form of assessment is an ongoing process, with the child's response to intervention determining the next step both in skill acquisition and in reduction of problematic behavior. As shown in Table 1.2, the Alpine Learning Group, the Lancaster–Lebanon IU 13 program, and the Douglass Developmental Disabilities Center all use the *Assessment of Basic Language and Learning Skills* (ABLLS; Partington & Sundberg, 1998) as part of their assessment procedures. Romanczyk and his colleagues at the Children's Unit note that they do a reinforcer preference assessment with their students to identify a hierarchy of potentially reinforcing items.

When managing behavior problems, it may be necessary to do a functional assessment to identify events that are linked to the behavior as antecedents or consequences. For example, systematic observation may indicate that Suzy is more likely to engage in self-injury when she is left alone, or that Tom becomes aggressive when he does not know the answer to a question. Those observations allow one to design an intervention to help the child learn alternative ways to manage these situations as well as ensuring that reinforcement for maladaptive behavior is not available. For example, Suzy might be taught to approach other people for attention, and Tom might learn to say, "I don't know."

Staffing and Administrative Patterns

Educational programs for children with autism typically maintain a large instructional staff in order to offer intensive teaching and low student-to-staff ratios. They also have support staff to provide specialized training and supervision. The teaching staff usually comprises professionals and paraprofessionals, who are involved in the direct instruction of the children. Administrators and supervisors are available to train the staff and to ensure the integrity of the specialized programming. Programs may also employ additional professionals to provide consultation or related services such as physical therapy and occupational therapy.

By contrast, the Princeton Child Development Institute describes itself as using a "generalist" rather than a "specialist" model of staff responsibilities, in which each staff member is trained to provide a range of services to the student. Similarly, the Alpine Learning Group does not employ speech–language pathologists, occupational therapists, or physical therapists and refers out children if those services are needed. In some programs, such as the one Andy Bondy and Kris Battaglini describe for the Sussex Consortium in Delaware and our own at the Douglass Developmental Disabilities Center, speech–language pathologists become integral members of the classroom, delivering therapy within the classroom, as well as using a pullout model when needed.

Staffing ratios, and the variety of professionals available to serve the students, vary from one setting to the next. Among the professionals most commonly involved are special and regular education teachers, along with speech–language pathologists and assistant teachers. Other professionals, including school and clinical psychologists, behavior analysts, social workers, and physical and occupational therapists, vary from program to program. At the Lancaster–Lebanon IU 13 Autistic Support Program, the Summit Academy, and the Sussex Consortium, many of these direct and support staff are used.

Some programs, especially those that exclusively serve individuals with autism, tend to have a large number of well-trained staff members who focus on the needs of students with autism; while programs that emphasize integrated placements will have fewer specialized staff members and rely more on outside consultants to address problems as they arise. For example, at the Sussex Consortium, the Pyramid approach, as described by Bondy and Battaglini, is being implemented under the guidance of consultants. Another consultation model is described in the chapter on the Douglass Developmental Disabilities Center.

Several programs, including the Valley Program and the Douglass Developmental Disabilities Center, report that they have board-certified behavior analysts and associate behavior analysts on their staff.

Curriculum

Programs for children with autism usually follow a developmental or a behavioral curriculum, and these may sometimes be blended. The developmental curriculum offers a standardized framework for constructing individual educational programs. Specialized behavioral curricula are designed to consider the learning characteristics of the child with autism, usually highlighting one particular area, such as communication. For example, a detailed description of the *Individualized Goal Selection Curriculum* (Romanczyk, Lockshin, & Matey, 2000), developed at the Children's Unit, is provided in Chapter 3. This curriculum is also used by the Lancaster–Lebanon IU 13 program, the Douglass Developmental Disabilities Center, and the Summit Academy. Other programs, like the Alpine Learning Group and the Princeton Child Development Institute have developed their own extensive collection of instructional materials. The programs also report using a variety of other commercially available instructional materials for teaching specific skills such as reading, arithmetic, and handwriting.

The TEACCH program places a strong emphasis on understanding the "culture of autism" in the development of instructional materials and teaching methods. Its approach is called "structured teaching" and places considerable emphasis on how one organizes the physical environment and on creating a reliable, predictable set of experiences for the student. The concept of visual schedules, now widely used by other programs, was first developed at TEACCH.

While goals and objectives regarding social, language, and cognitive development are emphasized in most curricula for students with autism, some programs may emphasize one area more than another or may vary the order of presentation. For example, in one program, children might be exposed to a developmentally based curriculum with adherence to such principles as "concrete to abstract" and "gross to fine motor"; students in another school may have educational plans that weight communication skills more than cognitive tasks. In Chapter 7, which presents the Sussex Consortium as an example of using the Pyramid model, the reader will find a description of the Picture Exchange Communication System (PECS; Bondy & Frost, 1994). The PECS system is also used by other programs in this book, including the Lancaster–Lebanon IU 13 program and the Douglass Developmental Disabilities Center. All the curricula described in this book provide systematic and planful teaching (National Research Council, 2001).

Primary Teaching Methods

In the last 2 decades, students with autism have greatly benefited from specialized teaching methods. Although variations exist, the programs described in this book all use teaching procedures that are carefully planned and typically research based. For example, behavioral models, such as those used at the Alpine Learning Group and the Princeton Child Development Center, and other programs described in this book, include the principles of applied behavior analysis (ABA); and programs using structured teaching, such as the TEACCH program described by Victoria Shea and Gary Mesibov, employ teaching techniques from the behavioral, developmental, psycholinguistic, and incidental teaching literature (Watson, Lord, Schaffer, & Schopler, 1989). All of the programs described in this book feature generalization and maintenance of responding as critical features.

Family Involvement

Family involvement is a universal feature of the programs in this book. The details differ, but the intention of teaching parents the skills they need to support their child at home and providing the interpersonal support parents need to work with their child from day to day and year to year was considered by all of the authors. Each author was asked to describe the ways and extent to which families are involved in the education of their children. Education for the student with autism goes beyond the school day and involves people in addition to professional staff. The home life and family contexts of these children not only present challenges for planning so that educational interventions mesh with the family's structure, but also provide opportunities for a rich set of learning experiences. Parents play many roles, including loving mom or dad, advocate, teacher, and nurturer. Their role as collaborator in their child's education can cement an important partnership with professionals. All of the programs train parents in the teaching methods used in their program (see Table 1.3). For example, at the Summit Academy, similar to the other programs in this book, various components of the program confirm the importance of collaboration between parents and professionals.

In addition to learning new skills, parents may need support in their roles as advocates, teaching collaborators, and nurturers of their child with autism, as well as facing the multiple other demands on their lives.

Grandparents and siblings also experience the child with autism on a variety of levels, and they too play many roles and present different needs. Meeting the complex needs of families is described in the chapter about the Douglass Developmental Disabilities Center, and each of the programs described in this book addresses the critical issue of family involvement. Most offer some family support, and several provide a specific program for siblings (see Table 1.3).

Integration with Typical Peers

An increasing number of children with autism are being prepared for integrated educational opportunities (Handleman, Harris, & Martins, 2005). Integrated experiences are varied and can range from simple parallel social activities on the playground to full participation in a general educational program, and they can involve either typical children or children with a disability of a different kind who are appropriate models. Some programs provide a range of experiences in nonspecialized or public schools, with support from trained "shadows" for older students. These

Table 1.3
Family Supports

Program	Parent Training	Parent Support	Sibling Support
Alpine Learning Group	Yes	Yes	Yes
Children's Unit for Treatment and Evaluations	Yes	Yes	Yes
Douglass Developmental Disabilities Center	Yes	Yes	Yes
Lancaster–Lebanon IU 13	Yes	Yes	
Princeton Child Development Institute	Yes		
Pyramid Approach	Yes	Yes	Yes
Summit Academy	Yes		
TEACCH	Yes		
Valley Program	Yes	Yes	

types of supported transitional experiences exist at the programs operated by the Alpine Learning Group and the Children's Unit. Programs located in public schools are at a decided advantage in providing ongoing contact with typical peers for students with autism who can remain based in their special classrooms for part of the day. The Valley Program and the Lancaster–Lebanon program provide examples of this ongoing use of a public school–based setting to create a range of integration experiences. In addition to the resources available within the school system, the Valley Program takes advantage of wider community resources and takes the children on regular outings to visit grocery stores, malls, and recreational facilities. The frequency of such trips increases as the child gets older.

Planning Transition from One Setting to the Next

As discussed in greater detail in Chapters 11 and 12, planning for the student with autism must reflect the many transitions that occur in a child's life. Transition means change, and often change can place the child with autism at risk for behavioral regression or the development of maladaptive behaviors. Both the simplest and the most complex transitions should be planned for in order to promote learning that is functional in focus and that will be maintained over time. For example, whether a child moves from one task to another or from one school to another, a transitional plan should be developed and systematically implemented. The Children's Unit sets as its goal the transition of the child to a less specialized setting within approximately 3 years after admission, and thus its staff is continually thinking of the transition process. The Douglass Developmental Disabilities Center uses a systematic transition process for movement to a new school or a new classroom, which includes a number of components: (a) assessing the proposed setting to identify an appropriate student–placement match (e.g., of students, teachers, curriculum, methodologies); (b) assessing the needs of the student for compatibility with the proposed placement (e.g., with school life, classroom life, curriculum); (c) conducting previsits to the proposed placement to confirm the choice of placement; and (d) developing a transition timeline (e.g., to occur over a 9- to 12-month period, to target skill deficiencies, to include gradual systematic inclusion, to be data driven). The highly individualized nature of transition planning is also described in the classes at the Summit Academy and the Valley Program. At the TEACCH program, considerable thought has been given to transitions from one activity to the next throughout the student's day.

All of the authors described ongoing efforts to assist their students in the transition to a less restrictive setting or one that provides a more advanced level of education than their current setting. They were all methodical about these transitions and anticipated the students' needs over an extended period of time.

Outcomes

Finally, we asked each author to provide us with information on the outcomes for the students they serve. What kinds of changes do they see in their students, and where do they go when they leave the current program? Some programs describe details of the skills mastered by their students, and others focus more on the placements for students at discharge or graduation. For example, the Lancaster–Lebanon program uses such indexes as the extent to which a student's IEP goals are met and the number of students who are transferred to less restrictive settings for some or all of the school day. The Princeton Child Development Institute has an independent evaluator judge, by very systemic criteria, the success of its teaching programs once a year. Among other measures, the TEACCH program looks at the rate of employment for its graduates.

With effective specialized education, students with autism are capable of learning a range of adaptive skills that will help them function in a variety of settings. For example, in the description of the Princeton Child Development Center, substantial increases in skill acquisition by the students are presented. As the result of that progress, one student may be able to be placed in a blended public school program that includes general classroom and resource room participation. Another child may attend a self-contained classroom for learners with communication challenges. In years past, with the exception of children with Asperger syndrome, children on the autism spectrum remained in special education settings throughout their schooling. More recently, our measures of outcome have expanded as the result of an exciting increase in placement options.

Common Themes

We hope that the reader will appreciate the complexity of the issues involving the education of school-age students with autism, as well as gain a sense of the similarities and differences among the various programs. For example, the education of students on the autism spectrum should begin with the earliest diagnosis and remain part of their lives as they mature and enter adulthood. Educational programs should include goals in the areas of cognitive ability, verbal and nonverbal communication, social responsiveness, and the reduction of challenging behaviors; and the generalization and maintenance of behavior change should be considered critical criteria for educational progress. In addition, approaches to the education of students with autism spectrum disorders reflect either a developmental or behavioral orientation. Educational efforts should span school, home, and community settings; and parents and professionals should collaborate in educational planning. The families of children on this spectrum face extraordinary challenges and can serve as important partners in the education of their children when they are provided with necessary supports.

Although the programs in this book differ from one another in many respects, some themes, consistent with the recommendations of the National Research Council of the National Academy of Sciences (2001) on the subject of the needs of the young child with autism, emerge. The Council proposed the following program quality indicators: (a) specific curricula, (b) highly supportive instructional environments, (c) maintenance and generalization strategies, (d) predictable routines, (e) functional behavior management procedures, (f) systematic transitional planning, (g) collaborative family involvement, (h) family supports, (i) low student-to-staff ratios, (j) highly trained staff, (k) comprehensive professional resources, and (l) staff supervision and program review mechanisms. Each of the programs described in this book reflects those quality standards, suggesting that the general standards recommended by the National Research Council hold true for older students with autism as well as for young children.

References

American Psychiatric Association. (2000). *Diagnostic and statistical manual of mental disorders* (4th ed., text rev.). Washington, DC: Author.

Bondy, A., & Frost, L. (1994). The Picture Exchange Communication System. *Focus on Autistic Behavior, 9,* 1–19.

Handleman, J. S., & Delmolino, L. (2005). Assessment of children with autism. In D. Zager (Ed.), *Autism spectrum disorders* (3rd ed., pp. 266–293). Mahwah, NJ: Erlbaum.

Handleman, J. S., & Harris, S. L. (Eds.). (2001). *Preschool education programs for children with autism* (2nd ed.). Austin, TX: PRO-ED.

Handleman, J. S., Harris, S. L., & Martins, M. (2005). Helping children with autism enter the mainstream. In F. R. Volkmar, A. Klin, & R. Paul (Eds.), *Handbook of autism and pervasive developmental disorders* (3rd ed., pp. 1029–1042). New York: Wiley.

Harris, S. L., & Handleman, J. S. (1994). (Eds.). *Preschool education programs for children with autism.* Austin, TX: PRO-ED.

Lord, C., Risi, S., Lambrecht, L., Cook, E. H., Jr., Leventhal, B. L., DiLavore, P. C., et al. (2000). *The Autism Diagnostic Observation Schedule–Generic:* A standard measure of social and communication deficits associated with the spectrum of autism. *Journal of Autism and Developmental Disorders, 30,* 205–223.

Lord, C., Rutter, M., & LeCouteur, A. (1994). *Autism Diagnostic Interview–Revised:* A revised version of a diagnostic interview for caregivers of individuals with possible pervasive developmental disorders. *Journal of Autism and Developmental Disorders, 24*(5), 659–685.

National Research Council. (2001). *Educating children with autism.* Washington, DC: National Academy Press.

Partington, J. W., & Sundberg, M. L. (1998). *The assessment of basic language and learning skills.* Pleasant Hill, CA: Behavior Analysts.

Roid, G. (2003). *The Stanford–Binet Intelligence Scales–Fifth Edition.* Itasca, IL: Riverside.

Romanczyk, R. G., Lockshin, S. B., & Matey, L. (2000). *The Individualized Goal Selection Curriculum.* Apalachin, NY: CBT Associates.

Schopler, E., Reichler, R. J., DeVellis, R. F., & Daly, K. (1988). *The Childhood Autism Rating Scale.* Los Angeles: Western Psychological Services.

Sparrow, S. S., Balla, D. A., & Cicchetti, D. V. (1984). *The Vineland Adaptive Behavior Scales.* Circle Pines, MN: American Guidance Service.

Tsai, L. Y. (2005). Medical treatment in autism. In D. Zager (Ed.), *Autism spectrum disorders: Identification, education and treatment* (3rd ed., pp. 395–492). Mahwah, NJ: Erlbaum.

Watson, L. C., Lord, B., Schaffer, B., & Schopler, E. (1989). *Teaching spontaneous communication to autistic and developmentally handicapped children.* New York: Irvington.

Wechsler, D. (1989). *Wechsler Preschool and Primary Scale of Intelligence–Revised.* San Antonio, TX: Psychological Corp.

Wechsler, D. (1991). *Wechsler Intelligence Scale for Children* (3rd ed.). San Antonio, TX: Psychological Corp.

Zimmerman, I. L., Steiner, U. G., & Pond, R. E. (1992). *Preschool Language Scale–Third Edition.* San Antonio, TX: Psychological Corp.

Alpine Learning Group

Linda S. Meyer, Bridget A. Taylor,
Kathryn E. Cerino, Julia R. Fisher,
Linda Moran, and Erin Richard

2

F ounded in 1988 as a nonprofit agency, Alpine Learning Group (ALG) opened its doors a year later as an approved private school for children with autism. The ALG program was developed in response to northern New Jersey's recognized need for a school program specializing in behavioral treatment and educational interventions for individuals with autism and pervasive developmental disorders. The program started in the basement of a church in Alpine, New Jersey (hence our name), with only four students. At the time, the mean age of our learners was 5 years.

Approved by the New Jersey Department of Education to serve children with autism ages 3 through 21 years, ALG's current enrollment is 27 students, with a mean age of 14 years. Since July of 1989, 44 children have been enrolled in the program; 7 (16%) have been female. The mean age of all children at time of enrollment was 46 months, with a range of 34 months to 93 months. Over the program's 16 years of operation, approximately 25% of the total adjusted enrollment have graduated and moved on to other educational settings (see Table 2.1.). As the statistics demonstrate, students transition to a variety of less restrictive settings with varying levels of support.

In July of 1995, ALG began to serve younger children diagnosed with autism through an outreach program. Through Outreach, toddlers and their families receive training, curriculum guidance, and supervision in the development and implementation of home-based educational programs.

The authors would like to recognize the contributions of the instructional staff, learners, parents, administrative staff, and board of directors of the Alpine Learning Group, whose ongoing commitment to quality and effective programming contributed to the development of this chapter.

Table 2.1
Statistics of ALG Graduates (as of 9/03)

Age at Graduation	Gender	Tenure at ALG	Graduate Placement	Support	Current Placement	Current Support
5.8	F	23 months	Public K	Self-contained with mainstreaming	Public high school	Resource room
5.5	M	22 months	Public K	None	Parochial high school	None
10	M	61 months	Public 3rd grade	Classroom aide	Vocational high school	In-class support
7.3	F	49 months	Public 1st grade	In-class support and resource room	Public high school	In-class support and resource room
8	M	47 months	Public 2nd grade	In-class support	Vocational high school	In-class support
5.9	M	22 months	Public K	In-class support	Public 7th grade	In-class support
9.6	M	72 months	Public 4th grade	In-class support	Public high school	In-class support
11.8	M	85 months	Public 3rd grade	Self-contained–mainstreaming	Vocational high school	In-class support
9.9	M	69 months	Private school for handicapped	In-class support	Private school for handicapped	
5.6	M	68 months	Public K	In-class support	Public 1st grade	In-class support

Note. ALG = Alpine Learning Group.

Approximately 14 families in the tristate area (New Jersey, New York, Connecticut) receive early intervention services through ALG's Outreach program.

ALG's oldest learner graduated from the school's program in June 2004 and is now participating in ALG's newly formed Adult Day program. Having maximized skill acquisition since his enrollment at ALG at the age of 6 years, this learner volunteers at several community sites, maintains part-time employment sorting and delivering mail at a local senior citizen's residence, and exercises regularly at a local health club. He continues to develop new skills at home and in ALG's adult learning program.

Currently, all of ALG's enrolled students are fully funded by the public school districts in which they live. During the school year 2003–2004, these learners resided in 21 municipalities representing five counties across central and northern New Jersey. The school year consists of 180 days from September through June and an extended-year program of at least 30 days in July and August.

Admissions

The majority of referrals for admission come from parents seeking placement for their children with autism, although the Child Study Teams and Special Services Departments of school districts (i.e., school districts' Individualized Education Program [IEP] committees) also frequently request information regarding placement. To be considered for admission, interested parents or professionals are required to visit ALG's program during a regularly scheduled visiting day and are asked to fill out a Request for Intake form. When an opening becomes available, intake forms are reviewed to identify a potential match to a current ALG learner's profile or a specific class. Information (e.g., records, videotapes) may be requested to determine appropriateness of the match, and a formal interview with the parents and child is conducted.

All learners enrolled in ALG's center-based program are educationally classified as eligible for special education and related services according to the classification system of New Jersey's State Education Department. As of July 1998, the New Jersey Administrative Code (6A:14-4-4.7) defines and identifies "special class" programs as serving students with similar educational needs in accordance with their IEPs. ALG's special class programs are designated Preschool Disabled (for learners younger than 5 years of age) and Autistic (for learners 5–21 years of age).

Instructional and Administrative Staff

Two instructional positions are available at ALG: classroom teacher and classroom instructor. A teacher must hold a certification as a special education teacher. In New Jersey, the mandated certification is as a Teacher of the Handicapped. An instructor must hold a bachelor's degree in a related field, usually psychology, sociology, or education. ALG's preschool and primary classrooms maintain a one-to-one staff–learner ratio. A typical primary classroom (ages 5–13 years) includes four or five learners, two full-time teachers, and two or three instructors. In secondary classrooms, five or six learners are supervised by two full-time certified teachers and two or three instructors. So the resultant staff–learner ratio is slightly less than the primary classroom's one-to-one ratio.

ALG's administrative staff consists of two nonteaching directors and two head teachers. All administrators are actively involved in the day-to-day programming with learners through supervision, educational clinics, staff training and evaluations, and family consultation.

ALG does not currently employ related service personnel such as speech–language pathologists, occupational therapists, or physical therapists. The school's curriculum comprises a wide variety of teaching programs that facilitate the development of both language and fine and gross motor skills. Instructional personnel implement these programs in the classrooms throughout the school day. The breadth and comprehensiveness of the ALG curriculum ensures that separate, pullout-related services are rarely necessary. In the event that occupational therapy or speech and language therapy services are deemed necessary, appropriate referrals or consultations are arranged by ALG administration.

Members of the instructional staff receive ongoing training and supervision in all teaching and intervention programs. A 40-hour training program consisting of didactic and hands-on training is conducted with each new staff member. Group training occurs at least once a year, usually in August, and all instructional and administrative personnel are required to attend training. Training topics include the following:

- an overview and history of applied behavior analysis
- fundamental principles of learning and reinforcement
- behavior shaping
- programming for generalization
- strategies for teaching language

- teaching language according to Skinner's analysis of verbal behavior (Skinner, 1957)
- use and implementation of various strategies such as errorless teaching
- script fading
- promoting language in natural environments
- incidental teaching
- stimulus shaping
- differential reinforcement procedures
- analysis and management of problem behavior

Training specifically emphasizes that teaching staff build relationships with learners through such techniques as providing noncontingent social reinforcement, pairing themselves with learners' preferred activities, and prompting reciprocal social interactions (e.g., compliments, comments, conversations). During the formal training week, learners are brought into the center and instructional staff members participate in hands-on training sessions to practice the skills learned in the didactic portion of the training.

The majority of training at ALG is ongoing and occurs throughout the year at regularly scheduled staff meetings and through classroom supervision. Regularly scheduled in-services and research meetings are held to enhance the staff's teaching skills. At these meetings, staff members review current and seminal research articles applicable to behavior analysis and the education and treatment of individuals with autism and develop research protocols to empirically assess novel interventions.

During the first 6 weeks of employment, staff members participate in an informal evaluation to assess skills in specific target areas (e.g., deliver prompts immediately and effectively, intermix learned targets with new targets, provide differential reinforcement appropriately). More comprehensive performance evaluations are conducted annually with each member of the instructional staff (McClannahan & Krantz, 1993). During the evaluation period, data are collected on the teaching behavior and professional skills of each teaching staff member (e.g., frequency of teaching opportunities provided, praise statements, and incidental teaching opportunities). Staff members are also assessed on their ability to address challenging behavior (e.g., implement procedures as described in formal behavior plans), to summarize and analyze data (e.g., data are graphed, data show change in the desired direction, graphs demonstrate phase changes when appropriate), and to use behavioral terminology appropriately (e.g., the instructor is able to describe the components of incidental teaching and the research supporting that intervention). In addition, staff members have the option of being rated by ALG colleagues in the areas of cooperation, communication skills, and effectiveness with learners (McClannahan & Krantz, 1993). These evaluations serve as tools to assess ALG's ongoing training programs and to determine the need for additional training of instructional personnel.

Assessment

Upon entry into the program, each learner receives a thorough skills assessment to determine functioning across a range of skill areas (e.g., social functioning, self-care, receptive and expressive language, play and leisure). The assessment procedure may also use published assessment protocols such as *The Assessment of Basic Language and Learning Skills* (Sundberg & Partington, 1998) or standardized assessment tools such as the *Vineland Adaptive Behavior Scales* (Sparrow, Balla, & Cicchetti, 1984), the *Peabody Picture Vocabulary Test–Third Edition* (Dunn & Dunn, 1997), or the *Stanford–Binet Intelligence Scale–Fourth Edition* (Thorndike, Hagen, & Sattler, 1986). In addition, curriculum-based measures may be conducted to determine academic functioning within the core academic areas (e.g., reading and mathematics) of specific published curricula. In collaboration with parents and sending school districts, each learner's IEP is then modified to outline goals for the school year.

Ongoing Identification of Objectives

When over the course of the school year a skill deficit is identified and prioritized for a specific learner, an individualized skill acquisition program addressing the deficit is obtained from ALG's curricular data bank, or a new program is written by a teacher, instructor, or director. Each of ALG's individualized skill acquisition programs includes a clearly defined target objective, a specific teaching procedure, a measurement procedure to evaluate the effectiveness of the intervention, and teaching steps that include procedures to promote stimulus and response generalization and maintenance.

Signature approval is obtained from the learner's parent, the learner's teacher, and the educational director prior to the implementation of skill acquisition programs. Approvals for each skill acquisition program are obtained annually to ensure that parents and ALG clinical staff are aware of (and agree to) the specific skills included in each learner's schedule. Once necessary approvals have been obtained, the program and data monitoring systems (e.g., graphs) are placed in the learner's data notebook for ongoing monitoring. On average, each learner at ALG has 25 active individualized teaching programs at any given time.

Curriculum

ALG's curriculum currently comprises approximately 1,100 individualized skill acquisition programs distributed across 21 specific curriculum areas. A sample of the school-age curriculum areas and examples of specific individualized skill acquisition programs are listed in Table 2.2.

Initial instructional objectives are individualized for each learner but typically focus on increasing a learner's ability to ask for desired items or activities, to approach adults to gain access to preferred materials, to sit and attend to instructional material, to play with toys, to initiate interactions with adults and peers, to use the bathroom, to increase responsiveness to spoken language, and to increase expressive language skills. Additional attention is directed toward replacing nonfunctional or disruptive responses (e.g., finger movements, tantrum responses) by teaching alternative, more appropriate responses (e.g., keeping hands in lap, asking for items appropriately, asking for a break). A representative example of a 7-year-old learner's program list can be found in Table 2.3.

Over time, and based on each learner's profile, emphasis is placed on skills required for participation in community and family activities (e.g., staying with an adult in the community, dining out with the family, going to the dentist). As learners approach 10 years of age, programming priorities expand to include goals necessary for participation in future supported volunteer sites. Such programs include completing tasks without the presence of an adult, monitoring appointments (e.g., taking a lunch break at 12:15), using a vending machine, and purchasing meals. Examples of published curricula targeting skills related to community integration include *Edmark Functional Words Series* (PRO-ED, Inc., 1990) for word recognition of common community terminology and *Basic Cafeteria Math* (PCI

Table 2.2
Sample School-Age Curriculum

Curriculum Area	General Skill Promoted	Sample Target Objectives
Attending	Orientation to visual or auditory stimuli	• Establishes eye contact in response to name • Waits appropriately for adult attention
Community	Participation in municipal resources and activities	• Stays with adult while walking • Checks out items from library
Expressive language	Nonverbal or verbal communication with others	• Requests/mands for preferred items • Asks for missing items to complete a routine
Fine motor	Small-muscle coordination	• Cuts using scissors • Types with correct finger placement
Gross motor	Large-muscle coordination	• Follows an exercise routine • Plays basketball
Handwriting	Graphomotor skills	• Prints name • Copies text from board
Imitation	Nonverbal imitative ability	• Imitates actions with objects • Imitates play response of peer
Leisure	Independent or group participant or spectator in recreation activities	• Sustains toy play • Plays video games
Mathematics	Numeration, computation, measurement, telling time, and money	• Tells time • Adds with a calculator
Prevocational	Skills needed to obtain employment	• Takes inventory • Cleans an area
Reading	Decoding and comprehension of written text	• Reads words • Answers questions about a sentence

(continues)

Table 2.2 *Continued.*
Sample School-Age Curriculum

Curriculum Area	General Skill Promoted	Sample Target Objectives
Receptive language	Understanding of oral language	• Identifies items by feature, function, or class • Follows conditional instructions
Science	Knowledge about self and environment	• Chooses clothing based on weather • Measures ingredients
Self-care	Independent personal hygiene	• Brushes teeth • Washes body in shower
Socialization	Social interaction skills	• Comments about play activities • Introduces self
Social studies	Knowledge of family, community, and country	• Answers general knowledge questions • Identifies functions of community helpers
Work studies	School-related work skills	• Follows written instructions • Raises hand to seek assistance

Educational Publishing, 1999) to teach "real-life" addition skills using realistic menus, along with visual worksheets for full-service restaurants. Table 2.4 is a sample schedule for one of ALG's 14-year-old learners.

Some published curricula have been adapted by ALG instructional personnel specifically for use with ALG learners. Published reading curricula include the *Edmark Reading Program* (Edmark Corporation, 1977) for word recognition and beginning comprehension, *Explode the Code* (1994) for phonics, and *Starting Comprehension* (Staman, 1998) for beginning comprehension. Expressive language and general knowledge skills have been taught using *Manual of Exercises for Expressive Reasoning* (Lingui-Systems, 1993), and numeration and currency skills have been addressed using the *Continental Press Mathematics* curricula (Gallivan, Greenburg, & Moss, 1980). Programs such as *Reader Rabbit's Toddler* (The Learning

(text continues on p. 32)

Table 2.3

Sample School Schedule for a 7-Year-Old Student: Mary

Program	Time	Instructor	Mon	Tue	Wed	Thu	Fri
• Answers questions • Completes time worksheets in *Continental Press Time Curriculum* • Relates past experiences to an adult or peer	9:00–9:45	Deirdre	X	X	X	X	X
• Labels absurdities • Solicits attention from adult or peer • Types with correct finger placement in the *Type to Learn Computer Program*	9:45–10:15	Shannon	X	X	X	X	X
• Identifies concepts in the *Concept Understanding Curriculum* • Prints words and sentences • Tells jokes	10:15–10:45	Jaime	X	X	X	X	X
• Spells words (fluency program) • Answers questions about past events • Engages in reciprocal conversation	10:45–11:15	Danielle	X	X	X	X	X
Lunch goal: Cuts with a knife	11:15–11:45	Shannon	X	X	X	X	X
Gross motor goal: Roller blades	11:45–12:15	Deirdre	X	X	X	X	X
• Group—follows conditional instructions • Completes an art project	12:15–12:45	Danielle	X	X	X	X	X

(continues)

Table 2.3 *Continued.*
Sample School Schedule for a 7-Year-Old Student: Mary

Program	Time	Instructor	Mon	Tue	Wed	Thu	Fri
• Describes similarities and differences among objects • Describes feature function and class of objects in view • Sings songs	12:45–1:15	Jaime	X	X	X	X	X
• Adds and subtracts on flash cards (fluency) • Describes actions with correct pronoun • Engages in scripted conversation	1:15–1:45	Dierdre	X	X	X	X	X
• Answers the telephone • Answers questions about a story • Monitors time-based appointments	1:45–2:15	Shannon	X	X	X	X	X
• Waits for attention • Maintenance • Initiates play with peer	2:15–2:45	Danielle	X	X	X	X	X

Table 2.4
Sample School Schedule for a 14-Year-Old Student: Paul

Program	Time	Instructor	Mon	Tue	Wed	Thu	Fri
• Adds using *Basic Restaurant Math* • Makes a list from dictation • Answers yes–no questions	9:00–9:45	Liz	X	X	X	X	X
• Reads words—*Edmark Level 2* • Laminates paper • Edits text	9:45–10:15	Amy	X	X	X	X	X
• Initiates scripted conversation with a peer • Writes in cursive • Maintenance	10:15–10:45	Trisha	X	X	X	X	X
• Instructs peers in a group • Completes tasks independently • Follows an exercise video	10:45–11:15	Liz	X	X	X	X	X
• Seeks assistance • Asks questions	11:15–11:45	Amy	X	X	X	X	X
Lunch: Orders from menu	11:45–12:15	Angela	X	X	X	X	X
Follows a gym routine	12:15–12:45	Staff	X	X	X	X	X
• Supported volunteer: Sorts mail at the hospital • Takes inventory	12:45–1:15	Trish	X	X	X	X	X

(continues)

Table 2.4 *Continued.*
Sample School Schedule for a 14-Year-Old Student: Paul

Program	Time	Instructor	Mon	Tue	Wed	Thu	Fri
• Supported volunteer: Sorts mail at the hospital	1:15–1:45	Trish	X		X		X
• Takes inventory				X		X	
• Writes in cursive	2:00–2:45	Angela	X	X	X	X	X
• Monitors appearance						X	
• Plays video game							

Company, 1997) have been used to teach functional use of a computer mouse (e.g., pointing and clicking), and *Words and Concepts II* (Wilson & Fox, 1993) and *Discrete Trial Trainer* (K. W. Smith, 2002) software have been used to develop receptive language concepts via the computer.

Teaching Procedures

Instructional strategies implemented at ALG are based on the principles of applied behavior analysis. Errorless teaching procedures may be used initially to promote responding during new or challenging programs (Touchette & Howard, 1984). Commonly used teaching interventions include time delay procedures (Taylor & Harris, 1995), discrete trial teaching (T. Smith, 2001), incidental teaching (Hart & Risley, 1975; McGee, Krantz, & McClannahan, 1985), contrived establishing operations (Sundberg, Loeb, Hale, & Eigenheer, 2002), video modeling (Charlop & Milstein, 1989; Taylor, Levin, & Jasper, 1999), photographic and textual activity schedules (Krantz, MacDuff, & McClannahan, 1993), script fading procedures (McClannahan & Krantz, 1993), observational learning, peer modeling, small group and paired instruction, shaping, prompting, and systematic prompt fading (Cooper, Heron, & Heward, 1987). Procedures to promote fluency (Binder, 1996; Kubina, Morrison, & Lee, 2002) are implemented in conjunction with specific programs to increase the rate and accuracy of a particular response. For example, several learners who participate in job sampling opportunities in the community are learning to sort mail at increased rates and with improved accuracy at school to enhance performance at the work site. Novel interventions such as the use of vibrating pagers to teach learners to seek assistance when lost in the community are evaluated empirically (Taylor, Hughes, Richard, & Hoch, 2004).

Challenging Behavior

Challenging behavior (e.g., tantrums, self-injury, aggression) is addressed by (a) conducting a functional assessment (Carr et al., 1999) or an analogue functional analysis (Iwata, Dorsey, Slifer, Bauman, & Richman, 1983) to determine the controlling variables (i.e., antecedents, consequences, and setting events) and (b) developing an intervention based on the results of the assessment or analysis. For example, if it is determined that the target behavior is maintained by escape from aversive stimuli (e.g., difficult task demands), instructional staff might be directed to teach the learner to use an alternative communicative response (e.g., to ask for a break), or to increase the density of positive reinforcement during the aversive situation (e.g., use preferred activities while implementing errorless teaching procedures), or to modify the antecedent stimuli (e.g., via curriculum modification) to decrease the learner's motivation to escape (Carr & Durand, 1985). Additional behavior reduction techniques that reflect current research findings in the behavioral literature are also used. Examples include extinction, differential reinforcement of low rates of behavior (DRL), response cost, and differential reinforcement of the nonoccurrence of behavior (DRO; Cooper et al., 1987). Parents, teachers, clinical administrators, and the building principal provide written consent before any behavior management procedure is implemented, and staff members are carefully trained prior to the use of and supervised during the implementation of all behavior management techniques. A human rights committee consisting of a senior behavior analyst, parents of present and previous learners, and education and legal personnel evaluates the effectiveness and social validity of all ALG intervention procedures.

Learning Environment

Two to five learners are enrolled in a given class and are typically grouped based on comparable skill levels. Although each learner has a designated desk and area where individualized teaching materials are located, teaching occurs in all areas of the school (e.g., kitchen, life skills bathroom, gross motor room, hallways, lobby) and in the community to promote generalization and responding in natural environments (Elliot, Hall, & Soper, 1991). For example, a learner may work on unpacking groceries in the kitchen or may learn to play a video game in the conference room. Similarly, a learner might practice purchasing items at a local convenience store or might run with a peer at a local high school track.

Teaching periods are 30 or 45 minutes in length. During each teaching period, an instructor or teacher is assigned to a learner and is responsible for teaching an average of three specific skill acquisition programs during that interval of time. Although staff is assigned specific programs to teach during each period, it is common for staff to mix programs in order that several targets may be worked on simultaneously to promote discrimination and task variation (Dunlap, 1984; Dunlap & Koegel, 1980).

If necessary, some teaching programs are targeted several times per day to allow for extra practice of a particular skill.

Most skill acquisition programs are taught during one-to-one teaching sessions. Teachers and instructors are responsible for ensuring response and stimulus generalization for each program they implement. Instructional sessions in pairs or small groups are scheduled throughout the day and provide opportunities to teach socially relevant behavior with peers, such as engaging in cooperative play, responding in a group, and learning novel responses through observation.

Each learner's skill acquisition programs are presented via a photographic or textual schedule (McClannahan & Krantz, 1999). For example, if a student is learning to identify colors, the schedule may present a photograph of the bin of the colored objects that the learner obtains to begin the teaching interaction. Learners are taught to attend to their schedules, to obtain the material depicted in the schedule (e.g., a bin of colored objects), and to initiate an interaction with an adult to begin the lesson (e.g., "Let's name colors"). Some learners are given opportunities to choose the order of their learning programs within their daily schedule.

Data Collection

To assess learner progress, data are collected during the implementation of all skill acquisition programs and behavior reduction procedures. Pretest and posttest measures assess performance of target responses in the absence of prompts and reinforcers. Interobserver agreement data are collected once per marking period (more often as necessary) and on all mastered objectives to ensure reliability of the data collected. Classroom teachers graph and review the data daily. The results of ongoing data analysis guide teaching interventions; for example, modifications in teaching strategies are implemented when data are variable or fail to show an ascending trend.

Educational Clinics

Once per month, learners, teachers, and parents participate in educational clinics supervised by either the director of educational programming or a head teacher. Clinics serve several functions: to assess the rate of acquisition of target objectives, to engage in collaborative problem solving when acquisition is slow or inconsistent, and to determine programming modifications or additions, if necessary.

Peer Modeling

ALG's peer modeling program provides opportunities for some learners with autism to gain peer-related social skills with typically developing peers (Taylor, 2001). Typically developing children are invited to attend ALG for part of the school day to participate in social interaction activities with learners with autism. Initially, the peers are taught to engage in a variety of social responses (e.g., how to share, how to direct play activities, how to persist to gain attention, how to offer choices of play activities) to increase their interactions with the learners with autism (Strain & Odom, 1986; Taylor & Jasper, 2001). Once these skills are established, the invited peers are paired with a target student with whom they engage in specific social interaction activities. In addition, learners with autism are taught specific skills (e.g., responding to a peer's question or direction, initiating social responses with peers) to increase their interactions with the typically developing children. For each participating learner, specific goals are developed and intervention strategies are identified and implemented. Data are recorded on specific responses (e.g., rates of initiations toward peers, percentage of prosocial interactions per play period) to document the effects of the social skills instruction.

Inclusion and Transition

ALG's inclusion program offers learners the opportunity to interact and learn with peers in less restrictive educational settings. A referral for participation in supported inclusion may be made by a parent, director, or teacher or by a sending school district team member. The decision for a learner to participate in an inclusion setting is made collaboratively. Each learner's academic and behavioral profile determines if and when he or she is able to benefit from such an inclusion placement (e.g., able to learn by observation). While participating in supported inclusion, the learner remains on ALG's roster and ALG receives full tuition.

Inclusion sites are typically located within the learner's neighborhood or within the local school district but may also be located close to ALG (Johnson, Meyer, & Taylor, 1996). Once a setting has been identified, training is offered to all inclusion site personnel (e.g., teachers, lunchroom assistants, gym teachers, building administrators) on subjects such as general information regarding autism, the principles of applied behavior analysis, and the development of measurement procedures to monitor behavior change. ALG staff members provide ongoing supervision and feedback to inclusion personnel to ensure continued behavior change for the learner with autism and to facilitate effective problem solving.

When inclusion is initiated, an ALG-trained support person accompanies the learner to inclusion until such a time as support is no longer required or until a school district–hired support person is identified and trained. Initially, a learner spends most of his school day at ALG and only part of the school day at the inclusion site. Over time, if data show change in the desired direction and the learner continues to master objectives in the inclusion setting, time in the inclusion site increases.

The ALG support person implements specific interventions to increase independence and specific responses (e.g., raising hand to seek assistance). Data are collected on specific responses to document the effects of the interventions. Goals targeted within the inclusion classroom may include the increase of overall independent functioning, social skills (e.g., responding to initiations from peers), and academic responses (e.g., completing grade-level mathematics). Skills are prioritized by district standards (successful completion of mathematics and reading curricula) as well as the learner's current educational status.

Once an ALG learner makes a full transition to a less restrictive setting, follow-up services may be provided in the form of ongoing consultation related to school, home, or community functioning. Some graduates may also attend ALG's extended-year program (i.e., the 30-day summer program) for additional instruction on target objectives (e.g., work study, social or academic skills).

Family Involvement

Parent participation and collaboration with families are an integral part of ALG's program. Prior to acceptance into ALG, families agree to 3 hours per month of school observation, attendance at monthly parent meetings, and home visits provided by a family consultant.

Family Consultation

ALG's family consultation has several goals: (a) to ensure stimulus gener-alization across settings and to novel persons (e.g., from school to home or community and from teacher to parent or caregiver), (b) to assist families in teaching functional skills in the home and community, (c) to address problem behavior that may be exhibited in home and community settings, and (d) to ensure that parents or caregivers can use the techniques nec-essary to increase skills and address problem behavior in the absence of ALG staff.

Upon enrolling in ALG, each family is offered weekly (or more, if nec-essary) home visits by a family consultant for the first year of enrollment. Newly enrolled families also participate in a didactic parent training course that covers the basic principles and common techniques associated with applied behavior analysis. During the second year, the family receives vis-its every other week. During the third year and throughout the learner's enrollment, the family receives at least one visit per month from a desig-nated family consultant (usually the learner's certified special education teacher) under the supervision of a head teacher or director. Provisions are made for additional visits related to crisis intervention or the imple-mentation of new or complex home- or community-based programs.

Assessment of Home and Community Functioning

At the time of enrollment, a comprehensive assessment of home and community skills is conducted by a head teacher or director via parent interview and direct observation. Domains assessed include self-care, domestic skills, leisure skills, receptive and expressive language, commu-nity skills, and problem behavior. Formal assessment protocols used may include the *Vineland Adaptive Behavior Scales, Interview Edition: Expanded Form* (Sparrow, Balla, & Cicchetti, 1984). Both standardized and informal assessment of home and community skills takes place an-nually to identify goals for the coming year. Family consultants work col-laboratively with the parents in prioritizing objectives and identifying rel-evant teaching strategies. The goals identified are then incorporated into the learner's IEP.

Once goals are established, a variety of skills may be targeted at a given time. For example, if parents are interested in including their child in a community recreation program, an ALG family consultant may be required to visit the recreation site to train relevant personnel in the implementation of specific objectives or instructional strategies (e.g., "Follows instructions of the dance teacher") and to supply general program development and assistance. Similarly, a family may be interested in implementing an activity schedule (McClannahan & Krantz, 1999) within the home to increase on-task behavior or leisure skills. In that case, a family consultant's assistance may be required to collaborate with the parents on identifying relevant activities to place within the schedule, to make materials for the schedule, and to teach the parents how to implement the activity schedule.

Data Collection

To document the effects of specific interventions in the home, parents are taught how to record data on their child's performance. Once objectives are identified, and before an intervention is implemented, the family is usually asked to record baseline data on their child's performance (e.g., the number of showering steps the learner completes without help). The family is then taught how to implement a specific teaching procedure or intervention designed to address the skill deficit or challenging behavior (e.g., how to provide prompts and reinforcers to teach a dressing program). During home visits, the family consultant may review the data that have been collected, observe the parent implementing the program, provide ongoing instructional feedback, or assist the family in modifying procedures or objectives. Interobserver reliability data are often collected by the family consultant during home visits to improve the reliability of data measures and to ensure proper implementation of procedures.

Because each family is unique in its strengths and weaknesses and in its ability and resources to implement specific procedures, ALG individualizes programs, interventions, and data collection procedures to match each family's needs and particular lifestyle. For example, one mother was unable to record step-by-step data on her son's showering program. As a result, the family consultant devised a rating scale judging the degree of prompts provided by the mother for her son to complete the showering routine (e.g., 0 = *no prompts required,* 1 = *a few prompts required,* 2 = *moderate amount of prompts required,* 3 = *almost fully prompted*). The mother found completing the rating scale more efficient and as a result was likely to complete the scale on a regular basis. These data, although not objective, served as feedback relevant for the parents' implementation of prompt fading procedures during the self-care routine.

Generalization

Some family consultation objectives are initially addressed at school, and then the skill or performance of the learner is systematically generalized to the home setting (e.g., a learner may learn to get dressed or brush his or her teeth first at school, and then the teaching procedure is transferred to the home and to the parent). One family, for example, was interested in teaching its teenage son to wake up in the morning using an alarm clock and to engage independently in a morning routine to get ready for school. Initially, at school, the learner was prompted to simulate sleeping (on a cot in the nurse's room) and to respond to an alarm clock by getting up, turning off the alarm clock, and referencing a textual list of steps to complete a morning routine (e.g., getting dressed, making breakfast, brushing teeth). Once the routine was fairly well established at school, the teaching program was transferred to the home. For a number of mornings, an ALG family consultant visited the home early in the morning to assist the learner's mother in implementing the teaching procedure for the morning routine. Eventually, the mother was able to implement the routine on her own and to record data to document her child's progress.

Addressing Problem Behavior

ALG assists families in identifying and reducing problem behavior at home and in the community. Each year, with the assistance of the family consultant, parents complete ALG's Problem Behavior Questionnaire. This questionnaire collects information on the display of problem behavior across typical family or community activities. Once specific behaviors have been prioritized, a functional assessment is conducted to arrive at hypotheses as to the potential functions of the problem behavior (e.g., is the behavior maintained by escape from demands or to gain attention from the parent?). ALG's staff then develop hypothesis-driven interventions (hypothesis driven with respect to the potential function and maintaining consequences of the problem behavior). With extensive support from ALG staff (e.g., three or four consecutive daily home visits), an intervention is subsequently implemented, and data are collected by the family to determine the efficacy of the treatment. For example, one ALG learner was observed to engage in tantrum responses when her mother talked on the telephone. A functional assessment indicated that the problem behavior was potentially maintained by attention (e.g., her mother got off the telephone to attend to her daughter when her daughter engaged in a tantrum). With the assistance of an ALG family consultant, this mother learned to successfully "ignore" the tantrum and provide differential reinforcement when her daughter was no longer engaged in a tantrum. The learner in question was further taught to ask for attention in a more functional way (e.g., instead of having a tantrum, she was taught to ask her mother to play with her).

Assistance for Extended Families and Siblings

ALG offers a variety of services to immediate and extended family members. For example, an annual lecture series is offered to grandparents, aunts, uncles, significant family friends, older siblings, and cousins. The lectures provide information about learning theory and basic behavioral principles so that extended family members can respond more effectively to a variety of situations encountered in the home and community. Siblings of our learners are likewise offered the opportunity to participate in ALG's sibling education and support groups and special sibling events (e.g., social outings with other siblings). Participation in these groups is voluntary and is left to the discretion of the family.

Parent Visits

ALG's open-door policy encourages parents to observe their children in programming as often as they like. Parents may observe their children at any time, unannounced, and may stay as long as they like. A minimum average of 3 hours of classroom observation is required each month and can include participation in monthly clinics, specially arranged training sessions, or general classroom observations.

During observations, parents are encouraged to adhere to observation policies and procedures to ensure that continuity of programming is maintained. Specifically, parents report to the office upon arrival and obtain a clipboard that contains a simple form with questions about their visit (e.g., "Did you achieve the goals of your visit?"). Parents are also asked to refrain from speaking to instructional staff members during these visits and to interact minimally with learners. Specific parent training sessions are scheduled separately from these observation hours.

Parents and teachers are in regular contact about a learner's education program and keep each other informed (e.g., report on learner's behavior over the weekend or performance on a specific program during the school day) via a daily communication book, e-mail, or through regular telephone contact.

Parent Meetings

Parents, directors, and teachers attend monthly group meetings. An average of eight meetings are held yearly. Topics include a review of ALG policies and procedures (e.g., how to provide feedback to teaching personnel, how to maximize your time at an IEP meeting), agency issues (e.g., the need for adult day services), current topics and issues (e.g., new state regulations, presentations from speakers on current research), and general programming issues (e.g., how to transfer skills to the home and community).

Consumer Evaluation

On an annual basis, parents are formally asked to share their concerns about or compliments to ALG programs by completing an anonymous consumer evaluation. Parents are asked to rate the overall effectiveness of intervention services, for instance, by responding to a written questionnaire about ALG's education and family consultation program, for example, "How satisfied are you with the amount of cooperation and assistance you have received from ALG administrative staff this school year?" (McClannahan & Krantz, 1993). The results of these evaluations are summarized and contribute to ongoing program development.

Preparation for Adult Years

Summaries of studies demonstrate that families' involvement in transition planning positively effects their children's future (U.S. Department of Education, 2000). Consistent with federal mandates (e.g., Individuals with Disabilities Education Act of 1990) and the New Jersey State Education Department Administrative Code, the IEPs of learners 14 years of age and older include a statement of transition needs, and therefore, educational goals for learners age 14 years and older focus on preparation for adult life (e.g., learning to function fully in community settings, developing relevant job skills, and increasing self-care and domestic skills). Some of the skills prioritized include the production aspects of a job, such as sorting mail or entering data into a computer, as well as skills to address successful integration into the work environment (e.g., use of a public restroom, taking a break). Such work-related goals are evident in the 21-year-old's program list shown in Table 2.5.

At the age of 14, learners enter ALG's supported volunteer or supported employment program. The program's goal is to help teenage learners acquire and perform age-appropriate, functional skills in a variety of integrated, natural community environments (e.g., public library, YMCA). A job sampling program is offered in which learners rotate through a series of positions at a variety of sites. By the time a learner graduates, at age 21, he or she may have sampled 12 or more volunteer positions. In some cases, job skills may be pretaught at ALG before being demonstrated at the work site. For example, a student may practice washing windows at school for several months before generalizing the skill to a local YMCA. In the case that deficits are observed at the volunteer sites, the skills in question may be practiced concurrently at school and in the community.

As in ALG's inclusion program, learners are accompanied to volunteer and job sites by ALG instructional personnel, who provide support in the form of discrete prompting and reinforcement. As soon as possible, accompanying personnel fade back in order to shift stimulus control to the setting, activities, and employees at the site. Problem behavior is addressed via systematic analyses and the development of interventions to ensure low rates of problem behavior within the community sites. Objective data measures document the effects of intervention and participants' success.

Potential employment sites are identified based on empirical data, which illustrate the learner's proficiency in a particular job, and anecdotal data regarding the learner's preferred work environment. For example, data may indicate that a learner performs better and displays fewer problem behaviors in a noisy setting (e.g., a packing warehouse) as opposed to a quieter one (e.g., a public library), or while sitting (e.g., alphabetizing medical files) as opposed to ambulating throughout a building (e.g.,

Table 2.5
Sample School Schedule for a 21-Year-Old Student: John

Program	Time	Instructor	Mon	Tue	Wed	Thu	Fri
• Follows instructions quietly	9:00–9:45	Michelle	X	X		X	X
• Makes copies							
• Initiates conversation					X		
• Supported volunteer							
• Asks questions and reports information	9:45–10:15	Maria	X	X			
• Cleans with a Swiffer							
• Maintenance							
• Supported volunteer						X	X
• Uses polite language in response to adult or peer comments	10:15–10:45	Maria	X	X			X
• Takes inventory							
• Supported volunteer					X	X	X
• Types with increased speed (without visual access to keyboard)	10:45–11:15	Erin	X	X			
• Types a variety of texts							
• Supported volunteer					X	X	X
Lunch goal: Engages in scripted conversation	11:15–11:45	Michelle	X	X	X	X	X
Gross motor goal: Follows an exercise routine	11:45–12:15	Meghan	X	X	X	X	X
• Plays solitaire	12:15–12:45	Amy	X	X	X	X	X
• Plays bingo with peers							
Monitors personal appearance	12:45–1:15	Meghan	X	X	X	X	X
Supported employment	1:15–3:45	Meghan	X	X	X	X	X
• Follows a recipe	3:45–5:00	Erin	X	X	X	X	X
• Purchases items using a list							

collecting recyclables). Further, the learner's affect may indicate preference for the noisy setting (e.g., smiles more often, shows more initiative in the setting).

Summary

ALG has changed substantially since opening its doors in 1989, continually expanding its programming in response to learners' needs, current behavioral analytic research, and steady advances in available technology. New methods and procedures have been assimilated into ALG's programming as they have evolved and their efficacy has been demonstrated. Technology has similarly offered new possibilities for teaching a broader range of skills in the school and the community. It is the student body, however, that truly defines ALG's progressive outlook. As successful educational and behavioral interventions equip our learners with larger and more refined skill sets, those learners develop new educational needs and embrace new challenges. By focusing intently on cultivating our students' futures, ALG ensures its own growth and development.

While striving to be responsive to scientific innovation and progress, ALG's commitment to the broad and fundamental principles of applied behavior analysis remains unwavering. Throughout 16 years of operation we have depended on data and experimental analysis to guide our decision making, the development of new interventions, and our implementation of those interventions. A dedication to addressing all aspects of a learner's development across a range of environments likewise remains central to our vision. The goals adopted in programming are individualized and socially significant and are developed in close collaboration with learners' families. As the science of autism treatment grows and expands, ALG will continue to broaden its own outlook and adapt its operations, but at the core, the organization will remain true to its first and most critical commitment: to the science of behavior and to the pursuit of lasting, meaningful changes for children with autism and their families.

References

Binder, C. (1996). Behavioral fluency: Evolution of a new paradigm. *The Behavior Analyst, 19,* 163–197.

Carr, E. G., & Durand, V. M. (1985). Reducing behavior problems through functional communication training. *Journal of Applied Behavior Analysis, 18,* 111–126.

Carr, E. G., Levin, L., McConnachie, G., Carlson, J. I., Kemp, D. C., Smith, C. E., et al. (1999). Comprehensive multi situational intervention for problem behavior in the community: Long-term maintenance and social validation. *Journal of Positive Behavior Interventions, 1,* 5–25.

Charlop, M. H., & Milstein, J. P. (1989). Teaching autistic children conversational speech using video modeling. *Journal of Applied Behavior Analysis, 23,* 275–285.

Cooper, J. O., Heron, T. E., & Heward, W. L. (1987). *Applied behavior analysis.* New York: Macmillan.

Dunlap, G. (1984). The influence of task variation and maintenance tasks on the learning and affect of autistic children. *Journal of Experimental Child Psychology, 37,* 41–64.

Dunlap, G., & Koegel, R. L. (1980). Motivating autistic children through stimulus variation. *Journal of Applied Behavior Analysis, 13,* 619–627.

Dunn, L. M., & Dunn, L. M. (1997). *Peabody Picture Vocabulary Test* (3rd ed.). Circle Pines, MN: American Guidance Service.

Edmark Corporation. (2001). *Edmark Reading Program, Level One.* Austin, TX: PRO-ED, Inc.

Edmark Corporation. (1990). *Edmark functional words series.* Austin, TX: PRO-ED, Inc.

Elliot, R. O., Jr., Hall, K., & Soper, H. A. (1991). Analog language teaching versus natural language teaching: Generalization and retention of language training for adults with autism and mental retardation. *Journal of Autism and Developmental Disorders, 21,* 433–447.

Explode the code. (1994). Cambridge, MA: Educators Publishing Service.

Gallivan, C., Greenburg, I. H., & Moss, A. R. (1980). *Continental Press Mathematics.* Elizabeth, PA: Continental Press.

Hart, B., & Risley, T. R. (1975). Incidental teaching of language in the preschool. *Journal of Applied Behavior Analysis, 8*(4), 411–420.

Individuals with Disabilities Education Act of 1990, 20 U.S.C. § 1400 *et seq.*

Iwata, B. A., Dorsey, M. F., Slifer, K. J., Bauman, K. E., & Richman, G. S. (1983). Toward a functional analysis of self-injury. *Analysis and Intervention in Developmental Disabilities, 2,* 3–20.

Johnson, S. C., Meyer, L., & Taylor, B. A. (1996). Supported inclusion. In C. Maurice, G. Green, & S. Luce (Eds.), *Behavioral intervention for young children with autism: A manual for parents and professionals* (pp. 331–342). Austin, TX: PRO-ED.

Krantz, P. J., MacDuff, M. T., & McClannahan, L. E. (1993). Programming participation in family activities for children with autism: Parents' use of photographic activity schedules. *Journal of Applied Behavior Analysis, 26*, 137–139.

Krantz, P. J., & McClannahan, L. E. (1993). Teaching children with autism to initiate to peers: Effects of a script fading procedure. *Journal of Applied Behavior Analysis, 26*, 121–132.

Kubina, R. M., Morrison, R., & Lee, D. L. (2002). Benefits of adding precision teaching to behavioral interventions for students with autism. *Behavioral Interventions, 17*, 1–14.

The Learning Company. (1997). Reader Rabbit's Toddler [Computer software]. Cambridge, MA: Author.

LinguiSystems. (1993). *Manual of Exercises for Expressive Reasoning, I and II*. Moline, IL: Author.

McClannahan, L. E., & Krantz, P. J. (1993). On systems analysis in autism intervention programs. *Journal of Applied Behavior Analysis, 26*(4), 589–596.

McClannahan, L. E., & Krantz, P. J. (1999). *Activity schedules for children with autism: Teaching independent behavior*. Bethesda, MD: Woodbine House.

McGee, G. G., Krantz, P. J., & McClannahan, L. E. (1985). The facilitated effects of incidental teaching on preposition use by autistic children. *Journal of Applied Behavior Analysis, 18*, 17–31.

New Jersey Administrative Code. (1998). NJAC 6A:14.

PCI Educational Publishing. (1999). *Basic cafeteria math*. San Antonio, TX: Author.

Skinner, B. F. (1957). *Verbal behavior*. New York: Appleton-Century-Crofts.

Smith, K. W. (2002). Discrete Trial Trainer [Computer software]. Columbia, SC: Accelerated Educational Software.

Smith, T. (2001). Discrete trial training in the treatment of autism. *Focus on Autism and Other Developmental Disabilities, 16*, 86–92.

Sparrow, S. S., Balla, D. A., & Cicchetti, D. V. (1984). *Vineland Adaptive Behavior Scales*. Circle Pines, MN: American Guidance Service.

Staman, A. L. (1998). *Starting comprehension: Stories to advance reading and thinking*. Cambridge, MA: Educators Publishing Service.

Strain, P. S., & Odom, S. L. (1986). Peer social initiations: Effective intervention for social skills development of exceptional children. *Exceptional Children, 52*, 543–552.

Sundberg, M. L., Loeb, M., Hale, L., & Eigenheer, P. (2002). Contriving establishing operations to teach mands for information. *Analysis of Verbal Behavior, 18*, 15–20.

Sundberg, M. L., & Partington, J. W. (1998). *Teaching language to children with autism or other developmental disabilities*. Pleasant Hill, CA: Behavior Analysts.

Taylor, B. A. (2001). Teaching peer social skills to children with autism. In C. Maurice, G. Green, & R. Fox (Eds.), *Making a difference: Behavioral intervention in autism*. Austin, TX: PRO-ED.

Taylor, B. A., & Harris, S. L. (1995). Teaching children with autism to seek information: Acquisition of novel information and generalization of responding. *Journal of Applied Behavior Analysis, 28*, 3–14.

Taylor, B. A., Hughes, C. E., Richard, E., & Hoch, H. (2004). Teaching teenagers with autism to seek assistance when lost. *Journal of Applied Behavior Analysis, 31,* 79–82.

Taylor, B. A., & Jasper, S. (2001). Teaching programs and activities to improve the social behavior of children with autism. In C. Maurice, G. Green, & R. Fox (Eds.), *Making a difference: Behavioral intervention in autism.* Austin, TX: PRO-ED.

Taylor, B. A., Levin, L., & Jasper, S. (1999). Increasing play-related statements in children with autism toward their siblings: Effects of video modeling. *Journal of Development and Physical Disabilities, 11*(3), 253–264.

Thorndike, R. L., Hagen, E. P., & Sattler, J. M. (1986). *The Stanford–Binet Intelligence Scale–Fourth Edition.* Chicago: Riverside.

Touchette, P. E., & Howard, J. S. (1984). Errorless learning: Reinforcement contingencies and stimulus control transfer in delayed prompting. *Journal of Applied Behavior Analysis, 17,* 175–188.

U.S. Department of Education. (2000). *Transition guidelines for parents and families: New Jersey Partnership for Transition from School to Adult Life for Youth with Disabilities* (Office of Special Education and Rehabilitation Services 2000 Project Award H 158A30013-958 CFDA 84.158A). Washington, DC: Author.

Wilson, M. S., & Fox, B. J. (1993). Words & Concepts II [Computer software]. Winooski, VT: Laureate Learning Systems.

The Children's Unit for Treatment and Evaluation

3

*Raymond G. Romanczyk, Stephanie B. Lockshin,
Linda Matey, and Jennifer M. Gillis*

· ·

The Children's Unit for Treatment and Evaluation (CUTE) at the Institute for Child Development (ICD) conducts Early Intervention, Preschool, and School-Age programs. In our school-age program, we serve children up to 12 years of age with autism spectrum disorders (ASDs), as well as a small group of children with developmental and emotional disorders. The CUTE is one of the three direct-service components (units) of the ICD and is located on the State University of New York (SUNY) at Binghamton campus, in a large, modern, single-story building recently built specifically for the institute. The CUTE was established in 1975 and was granted special status in 1977 through an act of the New York State Legislature, which allowed the unit to exist with a dual status as a fully certified New York State Education Department private school and at the same time as organizationally part of SUNY Binghamton. The bill permits school districts and other state agencies to contract directly with the unit.

The School-Age program is conducted between 8:45 A.M. and 2:15 P.M., 5 days per week, 12 months per year. Children may be admitted and discharged at any time throughout the calendar year. Referrals originate from a wide range of sources, including school districts, physicians, social services, family court, mental health professionals, and parental self-referral. Our catchment area is very large, with children who are transported daily up to 100 miles each way, from home to the institute and back again. Funding for student placement comes from each school district's Committee for Special Education, which approves placement. Parents are not responsible for any part of the tuition or fees.

As a New York State Education Department–certified private school, the CUTE must comply with regulations of the State Education Department with respect to child–staff ratios, age distribution, and programmatic as well as operational regulations, including such items as periodic on-site evaluations and yearly dual external fiscal audits. The program is also implicitly evaluated by the university each year with respect to the substantial physical plant that it occupies and other resources allocated to it.

Philosophy

The following is an excerpt from our program brochure:

> Our guiding philosophy is to employ intensive, child-centered, empirically validated educational and clinical procedures. Children who manifest developmental, learning, or emotional disorders impact not only upon themselves, but also their families and their communities, and this challenge must be met by a reciprocal intensity, quality, and precision of services. We firmly believe that providing a caring, warm, supportive environment that respects the dignity of individuals and celebrates their unique qualities and potential is the *minimum* starting point for services. Thus, our hallmark is the utilization, on a continuing basis, of well conducted educational and clinical research that appears in peer reviewed professional journals.

The CUTE was created to serve as a component in the continuum of services in our extended community of the southern tier of New York and northern Pennsylvania. That is, it is designed as an intensive short-term program and not as a parallel program in which children would remain for many years. Its focus is to achieve an approximately 3-year duration of placement that would result in sufficient change to permit children to function within the context of the services available within their local community. Because of this philosophy, the emphasis is on a focused rather than a balanced curriculum (Romanczyk & Lockshin, 1984). This focused approach, which may also be termed a deficit-oriented approach, seeks to identify the factors that are most crucial in preventing the child from benefiting fully from the continuum of services in the local community. By focusing on those deficits and problem areas, rather than attempting to provide a balanced curriculum, it is possible to provide in a brief span of time the necessary intensity of services that permits the relatively speedy transition to community-based services. Because of this focus on children's participation in services within their local community, and the focus on individual characteristics and skill deficits that are impeding such placement, the criteria for discharge from the program reflect a specific child–local community interaction. That is, because the unit serves children from scores of different communities (within a 100-mile radius), from urban to suburban to rural, and the resources available in these different communities vary to an extreme degree, an absolute level of progress is not used for discharge decisions. Rather, progress relative to what is required within the child's local community becomes the criteria. This approach allows maximum flexibility for families and their local school districts and service providers.

The philosophical underpinnings of the CUTE are rooted in child advocacy; family involvement; the use of empirically validated procedures; and the importance of training, research, and dissemination. Our model has evolved over time and is strengthened by research demonstrating the effectiveness of systematic behavioral interventions with difficult-to-treat populations. Further, the behavioral model provides a technology for effective teaching, ongoing assessment, and evaluation of treatment outcome based on precise and continuous behavior recording and analysis. Thus, our program is committed to a comprehensive, integrated, and state-of-the-art behavioral model of service delivery. We feel it is critical to point out that *ours is a philosophy derived from empirical research, rather than a philosophy in search of research support.*

Within the behavioral model, the objective assessment is the focus for treatment decisions. Therefore, extensive analyses are conducted to identify appropriate goals for intervention–habilitation. In addition to the administration of standardized tests, checklists, and skill inventories, formal behavior analyses are conducted to provide information regarding the frequency, intensity, and duration of target behaviors with respect to their eliciting and maintaining variables. Additional observations are conducted to determine controlling stimuli and the effects of environmental expectations and demands. Assessment of behavior assets is also conducted to determine their relationship to the behavior excesses or deficits, their relative strength, and the degree of stimulus control necessary to elicit responding.

From an administrative perspective, the problem of efficiently collecting, organizing, interpreting, and monitoring the myriad of information needed to fully implement our model is colossal and represents a continuing challenge.

Demographics

The CUTE typically serves an enrollment of about 42 children. Approximately 400 children have been enrolled to date, with 47% entering as preschoolers. In New York, a child's educational classification determines eligibility for special education services. It should be noted that an educational classification is not necessarily the same as a psychiatric diagnosis. Because we are a New York State certified school, it is not required for children to have a formal diagnosis of autism (given by a licensed psychologist or physician) for entry into the CUTE. However, approximately 90% of our enrollment meet the *Diagnostic and Statistical Manual of Mental Disorders–Fourth Edition–Text Revision* (DSM–IV–TR; American Psychiatric Association, 2000) criteria for autism or PDD-NOS. Given the importance of understanding a child's current level of functioning, we perform a comprehensive battery of both standardized and behavioral assessments periodically. Those assessments assist with selecting appropriate goals for a child and for monitoring child progress over time. Full diagnostic assessment is a separate service provided at the ICD.

The gender distribution of our school-age population of children with autism is 75% males and 25% females. For children meeting DSM–IV–TR criteria, scores at intake on *The Childhood Autism Rating Scale* (CARS; Schopler, Reichler, & Renner, 1995) average 40 (min 30, max 50), with 70% of our population classified by the CARS as "severely autistic." Average age at admission is 5 or 6 years (80% of our population), with less than 10% entering at 8 years or older, up to our maximum admission age of 11 years. Average length of participation in the program is approximately 3 years.

Staffing and Administration

Within a behaviorally based instructional program, staffing and administration considerations have been addressed and adapted to the needs and requirements of the mission of the program. As such, the organizational structure is a result of the needs of the direct care staff in meeting the needs of the children. The starting point, therefore, was to identify what functions, procedures, and personnel facilitate instructional effectiveness at different levels. Not surprisingly, resources are key to any discussion on how to structure an organization. In terms of human resources,

- the task and time required must not exceed the consistent ability of staff to maintain performance at a desired level of competency;
- the task must be defined by the needs of all parties involved with the child: family, school district, teacher, and so forth;
- the task must include checkpoints or safeguards to ensure that organizational goals are being met; and
- the timing and spacing of these checkpoints must be scheduled to facilitate rapid identification of child and organizational concerns.

In addition, equitable distribution and delegation of responsibilities, based on competence, across staff, by roles, are crucial. Our goal is to achieve a more horizontal than rigid and vertical organization structure. We separate our educational and psychological service personnel to allow a focus on child educational needs as well as a focus on family's needs. The convergence of these two subdivisions at the director level provides a structure where the overall organizational priorities can be addressed. Frequent communication between coordinators allows for joint programming to address the broad needs of the child.

Under educational services, we organize as teams focused on individual classrooms. Within each team,

- each staff member works with each of the children approximately four to five times a week;
- each child has an individualized weekly schedule that is implemented by the assigned staff, irrespective of role;
- time of day is recorded for all data collected; and
- child groupings within a team vary systematically.

This ensures that a child's behavior and performance reflect interactions with a variety of staff members and avoids the limited generalization that is often seen if there is a staff-static classroom. Likewise, the interaction of task and staff member can be evaluated, as well as the intra- and interactions in one learning group versus another.

By systematizing and recording these changes, results can be efficiently and time-effectively monitored and modified. There is also the benefit of having feedback from a number of staff members for trouble-shooting and identifying issues.

Procedural Safeguards

Crucial to our primary objective of maximizing rates of child progress is a set of procedural safeguards. As used here, procedural safeguards are mandatory steps in the organizational sequence, wherein more than one individual is involved in all processes and a senior staff member is required to give approval to move to the next step. Figures 3.1 and 3.2 taken together provide an example of a procedural sequence. They illustrate the tasks required of staff members when a child enters the program (Figure 3.1), through program implementation and evaluation (Figure 3.2). The figures illustrate our series of checkpoints, where consultation, analyses, and modifications are made. Although the sequence is not rigidly linear, it is organized so that the greatest length of time between checkpoints is 1 week.

With checkpoints in place to identify performance problems quickly, the work toward resolution begins at the staff team level. It involves

- initiation of consultation when a problem is identified at any checkpoint;
- discussion with team staff and coordinator or director;
- careful review of data and staff input;
- hypotheses development;
- development of a remedial strategy (e.g., in-service, supervision, resource reallocation); and
- follow-up based on information evaluated.

Professional Development

Another component of the staff and administrative aspect of the CUTE is professional development. Keeping current with research findings and technical updates as well as with unit policy and procedures is necessary to providing effective intervention and thus is a priority. The CUTE requires that all staff, no matter in what role or position, take a written exam, based on our policy and procedures manual. For the direct care staff, this occurs prior to involvement with the children. Then, weekly

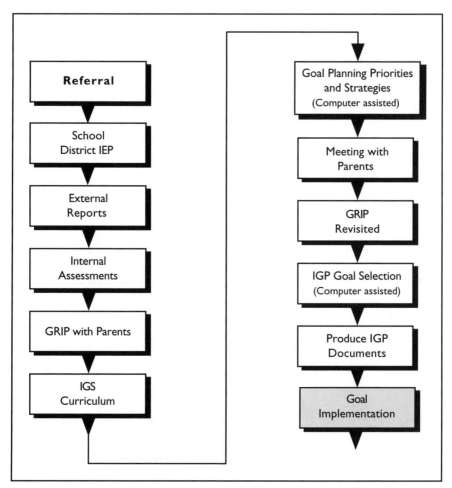

Figure 3.1. Flowchart of procedural checkpoints for a child entering the CUTE. *Note.* IEP = Individualized Education Program; GRIP = Growth, Relationships, Independence, Participation; IGP = Individualized Goal Plan; IGS = Individualized Goal Selection.

written evaluations of performance and skill competency are provided on an ongoing basis. Training in the form of internal and externally sponsored presentations is made available to all staff members, regardless of their role and responsibility. Attendance at, and participation in, relevant conferences is highly encouraged as a way of obtaining information about recent developments in the field.

Staffing and Administration Summary

Organizational structure facilitates good use of resources and adherence to policy. Well-trained staff members and procedural structure are necessary components of a well-run organization. Safeguards and checkpoints help to minimize error and inefficiency and prevent tasks from "falling between the cracks." Above all, however, the staffing and administration structure should be developed in response to program priorities and goals and must be flexible enough to rapidly change as priorities change.

Curriculum

The ICD uses the *Individualized Goal Selection* (IGS) *Curriculum* (Romanczyk, Lockshin, & Matey, 2000), which was developed over the last 25 years specifically for young students with ASD. The IGS curriculum is organized to address over 2,000 specific goals. Its organization allows for developing an individualized curriculum plan, tailored to specifically address a student's weaknesses and deficits. Student strengths are used to provide a foundation for the acquisition of new skills.

The IGS curriculum provides a reference for behavioral targets for applied behavior analysis intervention, although it is not methodologically based. Using the IGS provides a standardization of language in order to enhance communication among ICD staff members and between staff and parents. In addition, the organization of the IGS curriculum provides a structure for goal selection, in that goals and skills are developmentally sequenced, that is, they are arranged from simple to more complex developmental areas (e.g., from "imitates single action" to "imitates action sequence with two objects"). Given the extent of the domains in the IGS, a wide range of skills may be addressed. Figure 3.3 presents an overview of the IGS.

A computerized version of the IGS curriculum allows the generation of templates for writing detailed, habilitative behavior programs that can be evaluated and replicated. This version of the IGS curriculum also creates templates for data recording and graphing on the computer. The computerized version also provides data regarding designated priorities, timelines, and student progress both within and between goals.

The CUTE uses a comprehensive series of computer databases to organize each student's educational goal plan, specific habilitative goals, daily and monthly progress on each goal, graphs of progress, history of

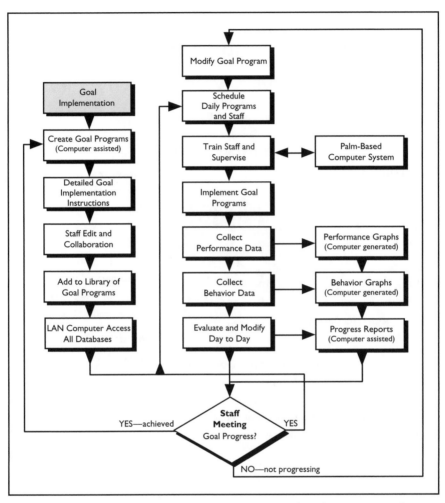

Figure 3.2. Flowchart of tasks, systems, and decision making for program implementation and evaluation.

educational goals, and evaluation of goals. The computerized IGS curriculum is connected to the databases, which allows the selected goals from the IGS to be imported into a student's Individualized Goal Plan (IGP) in the database. From this database, printed reports are generated. These reports include but are not limited to

- annual IGPs,
- monthly progress on current goals,

THE INDIVIDUALIZED GOAL SELECTION CURRICULUM

Habilitative Domains

I. Communication
II. Behavioral/Emotional
III. Social
IV. Preacademic/Academic
V. Life Skills

Instructional Level

I. Basic Skills Training
II. Integrated Skills
III. Functional Skills
IV. Independent

Goals

I. Explicit—Written
II. Individualized
III. Precise Data Collection
IV. Rigorous Evaluation

CHILD

Behavioral Expectations

I. Learning Readiness
II. Social Awareness
III. Social Norms
IV. Self-Regulation
V. Respect for Others
VI. Sensory Awareness
VII. Independent Learning

Required Resources

I. Large Group
II. Group
III. Small Group
IV. Individual
V. Multiple

Instructional Formats

I. Focused Instruction
II. Experiential Learning
III. Enrichment—Stimulation
IV. Skill Integration Activities

CURRICULUM AREAS

1. Maladaptive Behavior
2. Attentive Skills
3. Speech
4. Receptive Language
5. Expressive Language
6. Concept Formation
7. Gross Motor Skills
8. Self-Help and Daily Living Skills
9. Social Skills
10. Reading
11. Fine Motor Skills
12. Written Communication
13. Arithmetic
14. Cultural Skills
15. General Information
16. School-Related Skills
17. Life Relevant Skills
18. Leisure Skills
19. Emotional & Self-Control Development

Figure 3.3. Overview of the components of the *Individualized Goal Selection Curriculum.*

- goal planning summary analyses, and
- a detailed progress summary.

The database assists staff with monitoring current student goals; early detection of an increase, a plateau, or a decrease in progress; and generation of hypotheses for functional analyses and continuing assessments.

The Individualized Goal Plan

For an individual student, the IGS curriculum facilitates production of an IGP. The IGP can be thought of as a blueprint or map for sequencing skills to be taught across 19 areas of development throughout a designated span of time (i.e., a school year). The individualized goals in a student's IGP are sequenced to maximize student progress in the following ways:

- Staff members assign different priority levels to each goal within and across 19 areas of development.
- Goals that address fundamental learning skills are typically assigned a higher priority level than more complex goals within the same area.
- The IGP provides a framework for evaluating a student's progress.
- The IGP is intricately related to ongoing assessment (i.e., the expectation is that goals should be changed as objective data indicate progress is being made).

IGS Curriculum Structure

There are well over 2,000 specific goals (or tasks) in the IGS curriculum. These tasks are developmentally ordered and focus on specific skills. The purpose of the goal selection process using the IGS curriculum is to provide sequential and parallel skill development that is "branching" in order to focus on overall development. The IGS curriculum does not provide "cookie cutter" goal plans for students. Through efforts of the team, including the student's parents, a comprehensive IGP is developed.

There are several core issues that staff members address with parents when planning a student's IGP. First, goals selected are consistent with assessment data. That is, the goals are selected to be functional, age appropriate, and developmentally appropriate. Functional goals aim to result in a student's independent performance of tasks and activities.

Chronologically age appropriate simply implies that the materials, activities, and context are similar to those used or experienced by same-age peers. For a student's annual IGP, goals are sequenced so that each goal is addressed immediately, in 3 months, in 6 months, or in 9 months. Part of deciding in which sequence goals are taught depends on what we term the *horizontal and vertical integration of goals.* For vertically integrated goals, skills that are taught in the beginning or at one point will facilitate the mastery of more complex skills and activities that will be taught in the future. Horizontally integrated goals depend on skills taught in one curricular area that are also taught in another area. For example, a goal of greeting others, which might fall under the Social domain, might also be taught in the domain of Communication, as the student may learn to say hello, in addition to imitating an action of waving hello. Goals are often chosen to reflect cultural considerations, types of environmental demands, environments where the individual will be functioning, and accessibility to those environments. In this sense, some of the goals may be thought of as *community referenced,* which refers to teaching a skill to allow the student to function independently within his or her own community (Scheuermann & Webber, 2002).

GRIP

One of our first steps in developing a student's IGP is the GRIP process. GRIP is an acronym for Growth, Relationships, Independence, and Participation. It is the initial process for establishing communication, shared goals, and student expectations between staff members and parents. Parents, staff members at the unit, and the Educational Services Coordinator meet to discuss and modify a draft of the student's IGP. Through discussion, both staff members and parents revise areas of the IGP to achieve consensus as to goals selected, priorities, implementation strategies, and how closely the goals match the needs of the student.

Each family completes a GRIP worksheet as a first step to provide perspective for goal selection and prioritization. The following lists the content in a GRIP worksheet:

- Providing continuing and expanding positive physical, intellectual, emotional, and behavioral growth

- Developing and maintaining positive and sustained social and work relationships
- Developing the skills necessary to enable personal independence
- Developing the skills, motivation, and knowledge to permit active participation in the life of family and community

GRIP is used at many stages throughout a child's educational experience, because parent and child priorities and goals change over time, such as when a child makes progress in our program, as is illustrated in Figures 3.2 and 3.3, which underscores the dynamic nature of this process. A further example is provided in the section on transition.

Skill Acquisition

An elaborate computer-assisted learning program is available for all students, across a broad range of functioning levels. The computer learning program, called ICD Teach, can be easily programmed to provide individualized instruction for a variety of skill areas, from identifying sight vocabulary sounds and words, to identifying colors and shapes, to teaching elementary cause and effect. Additionally, the ICD Teach program allows different types of feedback for both correct and incorrect responses (e.g., video, sound clips of verbal feedback, music). Staff members can program ICD Teach to set how many trials are presented or how well a student needs to respond (e.g., with 85% accuracy) until the teaching program ends. For particularly difficult students to teach, ICD Teach permits a wide range of parameters to select from, to address their challenging needs (White, Matey, Gillis, Kashinsky, & Romanczyk, 2003).

The classroom and individual instruction and intervention methods incorporated at the CUTE include those that have empirical support, primarily applied behavior analysis, verbal behavior analysis, and behavior therapy. Discrete trial training; individual and small- and large-group instruction; experiential learning; social scripts; individual and small-group counseling; peer model instruction; systematic desensitization and exposure therapy; stress and coping strategies; augmentative communication systems; structured and nonstructured environments; and incidental teaching are all used at the CUTE.

Initial Response to Treatment

Based on clinical judgment and experience, we begin the student's initial acclimation to our program by using the least amount of structure and nonsocial reinforcement as seems appropriate. Given the student's initial response, we then go through a hierarchy of examining reinforcer preference assessment, teaching methods, prompts, degree of environmental structure, group size, instructional setting, and response modality preference.

Reinforcer Preference Assessment

We use three major types of reinforcer preference assessments: interview, sampling, and formal stimulus preference assessment. In the interview method, a paper–pencil form is sent home to parents requesting information about the student's preferences. The form can consist of checklists and open-ended questions. The interview method is time efficient but often not fully accurate. The second method is sampling. With sampling, a novel stimulus is introduced to the student to see if she or he responds. Usually, this method is used to probe additional stimuli to parent-suggested items and to confirm parent reports. The sampling method is relatively time efficient and improves the accuracy of the interview format, but it is more time-consuming and requires creativity and brainstorming. The last type is the formal assessment, which experimentally assesses the preferences of a student by asking the student to respond to a single stimulus or paired stimuli, which allows inference as to the stimuli he or she prefers. This method is more time-consuming than the previous two but very precise for ordering relative reinforcing value of stimuli.

Generalization

In order to generalize skill acquisition, staff members who teach the students are rotated, so that the student learns to learn with a variety of individuals. As specific skills are acquired, skills are taught in different settings and under varying demands in order to increase generalization. Simultaneously, materials used to teach specific skills are varied so that generalization of each skill is maximized for each student. The student's criterion environment is taken into consideration for skill generalization.

Thus, if a student is transitioning to an integrated classroom, the demands, setting, instructional materials, and so forth, characteristic of the integrated classroom will be taught prior to transition. As mentioned, an emphasis is placed on parallel goal development, which encourages generalization and assessment of progress and increases the extensiveness of a student's repertoire and spontaneous repertoire assembly.

Instructional Management

For each child's goals, a specific and detailed implementation program is designed. The program includes the goal (i.e., target behavior), operational definition of the target behavior, teaching approach, teaching procedure, and criteria for ongoing evaluation. Each program is written with enough detail to ensure consistency of goal implementation across teaching staff. When a teacher designs a student's program for an educational goal, the educational services coordinator must edit and approve the program prior to implementation.

The number of programs or goals per student varies such that some children may have 12 goals in place simultaneously and other children may have up to 26. This range does not reflect a student's progress or ability per se. But, typically, students who are higher functioning tend to have a higher number of goals. Some goals are also conducted parallel with each other. For example, a student may have one goal that addresses eye contact and one that focuses on matching colors that are conducted simultaneously during an art class.

Evaluation of Progress

Each week, students' progress is carefully evaluated at a staff or a team meeting. The staff meeting includes the educational services coordinator, classroom teacher, school psychologist, speech therapist, adaptive physical education teacher, teacher aides, and doctoral clinical psychology assistants. The team meeting typically includes the classroom teacher, educational services coordinator, and speech therapist. Both meetings are regularly scheduled to review completion of goals within a student's goal plan and to revise goals or teaching procedures as needed.

Additionally, each month, progress notes are completed for each student and sent to the student's parents. Three-, 6-, and 9-month progress meetings are also scheduled with the student's parents to review progress.

There are many times when a child's educational progress and ability to participate in classroom and social activities are compromised due to certain child characteristics, such as specific phobias, low frustration tolerance, inappropriate behavior, or deficit social skills. These are skill areas that are often neglected in most educational settings, simply because of lack of available resources and expertise. At the CUTE, there are two clinical psychologists, a school psychologist, and several doctoral clinical psychology assistants (i.e., graduate students in a clinical psychology PhD program). Given that our clinical psychology staff has the dual influences of applied behavior analysis (ABA) and behavior therapy, there is a strong clinical psychology influence on our program. Many of the clinical interventions, such as a graduated desensitization intervention for phobias, social skills groups, and anger management and coping skills therapy groups, have a strong behavior therapy approach and are integrated into our educational program.

Supervision to Achieve Procedural Integrity

Supervision of staff and undergraduates at the CUTE is an ongoing process that continues after staff members are initially trained in the implementation of ABA goals and have achieved a level of independence in teaching students with ASD. Typically, the initial staff training duration is 4 to 6 weeks.

When staff are hired, they are required to become knowledgeable about administrative policies and procedures, and all employees must pass a written exam that covers these areas. Teachers are trained in various assessment procedures, most notably the design and implementation of functional analyses. Teachers are also trained in procedures to identify the student's current level of performance across domain areas, goal selection, and prioritization of these goals. Teachers, the educational coordinator, and speech therapists work closely together with the student's parents to develop the most appropriate selection of goals for the student.

The goals of supervision include monitoring the integrity of the implementation of instructional programs, which, in turn, permits evaluation of program efficacy; monitoring the accessibility of data to enable objective measurement of student progress; identifying impediments to progress; monitoring the adequacy of instructional time; and monitoring student safety.

The aspects of goal implementation that are supervised include operationally defining the target behaviors, the selection of goals, and the choreography of goal sequence to maximize the student's functional repertoires. For each goal, supervision also takes place as to the specification of

- instructional materials
- instructional methodology (shaping, fading, etc.)
- consequences
- prompting procedures and prompt fading
- reinforcement parameters
- data collection procedures
- schedule for data collection
- program implementation

To facilitate supervision, we use a Palm-based monitoring system. The monitoring system manages a large amount of information easily, creates a supervision database that may be searched, provides a record of observations completed per staff member and per supervisor, provides summary data across observations, and provides printouts for staff to provide them with immediate performance feedback.

Classrooms

Each classroom is designed to address different functional levels and ages of the students. For example, one of the classrooms may be designed to accommodate more one-to-one instruction, and another classroom may look similar to a typical school-age classroom with chairs and desks for each child. The purpose is to provide an environment that will address the students' educational needs and prepare them for transition to other criterion settings when appropriate. A student may move between various classroom environments during the day to address different goals.

Throughout each day, students are exposed to many different teaching environments, even though the majority of their time is spent in their "home" classroom. Physical education classes are held in the multipurpose room, which serves as a gym, or outdoors. Art, music, snack time, and lunch are also all held in the multipurpose room. Depending on the student's social skills level, she or he may join other students from other classrooms for social skills group or counseling group sessions. The purpose is to provide opportunities for students to acquire skills in the most appropriate environments for teaching those skills. This promotes a smoother transition to criterion environments (e.g., when a student begins the transition process to a general education classroom).

Family Involvement

Parent involvement has always been an integral part of the program at the CUTE, and our staff continues to offer a menu of parent services. These can be grouped into the following eight major categories:

- routine home–school communication,
- involvement in goal selection and development of the IGP,
- parent education classes,
- daily homework assignments,
- progress meetings,
- consultation on specific home goals,
- parent counseling, and
- sibling support groups.

Despite the fact that parent services are increasingly mandated in the Individualized Education Programs (IEPs) that we receive from our students' sending school districts, we have seen a decline in the percentage of families that actively participate in these programs.

A number of factors appear to contribute to the underuse of our typical parent services. The first relates to economic factors. In upstate New York, recent economic decline has created financial hardship. These difficult economic times have made it necessary for many of our families to have two wage earners. With both parents working, there is little free time to participate in parent activities. Other families face different problems. With employment opportunities in some fields at a minimum, some of the parents in our program have found it necessary to seek employment outside of the local area. These families must cope with issues of separation and de facto single parenting. Other parents have returned to school to retool for new employment opportunities.

Another factor that has affected family participation in our array of parent services is the large catchment area served by the CUTE (a 100-

mile radius). This is the result of being located in a relatively rural area in which there are few programs for treating ASD. For parents in the farthest regions, factors such as travel time, poor driving conditions in the winter, and the cost of traveling (the result of higher gasoline prices) make participation very difficult.

A third factor relates to our admission practices. We do not screen parents for their ability or willingness to participate in our parent services. Some families participate in parent services to the fullest extent possible; others are apathetic and need our constant encouragement. Others decline even the simplest forms of communication such as phone calls and notes between school and home and have strained relations with the staff, despite our best efforts. In such cases, it is not unusual for social services to be involved, and, often, one or both parents are experiencing significant mental health problems.

Although we still aspire to provide parents with formal didactic instruction that involves education about ASD, instruction in behavior analysis methodology, consultation focused on the development and implementation of home programs, and in vivo supervision on home program implementation, we find that many parents are unable to participate in these programs.

Consistent with our commitment to families, we continuously evaluate parent use of services and generate alternative programs that might be more successful at meeting parent needs. The change in our conceptualization of how we provide services to parents has also been shaped by a shift in our thinking about how best to help our families.

We now address more explicitly the family context and how, through the selection of family-focused goals, we can have a more direct and significant impact on minimizing the effect of ASD on our families and, at the same time, effect positive behavior change for our children. The mechanism that drives the implementation of this conceptual shift is the Family Individualized Enhancement Plan, or FIEP. The FIEP, as might be expected, is similar to the IEP in that it identifies goals for family wellness and positive behavior change. Thus, we urge families to evaluate their specific needs and to generate both short-term and long-term goals that address these needs. Child-centered goals that emerge from this process focus on the reduction of maladaptive behaviors that prevent the family from more normative functioning (e.g., establishing and maintaining social networks, participating in community events, benefiting from respite services), improve social functioning, and increase the child's ability to perform activities of daily living at age-appropriate levels.

Family-centered goals that emerge from this process can include the following: increase communication about individual and family needs; prioritize needs within the family; and increase cooperation, with a focus on achieving goals that benefit the family.

Embracing this model of conceptualizing parent services has also had an impact on the assessment of parent needs. We now routinely ask parents to

- realistically appraise the amount of time they have to devote to conducting teaching programs at home;
- evaluate the availability of resources to determine who can help with program implementation or who can "man the fort" while parents are involved in direct teaching activities;
- evaluate their willingness to schedule activities at home (some parents report increased stress when they are asked to adhere to a specified schedule at home);
- consider having their child participate in school-based programs designed to decrease heightened emotional responses to essential activities such as doctor's visits, haircutting, washing and grooming, and toileting (i.e., desensitization and graded exposure procedures);
- realistically appraise their availability for participation in generalization procedures so that skills learned at school can be transferred to home and community settings;
- identify tasks that they would like their children to participate in to help them use their free time productively (e.g., independent play, daily homework, computer use); and
- identify tasks or chores that they would like to have their child participate in at home (e.g., helping prepare food, setting the table, making beds, sorting or putting away laundry, washing the car, weeding the garden); we have found that when children are actively involved in "helping" with chores that they can complete with relative ease, supervision issues are reduced.

The information obtained from these types of assessment questions helps us determine the breadth of services desired by a particular family and the best methods for providing those services, thus increasing family participation. We then help parents select from an array of participation options, as follows:

- participation in our standard parent education program;
- self-study: reading our parent manual independently, completing self-study questions, and meeting with staff for a tutorial on how to read and implement home programs;
- intermittent consultation versus intensive home teaching;
- selecting behaviors to target first in the school setting and then being involved in the process of generalizing skills to the home setting (e.g., complying with functional directions and directions to decrease safety risks, informing adults where they are going when they leave a room, remaining at the table for the duration of a meal, toilet training, improving behavior during transport to school, using toys appropriately and following a play schedule to occupy their free time, participating in age-appropriate chores, independently completing dressing and grooming skills, preparing simple food, using checklists and schedules to complete activities independently, participating in play groups or age-appropriate leisure activities with others, waiting skills, language skills to improve ability to communicate appropriately about wants and needs, recognizing physical boundaries and asking permission before using or taking the possessions of others, relaxation and coping skills to help manage affect, using picture schedules to anticipate a sequence of planned activities and to tolerate deviations from the plan); and
- generating home–school reinforcement programs.

The following case example demonstrates implementation of the principles discussed in this section.

Sam is a 6-year 5-month-old boy diagnosed with autism. The results of standardized testing indicated that he exhibited severe deficits in expressive and receptive language. His overall communication ability was estimated at the 1-year 6-month level, and his age equivalent on a measure of adaptive behavior was at the 1-year 8-month level. Sam lives with his biological parents and one older sibling. Both parents work; Sam's father works nights and sleeps during the day. Sam's mother provides most of the childcare. According to parental report, the family has a limited social network and financial constraints that prevent them from hiring additional help. Sam's mother reported that she has little time for herself and expressed a desire to spend more quality time alone with each of her children. One major issue that prevented her from "stealing" a few minutes for herself during routine activities was Sam's insatiable need for continuous maternal attention.

Discussions with Sam's mother generated the following goals:

- Increase the amount of time that Mom has to spend with each child alone.
- Increase the amount of time that Mom has to herself.
- Minimize interruptions from each child when Mom is busy (i.e., help them to wait appropriately).
- Teach Sam to occupy his free time when Mom is unavailable.

Prior to implementation of the home program, Sam was taught to follow a simple picture schedule at school and then at home. The home intervention involved construction of a "Mommy Schedule" that consisted of pictures of the two children and pictures of Mom. At specific time intervals on the schedule, Mom's picture was paired with Sam, his sister, or neither of the two (i.e., Mom alone). The presence of Mom's picture adjacent to one of the children indicated that for that time interval, Mom was scheduled to spend time with that child. The other child was expected to occupy him- or herself independently. When no child picture was paired with Mom, the interval was designated as her personal time.

In the initial stages of program implementation, Sam was taught how to interpret the schedule, and he was reinforced for minimal interruptions when Mom was "busy" (i.e., for 5-minute intervals). During this stage, Sam also received instruction in appropriate toy use both at school and at home.

Once criterion was reached on the first step, pictures were added to the schedule that depicted a choice of play activities that Sam could engage in while his mother was busy. During this phase of the program, Sam was reinforced for appropriate toy play and minimal interruptions.

Data collected by Sam's mother at home indicated that Sam learned to occupy his time appropriately when she was busy with his sister or personal or household tasks. Sam's mother also taught Sam's sister to follow the schedule, as she, too, had a high need for parent attention. Once Sam met criteria on the first two steps of the program, his mother opted to gradually increase the time interval for independent activity. In addition, she taught him to perform simple chores and added these to the picture schedule.

Transitions

Transition requires preparation. This is because when children move from one setting to another, they are confronted with numerous changes. All that had been familiar is novel—the physical setting; relationships with teachers and peers; and the demands placed on them for achievement, independence, self-regulation, and cooperation. Although transitions can be difficult for all of us, transitions are particularly difficult for children with ASD. The criteria used for diagnosing ASD alerts one to the fact that the transition from one educational setting to another is not likely going to be smooth. Children with ASD have marked impairment in communication and their ability for social interactions, and they tend to exhibit patterns of behavior that are restricted, repetitive, and stereotyped (i.e., preoccupation with one or more stereotyped and restricted patterns of interest that is abnormal either in intensity or focus and inflexible adherence to specific, nonfunctional routines or rituals). These characteristics have a significant impact on their interactions with familiar people in familiar environments and are likely to be exacerbated by the stress associated with change.

Most people respond best to change when they have time to prepare. The same is true for children with ASD, except that preparation is often a more lengthy process and actually begins at the outset of their educational careers.

When students enter the educational system, service providers should be thinking about immediate and short-term goals within the context of long-term goal planning. That is, the immediate goals addressed should serve as the foundation or building blocks that will be linked with other goals to create rich and elaborate functional skill repertoires over the course of the child's educational career. Brown, Nietupski, and Hamre-Nietupski's (1976) concept of the "criterion for ultimate functioning" is relevant here, as that concept should drive both short-term and long-term goal selection. These authors define the criterion of ultimate functioning as "an ever-changing, expanding, localized and personalized cluster of factors that each person must possess in order to function as productively and independently as possible in social, vocational, and domestically integrated, adult community environments" (p. 8). The implication is that IEPs should be continuous and should involve both longitudinal (i.e., sequencing of skills from the simple to the complex) and horizontal planning (i.e., cross-curriculum programming that explicitly creates opportunities for children to use skills within functional contexts). Continuity across IEP years advocates for a plan for systematically building skills, so that each successive year, the child's repertoire becomes richer, more complex, and more functional.

At each level of goal planning, consideration must be given to preparation for the next educational environment. Thus, it is important that assessments target not only a child's current level of functioning, but also the skills, behaviors, and knowledge that the child must possess in order to function satisfactorily in the next educational environment. These ecological assessments are a crucial component of assessment, as they identify goals that are essential for the transition process.

Given our mission as a short-term, intensive treatment program, explicitly designed to remediate the deficits that prevent children from participating in programs offered by their sending school districts, these issues are continuously at the forefront of our thinking about educational planning.

Using the GRIP as the starting point for goal selection (as described earlier), we help parents select broad goals that form the core of our planning for transition. As mentioned, the letters in the acronym stand for

Growth,

Relationships,

Independence, and

Participation.

Examples of the types of goals targeted in each of the GRIP components and annual goals associated with each for children transitioning from elementary to middle school are specified in Table 3.1.

Although the CUTE does not operate a continuum of educational classrooms within the community, the overall structure of our program was designed to address the issue of gradually shaping the skills required for transition. Throughout a child's tenure in the program, group size is systematically increased to approximate that of classrooms to which the child is likely to transition. The degree of structure is also varied to give the child experience with managing behavior, affect, and attention under varying levels of supervision and individual attention. Social contexts are varied to give the child ample opportunity to participate in small- and

Table 3.1
GRIP Components and Associated Annual Goals for Children
in Transition from Elementary to Middle School

GRIP Component	Possible Annual Goals
Growth	• Manages affect with minimal assistance from staff • Uses coping strategies to manage affect/behavior • Accepts consequences for behavior • Tolerates delays in reinforcement (i.e., manages behavior well with token reinforcement) • Begins to identify triggers for challenging behaviors
Relationships	• Competently states wants and needs • Works cooperatively with others on leisure or academic projects • Shares and participates in reciprocal, give-and-take exchanges. • Has basic awareness of how to initiate and terminate social interactions • Identifies problems when they occur and seeks assistance with resolution • Respects the possessions of others (asks to borrow and accepts restricted access)
Independence	• Follows a daily schedule • Travels in the school building with minimal supervision • Manages all self-care activities needed within the school • Manages personal possessions • Completes routine assignments with minimal assistance
Participation	• Follows classroom instructions • Makes transitions between activities easily · • Tolerates changes in daily schedule • Attends for the duration of instructional period • Occupies free time appropriately • Participates in community or extracurricular activities

large-group social situations that place different levels of demand on social participation, attention, cooperation, and interaction. Furthermore,
the staffing pattern at the CUTE provides our students with extensive
practice in working with multiple individuals to promote generalization.

Formal preparation for transition requires establishment of a cooperative working relationship with the administration and teaching staff of the
receiving school and the child's parents. The quality of the relationship
must exceed the buzzwords that are often used to define collaboration and
cooperation. In other words, it is not sufficient to agree to a cooperative
venture and then not provide the supports needed for follow-through. All
parties involved must be willing to communicate openly about resources
and biases and maintain an objective view of the process. It is also important that the participants not feel threatened or intimidated by the input
of others on the transition team, as those emotional reactions have a negative impact on the process. Additional assurances include the following:

- willingness of the receiving school to allocate teacher time
  for preparation,
- willingness of the school district to make special concessions
  for transportation during the transition period,
- willingness of teachers to work cooperatively with unit staff,
- commitment of the unit staff to provide follow-up consultation, and
- availability of support staff to address issues that arise both during
  and after completion of the transition process (counseling, continued involvement in social skills training, academic assistance, etc.).

We conceptualize the transition as a four-stage process that involves
planning and identification of need, development of the transition plan,
implementation, and follow-up:

Planning and Identification of Need
- Develop a transition team.
- Invite parents and staff (and the child, when appropriate) to visit
  possible classrooms for transition to determine best placement
  options.
- Update standardized assessments.
- Bring receiving school personnel who participate on the transition
  team to observe the child at the CUTE and learn about the child's
  strengths and weaknesses, as well as the programmatic supports
  that have been successful in eliciting and maintaining appropriate

behavior and expected classroom performance (e.g., reinforcement programs, schedules, social scripts, coping strategies, classroom accommodations).

• Send the transition team to observe in the receiving classroom and complete an ecological assessment.

• Meet with the receiving staff for the purpose of transmitting information about how best to modify the support structure to fit the new setting; specific procedures to manage problem behaviors and adapt them to the new setting; and development and implementation of procedures to enable parents to support transition.

Development of the Transition Plan

• Identify the tools and strategies that will transition with the child and train staff in their implementation, if needed.

• Formulate a schedule for transition. Ideally, the plan will allow for gradual integration into the new setting (e.g., part-time placement in the new environment, with additional time added contingent upon success).

Implementation of the Plan

• Continue to evaluate the transition schedule. If the child is adapting well to the new setting, the integration schedule could be expedited. If not, extra time at the CUTE may be needed.

• Communicate weekly about successes and areas of concern.

• Continue to work on areas that remain problematic at the CUTE.

To "follow up" means to provide ongoing consultation after integration is complete.

Integration

The successful integration of children into their district schools, community, and family lifestyle is of highest priority at the CUTE. So much so that each intake interview includes a discussion specific to the exit behaviors and skills required for transition to community-based services. The criteria that emerge from that discussion are then used to select goals that will form the exit criteria for the child.

With exit goals established, priority is placed from the start on the required prerequisite skills. Frequent monitoring, review, and fine-tuning of the child's progress toward these exit criteria are ongoing. Concurrently, generalization and maintenance of acquired objectives are conducted to ensure that the skill in the child's repertoire is not limited to the setting and requirements of the acquisition program, but is functional in those environments where the skill is to be used.

This approach requires high levels of individualization, which is seen in goal selection, program development, program implementation and monitoring, assessment, and evaluation. In addition, a child's daily and weekly schedules reflect the child's priority areas at any given time by specifically programming the *proportion* of the child's instructional time to be spent on each target area, not just the actual task being taught. In this way, the child receives the greatest amount of instruction on the specific goal area that is of highest priority at a given time.

When the final stages of the exit criteria are nearing completion, transition plans begin. Family, along with district and the CUTE staff, meet to determine the best transition placement and sequence. The family provides the goals they see as highest priority in written form (GRIP). The CUTE staff provides a progress review, with specific emphasis on the aspects of the child's skills that require continued emphasis. This typically includes setting specific recommendations such as staff-to-student ratio, level of structure, learning style, and support requirements. The district then identifies potential placements that include those characteristics. Through visits and discussions with potential staff, a site selection is made. When agreement is reached, the following activities and discussions begin:

- Transition (new) classroom staff are invited to the CUTE to observe the child and speak to the staff.
- CUTE staff members observe the transition classroom to identify areas that may need to be addressed or strengthened to maximize the child's success.

Next, the following questions are asked to allow for a successful transition plan:

- Will there be an aide in the transition classroom?
- Will that aide or other classroom staff need to be trained, and by whom (the CUTE or district)?
- Will there be need for CUTE consultation during or after transition?

Then, transition schedules are considered to optimize the child's transition from the CUTE to the child's new classroom. The following are a few transition schedule options:

- A full, complete transition occurs on a specified date.
- A partial-day transition, with gradual increases in the number of days and weeks or hours and days, may occur.
- A schedule that allows for a child's attendance at the transition classroom to be contingent on the child's specific prosocial behavior at the CUTE.

Multiple permutations of this result, and the flexibility inherent in these options, allow for modifications along the way. An advantage of the gradual transition is that both sites have contact with the child regularly, and communication between sites is frequent and based on current issues. Shaping of skills that are emerging, or functional use of acquired skills, can be addressed across settings. This time allows for the transition site to become familiar with the child while the CUTE is there for support and information.

Posttransition consultation is an ongoing part of the transition process at the CUTE, to assist in identifying and addressing problems before they influence the child's placement.

Social Skills: Essential for Integration

Many times, children with ASD who are socially motivated attempt to use acquired skills with typical peers and fail. Separate from other skill building areas, social skills require recognition of and reaction to multiple layers of subtle, often unspoken cues. Children with ASD have difficulty recognizing social innuendos, emotions, or intent as gradients and instead identify a situation dichotomously, based on a narrow range of criteria. Thus, for example, vulnerability and inappropriate responding result from a lack of ability to discriminate a sarcastic remark from a friendly one, because in both situations the speaker is smiling.

Social interactions are particularly difficult because they are typically

- unrehearsed,
- unpredictable,
- unstructured,

- unique, and
- require consistent reciprocity.

It is thus not possible to teach simple responses to attenuate these difficulties. In fact, the very nature of the components listed above conflict with simple response-based teaching.

Defining and Measuring Social Success

Unlike skill and fact acquisition, which can be identified as accurate or inaccurate, social success depends on the response of both social partners, not only the response of one child. If the social partner does not react favorably or reciprocally, it does not matter whether a child has responded exactly as taught or coached: The interaction was not successful.

What is a successful social interaction? Kennedy and Itkonen (1996) offered the following parameters of social interaction: proximity (physical closeness, technologies that allow two people to communicate [e.g., phone, e-mail]); mutually reinforcing events (seeing a game or movie, working together on an assignment, reinforcing to both children, cooperation is needed to receive the reinforcer); and reciprocity (exchange of reinforcers between two individuals).

Thus, the positive result of an interaction between one child and another depends on much more than the child's ability to perform the skill; the child's appropriate use of the skill; and the timing, fluency, variety, and spontaneous nature of the response.

If the peer accepts the response or interaction, it is a successful interaction. If not (no matter how well performed), the response or interaction was not successful in providing the child with social acceptance from a peer. In both definitions above, the emphasis is on the interaction outcome, not the individual. Thus, the criteria for a social interaction includes the child's response and the interaction of the social partners. Critical to accurate assessment and evaluation is measuring the outcome, not just the response.

What Typical Peers See

When assessing a child's ability to integrate with peers in social situations, a very important component is the behavior and reactions of the social peer. The examples below are taken from actual samples of integrated playgroups. Notice that many of the characteristics of ASD are easily identified by peers spontaneously.

- "Why does he only talk to you?"—reflects that children with ASD often do not address peers directly.
- "Hey, move over, you're squashing me!"—reflects that children with ASD often do not recognize personal boundaries.
- "Why do you always say/do that?"—reflects that children with ASD often have rigid, rote presentation styles and a narrow range of responses.
- "You talk weird, like my grandma"—reflects that children with ASD often show little or no use of typical "kid speak."
- "But we already played basketball 3 days in a row—it's my turn to pick the game"—reflects that children with ASD often do not engage in social reciprocity.
- "Look, let me show you again—do it like this"—reflects that children with ASD often do not imitate their peers.
- "What do you mean you like the spider? Good Charlotte is a music group"—reflects that children with ASD often do not have a common information base.

Recognition of the complexity of social interaction skills and the importance of the reaction of peers led to the development of a peer-based social skills group called the Buddy Group. This group pairs children with ASD with typical peers, which provides the following advantages:

- frequent contact and interaction with a peer group;
- for children, appropriate models and exposure to social interaction situations;
- for our staff, a reminder of typical child behavior; and
- the opportunity to observe a child's behavior relative to a peer group, for ongoing assessment on strengths and obstacles to achieve social success as determined by the peer group.

For a model of this type to work, however, the typical peers must be free to be a peer, not a counselor, babysitter, or teacher. The role of the buddies is defined explicitly:

- to **relate** to children as peers,
- to **model** appropriate social interactions and problem solving,

- to **emphasize** age-appropriate reactions to social situations, and
- to **encourage** the practice of new or alternate social skills by being supportive of the child's need for repeated exposure to social situations.

Within the Buddy Group, all skill-building procedures use a multilevel approach in which the focus is simultaneously and continually divided between learning and reacting to skill opportunities functionally. This process provides contextual and functional use of skills at each step, provides ongoing assessment of the effects of structured teaching on generalization of skills within the criterion environment, and allows for continual analysis of the quality of the children's reactions and interactions with particular attention to spontaneity and reactions of peers.

Critical Aspects of Social Integration

Critical aspects of social integration must be considered when implementing any social skills–building intervention, including a program such as Buddy Group. These critical aspects include, but are not limited to, discriminability, rote response versus skill acquisition, and goal selection. We start with the concept of discriminability, or the ability to discriminate. How much or how clearly do our children appear different or odd in comparison to the norm? The answer to this question provides a baseline or initial assessment of the skills that need to be taught. Response versus skill acquisition refers to the difference between learning a rote response to a social question, such as the responses taught via a social script, and learning the social skill of figuring out a personal, unscripted response. Although social scripts may provide a reasonable starting place, responses are often few, and variability is not addressed. The result is a limited repertoire that will most likely be overused by the child, resulting in the type of response that is immediately identified as atypical by peers. If the goal is to have the child become successful in interacting with peers, it is important to teach the skill of social conversation, not simply provide a rote response. An example of the difference between a rote response and social skill when a person asks, "How are you?" follows:

- Rote response (the same response is provided each time): "I'm fine," or, "I'm good."

- Skill (recognizing that the response varies based on the referent, having a repertoire of responses to draw upon, having the ability to interpret the actual meaning of the question): If the teacher asks, a possible reply might be, "I'm fine. Thank you." If a peer asks, a possible reply might be, "Not bad." Or, "I'm cool. You?"

The specific goals that are selected depend on the information gathered during the assessment of discriminability and response versus skill acquisition of specific social skills. Goals are tailored to the individual's learning style and current skill level. Emphasis is placed on age-appropriate normative peer group social skills.

Table 3.2 provides possible goals to teach for social skills success.

Preparation for Adult Years

Although the CUTE does not provide services for children beyond the age of 12 years, our program clearly prepares our students for the challenges of adolescence and adulthood. Consistent with our mission of short-term, intensive placement, our interventions tend to focus on behavioral and emotional development, social skills development, basic attentional skills, and communication skills. Although we emphasize daily living skills (i.e., mastery of age-appropriate skills in the areas of self-feeding, toileting, dressing, grooming, personal hygiene, cleanup, and simple meal preparation) within the school setting, we work exclusively on those types of goals only when the following conditions are present:

- when toileting is a high priority for parents, and progress has not been seen;
- when the child will be excluded from subsequent learning opportunities if toilet training is not completed;
- when behavioral issues prevent instruction in specific daily living skills.

In these cases, our staff takes on the challenge of resolving issues that interfere with the teaching process and then teach parents how to manage the interfering behavior and teach the new skills. Otherwise, we tend to invest our time educating parents about how to expand independent self-care repertoires and consulting on program development and

Table 3.2

Possible Goals To Teach for Social Skills Success

Goal	Explanation
Decrease overselectivity by increasing the number of variables used to increase social comprehension	One aspect of rigid, out-of-context responses may be the limited number of cues, stimuli, or conditions that define the social situation for the child.
Increase auditory awareness	Teach children to attend to the relevant instructions in contexts where the instruction is spontaneous and highly variable.
Decrease social anxiety and inappropriate behavior when entering a social situation	One of the more difficult skills for many people, children and adults, with and without disabilities, is entering a social situation that is already in progress.
Increase independence with the use of supplemental supports	While a child may be able to perform the skills of an activity, there may be social cues or unspoken expectations that need to be addressed.

implementation within the home setting. This is largely because we have so much to accomplish within such a short amount of time.

Conceptually, our method of preparing students for adulthood is closely related to Brown, Nietupski, and Hamre-Nietupski's (1976) concept of the criterion of ultimate functioning. That is, we anticipate the skills that our children will need to successfully navigate adulthood and then systematically select and choreograph goals (applying the principles of horizontal and longitudinal goal selection) to achieve mastery of skills. Of course, the skills selected are consistent with the child's age and developmental level. By providing our students with strong, flexible, and rich repertoires in the areas of behavioral and emotional control, social skills, and communication, we maximize the likelihood that our students will be successful in the educational environments that will elaborate upon the skills that they will need to be successful adults.

Table 3.3 provides an example of the types of goals we expect our children will need to succeed in adolescence and adulthood. We must temper the number and extent of the goals within the context of our short-term, intensive treatment model. Although communication skills are always addressed, the social aspects of communication expected at the adult level have been included within the social skills development domain.

Table 3.3

Types of Goals Needed To Succeed in Adolescence and Adulthood

Curriculum Domain or Curriculum Area	Goals To Be Addressed
Behavioral or emotional development	• Decreases fears related to people (interacting with unfamiliar persons)
	• Decreases fears related to performance and behavior (criticism, tests)
	• Decreases fears related to medical procedures (e.g., basic physical examination)
	• Accepts everyday variations in the environment
	• Recognizes when assistance is needed and asks for help appropriately
	• Maintains high levels of appropriate prosocial behavior to access reinforcers
	• Adheres to promise or commitment for extended time periods
	• Understands the relationships between behavior and consequences
	• Uses self-monitoring and self-control techniques independently
	• Retains and adheres to specific rules
	• Appropriately asserts self to persevere in completing activity or goal
	• Is able to wait appropriately to participate in preferred activity
Social skills development	• Greets and addresses others by name
	• Notices absence of others and inquires about their whereabouts
	• Works and plays cooperatively with others using common toys and materials
	• Negotiates turn-taking sequences with others
	• Participates in a plan for achieving a goal
	• Negotiates differences of opinion that arise in the process of goal attainment

(continues)

Table 3.3 *Continued.*

Types of Goals Needed To Succeed in Adolescence and Adulthood

Curriculum Domain or Curriculum Area	Goals To Be Addressed
Social skills (*continued*)	• Takes responsibility for own belongings with age-appropriate cues
	• Treats the property of others as if it were personal property
	• Takes responsibility for reporting damages to property and offers to make appropriate reparative efforts
	• Focuses attention in the general direction of the conversational partner for the duration of a short conversation
	• Makes comments and asks questions related to the content of partner's verbalizations during short interchanges
	• Looks at others to check emotional reactions
	• Visually and verbally checks another's reactions to behavior
	• Responds appropriately when an individual expresses an emotional state either verbally or nonverbally
	• Accepts constructive feedback from social partners
Preacademic/academic skills	• Maintains attention on preacademic/academic worksheets for a lesson period
	• Reestablishes attention after an interruption
	• Remains in the instructional work area

Outcome

The question of outcome is a complex one for our evolving field. In the past, typical measures of outcome for clinical populations have included employment status, independent living status, and school placement, as well as traditional standardized achievement and intellectual instruments. Formal research projects on outcome use a battery of assessments, and participants have a consistent "dose" of the intervention, typically measured by hours per week for a set number of months.

Now, as contrasted to the past, simple status measures, such as school placement after exiting our program, are difficult to interpret, as they interact with community resources and parental requests. Placement in a typical classroom no longer necessarily conveys information about a child's skill level. The range and diversity of school placements have increased dramatically over the past 15 years; thus, we are cautious in presenting outcome from a nonresearch, clinical program. In our program, children are accepted based on need and not fixed criteria (as in a research project), and periodic standardized assessment is based on school district initiative and requirements. Such assessment must be accomplished with normal school resources, as we are funded through public funds, not research funds. Further, given the large number of school districts we serve, from urban to very rural, and the fact that some districts have few placement options, while others have a moderate range, exit criteria become essentially case-by-case decisions. As stated, we are a short-term program, and our primary goal is to have the children return to their school districts, which vary widely in services offered.

With these caveats in place, we present information from the past 10 years of our school program in Table 3.4. The table shows that when they have acquired the appropriate skill level for the planned transition setting, approximately half of the children move to general classroom settings. There is an equal split between transition to mainstreaming and transition to self-contained settings. Interestingly, for the unplanned transitions, there is an equal (but small) split between placements in typical, mainstreaming, and home-schooling settings, with the majority of children placed in self-contained settings. The differences between those two categories of transition are thus clear: It is critical to actively teach skills to prepare the child for the intended transition setting. The last two categories of transition, lack of progress and the "aging out" of a child, reflect problems with acquisition rate, and, not surprisingly, the majority of children are placed in self-contained classrooms.

Knowing that children with ASD present with a wide range of symptoms, it is important to remember that a typical classroom setting may not be the least restrictive or most appropriate placement for educational purposes. As an example, upon entry to the CUTE, a transition to a self-contained classroom may be the appropriate goal for a child who has been unable to continue to participate in the services provided by his or her local school district's self-contained classroom options. This may be due to a variety of factors, such as intensity of behavior problems, severe difficulty in skill acquisition, and limited social and communication development.

Table 3.4
Parent and School District Agreed-Upon Transition Setting

Reason for Transition	General Classroom	Main-streaming	Self-Contained	Home School
Child skill level appropriate for planned transition	54%	23%	23%	0%
Unplanned transition (parent withdrawal)	14%	14%	57%	14%
Transition due to lack of child progress	0%	0%	100%	0%
Transition because child aged out	8%	17%	75%	0%

Given that we have a short-term program and given the difficulty of addressing these types of deficits, a specific transition goal for such a child may be appropriate in consideration of parental priorities and school district options.

These types of factors (parent priorities, school district placement options, child age, type and severity of behavior problems, skill deficits, and degree of difficulty of acquiring new skills) are difficult to parse out for determining a priori the appropriate transition setting. This is also true for evaluating outcome. Parsing the variables influencing outcome is beyond the scope of a nonresearch-based clinical setting. As mentioned, true outcome data can come only from well-controlled formal research studies.

However, with respect to a clinical setting, it is nearly impossible to determine which specific factor or combination of factors is the most influential in producing a positive outcome. We must bear in mind that the goal for the children and families we serve is to transition to their home school districts and to function within their communities, and that the specifics of that transition are different for each child. Because of the complex variables, it is important for clinical programs to use the results of well-conducted research studies in guiding their clinical practices.

Summary

The CUTE program at the ICD provides comprehensive services for children with an autism spectrum disorder, between the ages of 1 and 12 years. The CUTE is a behaviorally oriented, empirically based, school-age program that focuses on development of the child across all areas of development. Additionally, family involvement and participation is a key component of the program. Within the CUTE, numerous specialty services and interventions are implemented to promote the development of necessary skills. One of the most important emphases at the CUTE is to rapidly provide (i.e., an average of 2.5 years) each child with the skills needed to transition to his or her community setting.

References

American Psychiatric Association. (2000). *Diagnostic and statistical manual of mental disorders* (4th ed., text rev.). Arlington, VA: Author.

Brown, L., Nietupski, J., & Hamre-Nietupski, S. (1976). Criterion of ultimate functioning. In M. A. Thomas (Ed.), *Hey, don't forget about me!* Reston, VA: Council for Exceptional Children.

Kennedy, C. H., & Itkonen, T. (1996). Social relationships, influential variables, and change across the life span. In L. Koegel, R. Koegel, & G. Dunlap (Eds.), *Positive behavioral support: Including people with difficult behavior in the community*. Baltimore: Brookes.

Romanczyk, R. G., & Lockshin, S. B. (1984). Short-term, intensive services: The deficit oriented, focused model. In W. P. Christian, G. T. Hannah, & T. J. Glahn (Eds.), *Programming effective human services*. New York: Plenum Press.

Romanczyk, R. G., Lockshin, S. B., & Matey, L. (2000). *The Individualized Goal Selection Curriculum*. Apalachin, NY: CBT Associates.

Scheuermann, B., & Webber, J. (2002). *Autism: Teaching does make a difference*. Belmont, CA: Wadsworth Thomson Learning.

Schopler, E., Reichler, R. J., & Renner, B. R. (1995). *The Childhood Autism Rating Scale*. Los Angeles: Western Psychological Services.

White, S., Matey, L., Gillis, J., Kashinsky, W., & Romanczyk, R. G. (2003, October). *Organizational decision making regarding instructional strategies in behavioral intervention for children with autism*. Presented at the annual meeting of the New York State Association for Behavior Analysis, Saratoga Springs, NY.

The Douglass Developmental Disabilities Center

Jan S. Handleman, Sandra L. Harris,
Maria S. Arnold, Marlene Cohen, and Rita Gordon

T he Douglass Developmental Disabilities Center (DDDC) was founded in 1972 by the authority of the Board of Governors of Rutgers, the State University of New Jersey. The Douglass School, the original unit of our School Program, was approved as a college-operated program by the New Jersey State Department of Education that same year. The Douglass School has since become part of the School Program as the center has expanded steadily for 3 decades to include four divisions: Douglass Outreach, the Division of Adult and Transitional Services, the Division of Educational Services, and the Division of Research and Training.

From its inception, the Douglass School used the principles of applied behavior analysis (ABA) to serve a full range of students with autism. As the program developed, a specialized preschool component was created with three classes: a Prep class, providing exclusively one-to-one teaching; a Small Group class, offering instruction in pairs and small groups; and an integrated class, known as Small Wonders, where children with autism attend school with typically developing peers. A detailed description of the Douglass School preschool program is presented in Handleman, Harris, Arnold, and Gordon (2001). In addition to these classes, the Douglass School has an upper-school component for older students, ages 5 to 21 years, and that program is described in this chapter.

In order to meet the lifelong needs of a broad range of individuals with autism, we expanded the School Program to include the Elementary Satellite in 1994 and the Secondary Satellite in 1998. Classes in the satellites provide intensive one-to-one support for young children and adolescents with autism who pose learning and behavioral challenges, and specialized services for older adolescents with Asperger syndrome. Additional related educational services of school consultation, home intervention, and assessment provided to students ages 5 to 21 years by Douglass Outreach are also described in this chapter.

The Douglass School is located on the Douglass College Campus of Rutgers University, in New Brunswick, New Jersey. The Elementary and Secondary Satellites are in a separate building on the same campus. Tuition for all School Program classes is paid by local school districts. The children attend the School Program 5 days a week, 5½ hours a day, including a 7-week extended-year summer program, for a total school year of approximately 217 days.

Common Features

The center was established to meet the needs of people with autistic spectrum disorders (ASD), their families, and the professionals who serve them. As it is an ABA program, behavioral principles guide the primary technology for instruction. A broad range of methods are used, including discrete trial teaching, the verbal behavior classification system for language (Sundberg & Partington, 1998), fluency-based instruction, functional assessment, functional communication training, and the use of a variety of incidental and naturalistic strategies to promote learning that can be maintained and generalized to a variety of settings. We also recognize that it is our responsibility to work collaboratively with the families of the students and clients, and with the agencies that fund their education and treatment. As a university-based program, we have a commitment to the education of undergraduate and graduate students and to the dissemination of knowledge through research, training, and consultation services. The DDDC also provides information about ASD to the entire professional community and to the general public.

Population Served

Each program operated by the DDDC serves individuals with ASD. Classes in the School Program have limited enrollment based on State Department of Education regulations (i.e., six or seven children in a class, depending on age). Children are referred by local child study teams or parents, and applications are reviewed year-round; however, openings are typically for the beginning of the school year. Although the focus of this chapter is on the school-age child with autism, the DDDC currently provides services to children age 3 years to adult and is developing a program for children younger than 3 years.

Teaching and Administrative Staff

The executive director, a clinical psychologist and founder of the DDDC, and the director, who holds a doctorate in special education, address administrative issues and supervise the delivery of services and activities by all divisions. Each division director consults with the executive director and the director of the center in planning and implementing major policy decisions. The directors of the divisions collaborate with their assistant directors on daily operations and supervise all direct service staff. Currently, each director and assistant director is a board-certified behavior analyst (BCBA; in one case, BCABA [board certified associate behavior analyst]). Each division also has coordinators, who support the efforts of the senior administrators. The executive director, director, division directors, assistant directors, and the business manager constitute the Development Committee and meet monthly to review policies and procedures. In addition, division directors attend a monthly group meeting and individually meet with the director of the center to discuss its operations.

At the DDDC, the teaching staff is always learning. Teachers, speech therapists, home–school consultants, assistant teachers, program coordinators, consultant–tutors, and job coaches all participate in professional development activities. Initial staff training occurs each fall, with additional training provided through in-service activities and required attendance at yearly conferences and workshops, including the annual statewide conference on autism sponsored by the New Jersey Center for Outreach and Services for the Autism Community (COSAC). Many of the staff present workshops at an annual conference for educators that is sponsored by the DDDC. In addition, many have coauthored posters and research papers and have presented at local, state, and national conferences. The research active faculty at the DDDC, in conjunction with the Center for Applied Psychology and the Graduate School of Applied and Professional Psychology at Rutgers University, offer graduate-level ABA courses and continuing educational opportunities that are required for BCBA certification and New Jersey teacher certification.

The Division of Research and Training provides support to the center's many services. The staff of the Division of Research and Training includes three doctoral-level clinical psychologists and five graduate students from the Rutgers University Graduate School of Applied and Professional Psychology and the Graduate Program of the Department of Psychology. Two master's-level trainers with BCBA credentials are also on staff. The division provides behavioral consultation services, assistance with staff training, and opportunities to participate in applied research. Each division at the DDDC also has an office staff, and the programs share a full-time nurse and business manager.

The center's Division of Educational Services also provides the DDDC community with various supports for curriculum design and professional development. This division is responsible for the annual Professional Development Plan and coordinates all statewide testing for the School Program, including the Alternate Proficiency Assessment. Compliance with government regulations is also monitored by the Division of Educational Services.

As a university program, the DDDC provides practicum experiences to approximately 100 undergraduate students each year. These student interns are enrolled in a Fieldwork in Psychology course, work one day each week in a classroom, and attend one lecture a week. Every major in special education at Rutgers University is required to take the fieldwork course, and many psychology majors enroll, as well. In the classroom, the teachers closely supervise the students, and the weekly seminars provide supporting academic assignments.

Curriculum

All classes share the same DDDC behaviorally based, developmentally organized curriculum for students from preschool to young adult years. Individualized Educational Programs (IEPs), and quarterly progress reports at the center, are based on the *Individualized Goal Selection* (IGS) *Curriculum* (see Chapter 3; Romanczyk & Lockshin, 1982). The curriculum is language focused and includes the general areas of attention, speech–language, cognition, fine and gross motor abilities, socialization, self-help, and adaptive behavior. Each area also includes specific categories. For example, goals and objectives in the area of socialization focus on affect, peer and adult interaction, self-concept, and play; and those in the cognitive area emphasize readiness skills, early concepts, and reasoning. For older students, community participation, prevocational training, and work-oriented instruction are featured. Curriculum planning progresses from instruction in fundamental skills to training in all developmental areas. Initially, a child might be taught to request desired items, or to attend to and comply with small demands. As the student becomes more cooperative, instruction expands to language development, socialization, and adaptive skills. If a child encounters difficulty in any area of the curriculum, we assess the learner's skills to determine whether there are missing prerequisite skills that must be taught before moving ahead. The curriculum is also supported by a blend of commercial products and teacher-made materials from companies such as Communication Skills Builders, Crestwood, Ebsco Curriculum Materials, Flaghouse, and Lakeshore Learning Materials.

Nowhere is state-of-the-art ABA technology more essential than when addressing the behavioral challenges of some individuals with autism. Behavior management policies at the DDDC reflect a broad continuum of empirically based options, and our choices of specialized strategies are consistent with appropriate clinical standards as determined by the results of efficacy and effectiveness research. In addition, ongoing monitoring and evaluation of these policies ensure continual compliance with changing professional and legal guidelines.

Behavior management issues are considered within the context of a student's total educational program, and each program at the DDDC follows a strict protocol when designing and implementing behavioral interventions. Individual interventions are initially based on a thorough functional assessment and are selected from a hierarchy of strategies. Often these consist of environmental or teaching modifications. Next, the least intrusive but potentially effective procedure is paired with positive strategies, in order to guarantee a rich schedule of reinforcement and functional alternative responses. Behavioral consultation services are available to each program from the Division of Research and Training, and a clinical committee, composed of center administrators, meets regularly to review behavior management programs.

Integration and Transition

Experiences that promote mainstreaming and inclusion are important components of our School Program. An initial segregated experience for some students often increases their ability to benefit from subsequent integrated experiences. Activities are arranged with the goal of teaching the fundamental skills that will eventually promote responsiveness to normalized and community-based living.

Education during the elementary and secondary years includes many well-planned transitions for our students. For example, movement from the preschool program at the DDDC to the upper-school classes occurs through a systematic transition process. Subsequent progression through the elementary and secondary classes is also carefully planned, in order to promote maintenance and generalization of skills and to avoid regression.

The transition to a less specialized school also involves careful planning and the implementation of a systematic transition plan. Initially, the staff of the center work collaboratively with parents and school district representatives to identify a more normalized setting, whether a self-contained classroom or full- or part-time experiences in a general class. This effort involves the assessment of variables such as staff–student ratio, contingencies, school–life activities and classroom structure, and brief visits to the class by the student in order to confirm a student-placement match. Often, the transition process begins 12 months in advance of the change of placement and first includes further assessment of the requisite skills necessary for successful adjustment to the new class, and the subsequent remediation of skill deficiencies. Efforts to approximate final programming at the DDDC with the components of the new placement often conclude with increasing visits to the new class by the student and cooperative planning by current and new staff. Formal follow-up services are offered after graduation, as well as preparation of parents for the new placement. Often, the family supports found in a specialized setting are not available in more typical educational settings, and parents are encouraged to become more independent problem solvers, strong advocates for their children, and full participants in the educational process.

Parental and Family Involvement

Education at the DDDC is viewed as a collaborative process between the staff and the family. Staff members are encouraged to be sensitive to the needs of the family as a system, and families are invited to actively share in the partnership. After participating in parent training sessions when their child is first enrolled at the DDDC, a family receives visits approximately twice a month from a home–school consultant, who is responsible for providing ongoing support and training. Training sessions focus on the principles of ABA, and home visits provide an opportunity to elaborate on behavioral teaching and to tailor programming to the home setting. For example, the home–school consultant helps parents prioritize goals, develop skill acquisition programs, and address challenging behaviors. Parents are provided with numerous resources to enhance home programming, such as *Steps to Independence* (Baker & Brightman, 1997), *Children with Autism* (Powers, 2001), and *Behavioral Intervention for Young Children with Autism* (Maurice, Green, & Luce, 1996). The home–school consultants continue to provide training in ABA principles, as well as conducting generalization checks of mastered skills and providing the students with community-based learning experiences.

Weekly phone calls and exchanges of data, along with monthly clinics, provide the staff and families with many opportunities to meet, discuss, plan, and monitor a child's educational program. In addition to these efforts to promote active involvement by the staff and parents, the center also offers support services to families. For example, afternoon and evening discussion groups are scheduled to provide parents with the opportunity to share with one another their feelings about the special demands in their lives and their methods of coping with those demands. Similar age-appropriate sibling groups have also been a useful service. These voluntary groups provide a valuable source of support for families. Approximately four times a year, parents come together for an evening meeting to discuss topics of concern with an invited speaker. In addition, a yearly conference is sponsored by our parent–professional organization, DOORS (Douglass Organization for Occupational and Related Educational Services). These conferences involve nationally distinguished speakers and provide a source of income for the parent group, as well as informing parents of current developments in autism.

Research and Training

In order to ensure that the DDDC provides state-of-the-art services representing data-based "best clinical practice," we maintain ongoing research and training activities. These activities are the responsibility of the Division of Research and Training and are provided to all divisions of the center.

The Division of Research and Training is responsible for the development, implementation, and evaluation of the center's research. Undergraduate and graduate students in the division participate in ongoing studies comparing various educational interventions and behavior management techniques. Graduate students in the Clinical and School Psychology doctoral programs of the Graduate School of Applied and Professional Psychology and the Graduate School also receive intensive, individualized research experience as part of their training. All of our research is conducted within the guidelines of the Institutional Review Board of the Office of Research and Sponsored Programs at Rutgers University and includes fully informed parental consent.

The Division of Research and Training offers training services to new and continuing staff. A variety of training programs is offered throughout the year on a full range of topics relevant to autism and ABA. Two full-time staff trainers provide hands-on training, and each year several graduate students in psychology serve as behavioral consultants to program staff under the supervision of BCBAs. The division also provides community education opportunities that include an annual conference for public school employees, as well as a number of training institutes. The faculty offers a sequence of five courses in ABA that meet the academic requirement to sit for the BCBA examination and, in collaboration with the Douglass Outreach, provides mentorship and continuing education opportunities. In addition, the Research and Training staff, along with classroom teachers, teach the undergraduate interns the techniques and educational strategies used with students with autism.

The Douglass School

The Douglass School has four classes for school-age children. The level I, II, III, and IV classes each have six or seven students, grouped according to a 4-year age range, and have available a one-staff-to-two-student ratio. Certified special education teachers work closely together, and additional staff support is provided by paraprofessionals or university interns. The curriculum balances functional academics with prevocational training and community instruction, and culminates with work-oriented activities. The program provides transitional planning at all ages. For example, an 8-year-old boy may be placed in a special educational setting in his or her local school district, or a 21-year-old student may graduate to an adult program.

Population Served

During the 2004–2005 school year, there were 27 children in the upper-school program, 26 boys and 1 girl. Twenty-three children were Caucasian, 1 was Native American, and 3 were Asian. With the exception of 14 students, all had attended the preschool program at the DDDC and upon initial admission had been diagnosed as having a condition on the spectrum of autism, according to the *Diagnostic and Statistical Manual of Mental Disorders–Fourth Edition–Text Revision* (DSM–IV–TR; American Psychiatric Association, 2000). A speech and language assessment done at admissions, using the *Preschool Language Scale–Third Edition* (PLS–3; Zimmerman, Steiner, & Pond, 1992), resulted in scores ranging from 24 months to 4 years. Both the *Autism Diagnostic Interview–Revised* (ADI–R; Lord, Rutter, & LeCouteur, 1994) and the *Autism Diagnostic Observation Schedule* (ADOS; Lord, Rutter, DiLavore, & Risi, 2001) were added to the preschool intake in the past few years, and those scores are available for some of the younger upper-school students.

Many of the children in the upper-school classes are graduates of the preschool program who continue to require highly specialized supports. Some youngsters also remain at the center until there are appropriate programs in their local school districts. For example, during the 2003–2004 school year, two children participated in a highly systematic transition process, spending increasing amounts of time in local elementary schools.

Assessment Procedures

Children who enter the upper school from the preschool have already undergone an extensive evaluation at the time of admission to the preschool. On those less frequent occasions when school-age children enter the upper-school program directly, they typically have already received an extended battery of tests from their school, child study team, and consultants. As a result, our intake assessment with these youngsters focuses primarily on an assessment of their readiness for our curriculum and of their goodness of fit with our available openings. That includes observation of the child in the classroom being considered and may include videotapes of the child in other settings and visits to the child's current placement. During the first few weeks of school, a newly admitted child is evaluated by the classroom teacher on all areas of the DDDC curriculum. Functional behavioral assessments and preference assessments are conducted as needed to develop the child's individual educational program. Results from these initial assessments provide a profile of a child's strengths and challenges and become a baseline from which to measure progress. In addition, mastery, maintenance, and generalization data are collected and charted on a daily, weekly, and quarterly basis to monitor growth and fine-tune programming.

Regularly scheduled clinics provide an additional opportunity to review goals and objectives and to monitor programming. Attended by the supervisor, teacher, speech–language pathologist, home–school consultant, and parent, these meetings allow members of the planning team to remain current regarding educational programs, to fine-tune interventions, and to ensure consistency between school and home programming. At many meetings, the child is also present in order to provide an opportunity to introduce new programs and model changes in current programming. Regular phone calls and exchange of data between school and home also contribute to consistency of programming.

Teaching and Administrative Staff

In addition to the director and assistant director of the Douglass School, a coordinator of curriculum and instruction provides support to the upper-school classes. Each classroom is staffed by a certified special education teacher and at least three assistant teachers, as well as at least one undergraduate intern. Additional paraprofessional staff members are available, depending on the individual needs of the students. For example, if a student is presenting a particularly challenging behavior, an additional assistant teacher might be assigned on a temporary basis. For Levels I and II, a minimum of a one-staff-to-two-student ratio is maintained, while the goal for Levels III and IV is to increase the ratio in order to promote small-group programming. Supplemental staff members are also available for Levels III and IV, in order to provide supervision during community events such as job sampling and training. Individual teaching can be provided for any student if a need is determined.

Teachers are responsible for assessing students' progress, coordinating the development of educational plans with parents and child study teams, designing and implementing educational programs, organizing class and staff schedules, training fieldwork interns, and collaborating with parents and other professionals. In addition, each class is supported by a half-time speech–language pathologist who provides individual and small group instruction, as well as consultation services to classroom teachers, including augmentative systems of communication, when used. An adaptive physical educational teacher also instructs the students each week and serves as a liaison to consulting professionals such as occupational and physical therapists.

In order to provide support beyond the school day, our home programming staff assists teachers and parents in promoting the generalization and maintenance of learning to the home and the community. These home–school consultants help teachers identify goals for home and community programming and work with families to establish priorities and develop programs addressing self-help skills and challenging behaviors. Home–school consultants typically visit each home approximately twice a month, and they may also provide crisis intervention if needed. In addition, home–school consultants may assist parents in obtaining services such as respite care from local and state agencies.

The educational staff of the center is regularly supervised to ensure that the students are receiving the best available clinical practices. Classroom teachers provide supervision for assistant teachers and student interns through daily meetings and classroom observation. A certified supervisor of education meets with new teachers twice a month and more experienced teachers once a month to discuss all activities of the teacher, including the development of educational plans and the monitoring of student progress. This supervisor conducts monthly classroom observations, reviews program books, and attends students' clinics. Both formative and evaluative oral and written feedback is provided to the teachers by the supervisor. Similar supervision is provided for speech–language pathologists and home–school consultants.

The Curriculum

Individual goals are determined according to the results of formal and informal assessment measures (e.g., *Assessment of Basic Language and Learning Skills,* ABLLS; Partington & Sundberg, 1998); classroom observations; and input from parents, child study teams, and support staff. Instructional experiences are then designed to capitalize on a student's strengths while addressing weaker areas of development. A broad range of

ABA techniques is used in programming at the DDDC. For example, if a child entered the upper school without a capacity to make spontaneous requests, one of our initial programs would be mand training to establish this vital skill, and other natural environment training methods for teaching verbal behavior would follow (Sundberg & Partington, 1998). Discrete trial instruction is used to help a student learn foundational skills such as tacting (naming). As the child shows initial skill acquisition, ongoing work promotes generalization outside of the classroom. Fluency-based instruction is implemented to increase the ease and comfort with performing a motor task, as well as some verbal and social behaviors. Antecedents of behaviors are considered in the design of behavior management programs. This blend of more traditional developmental programming with the innovative verbal behavior techniques allows the staff to individualize a student's program.

Meeting the needs of the older student is accomplished by focusing the curriculum on functional and independent behavior. Maintaining an emphasis on functional programming that is attuned to the student's needs and abilities provides the learner with a repertoire of behaviors to use in a variety of settings, including the home and community. As the student gets older, providing prevocational and work-oriented experiences begins the preparation for the adult years. Use of a photographic or written activity schedule allows all programming to be linked in an effective way that promotes independent functioning.

The involvement of the speech–language pathologist provides additional support for the design and implementation of programs in the area of communication. In addition to individual sessions, the speech–language pathologists spend time in each classroom. They provide integrated speech services to support language instruction in a functional context, especially in the community. This integrated approach enhances coordination of programming by allowing the teacher and assistant teacher to observe instructional strategies and to collaborate in planning.

Integration and Transition

Students in the upper school have the opportunity to participate in weekly community activities. Whether going to a restaurant for lunch, shopping for food to make lunch, or working at a local store, these experiences are systematically increased as the student progresses through the program. For example, students in Level IV are in the community at least three times a week. The opportunity to interact with typical peers is also a focus in the upper school. An optional after-school program provides many of the children with weekly social and recreational activities. As the students grow older, the Rutgers University's undergraduate students also provide a source of normalized interactions with same-age peers.

For the older student, planning for the transition to a community-based adult program begins early. For example, student-centered planning guides home and community programming in the Level I class. This emphasis on the individual interests and abilities of the student continues throughout the older classes and expands to planning for prevocational and work-oriented activities. The joint efforts of the classroom teacher and the home–school consultant focus on collaboration with State of New Jersey agencies and parents to identify potential programs after graduation. If a placement can be confirmed sufficiently in advance of graduation, a systematic transition plan is initiated. Requisite skills are assessed, and programming is included to target deficient areas. When possible, similar experiences in the community or part-time participation in the new program are provided and are increased as the student approaches graduation.

Parental and Family Involvement

All programs at the DDDC promote a full partnership between the families and the professionals who serve them. Parents are encouraged to be equal collaborators in their child's education at all levels, including curriculum planning and home programming. In addition to daily notes and weekly phone contacts, parents are invited to attend regular "clinics" with the educational team, in order to fine-tune programming and demonstrate new teaching strategies. Parents are also expected to participate in training sessions on ABA, focusing on teaching skills, managing behavior, and increasing communication. In addition, support groups for family members, including parents, siblings, and grandparents, are provided to the families by DDDC staff members.

Outcome

The goal of the upper-school program is to prepare students for independent, productive living in the least restrictive environment. The challenge for many of our older students is finding appropriate placements for them as they approach adulthood. Community resources for adults with autism are much less adequate than those for school-age students, and many families find they must compromise in accepting placements on behalf of their young adult. The contrasts across the age span are striking. For the preschooler with autism, community options have grown considerably in recent decades, thus providing many more opportunities for transitions than for older students. For example, since 1994 among the 39 students who completed the preschool program, only 12 have continued in the upper-school program. In the last 10 years, 9 students graduated from the upper-school program and were admitted to the center's adult program. One graduate now has a full-time job at a local restaurant, and 8 are working at least 3 days a week in local businesses. Since 1994, 2 students in the upper school transitioned to public school settings, and 4 were enrolled in other specialized schools. One student was admitted to a residential program.

Elementary Satellite of the School Program

The Elementary Satellite includes two classes that provide one-to-one treatment for young children whose parents or school district wishes to offer the benefits of a highly individualized home-based program but are unable to accommodate that goal at home or within the district. For example, a family in which both parents are employed may elect to have their child's initial instruction provided in one of the satellite classes; or a small school district that does not have the resources, or demand, to offer a full spectrum of services for children with autism may elect a short-term placement for an older child. For these children, the Elementary Satellite becomes a "home away from home." The children range in age from 5 to 9 years and are typically placed with us for 2 to 5 years before being moved into another setting. Most of these children are at the young elementary level. To be accepted into the satellite classes, the child must have a diagnosis on the autism spectrum including autistic disorder, PDD-NOS, or Asperger syndrome. In the past 5 years, all 15 of the school-age children served had a diagnosis of autistic disorder.

The instructional staff includes a certified teacher who oversees each child's programming and assistant teachers who provide a one-to-one instructional ratio, as well as a lead teacher who is responsible for clinical oversight and training. Speech therapy and adaptive physical education are also provided. During the 2004–2005 school year, there were four New Jersey–certified teachers, four full-time teaching assistants, four part-time teaching assistants, two speech–language pathologists, two administrative support staff, and a school nurse and an adaptive physical education teacher who are shared with the other classes of the School Program. The director of the satellite and one teacher have their BCBA, and the assistant director and another teacher have their BCABA. As of the winter of 2004, another three staff members were enrolled in courses for BCBA certification. Classes in the Elementary Satellite use the DDDC curriculum and feature a verbal behavior approach to organizing language instruction (Sundberg & Partington, 1998), discrete trial instruction for material that requires repeated rehearsal, incidental teaching to support the naturalistic use of language and social skills, and fluency-based instruction (Binder, 1996) to ensure the smooth, integrated use of skills. Shortly after a child enters the program, skill level is assessed using the *Assessment of Basic Language and Learning Skills* (ABLLS; Partington & Sundberg, 1998), the *Preschool Language Scale* (PLS; Zimmerman, Steiner, & Pond, 1992), the *Pace and Fisher Preference Assessment* (Fisher et al., 1992; Pace, Ivancic, Edwards, Iwata, & Page, 1985), and the DDDC Curriculum Checklist. The child's progress through the curriculum is monitored by the director, the lead teacher, the classroom teacher, and the speech–language pathologist at regular weekly meetings, as well as at monthly clinics attended by both the educational staff and the parents.

Because placements in the Elementary Satellite classes are viewed as short term and typically do not last longer than 4 to 5 years, there is an emphasis on transition planning for movement to the next, less restrictive setting. We also work to ensure that the child can employ newly learned skills in other important environments, including home and community. Parents are provided with home consultation services that include behavioral parent training and consultation to develop programs for use at home as well as ensure a close integration with school programming. In the last 5 years, four children have returned to their local public school districts, two have entered the DDDC upper-school program, and one has enrolled in a private school for children with a range of disabilities.

Secondary Satellite of the School Program

The DDDC Secondary Satellite includes a specialized service for youths with autism age 14 years or older who pose very substantial behavior problems that preclude their being placed in other, less restrictive settings. These young people all have significant, long-standing challenging behaviors such as aggression or self-injury and have not responded favorably to previous treatment efforts. Many, but not all, have mental retardation along with a diagnosis of autistic disorder. We also serve students with average or better intellectual functioning and a diagnosis of autistic disorder or Asperger syndrome who have engaged in seriously maladaptive behavior. These students have the opportunity to work toward their GED. Both of these classes share the supports and services of the DDDC. The goal of the Secondary Satellite is to prepare students to live and work in the community. Some students may return to a less restrictive school placement after one or more years in the program, and others may move from the school program to our adult services program. Since the opening of our first class in 1998, the Secondary Satellite has served 11 students ranging in age from 14 to 21 years. Among these students, 3 have been discharged to the Douglass Adult Program and are training for a community job placement. Currently, 6 students are being served at the Secondary Satellite.

In order to address the very serious behavior problems of the students, the Secondary Satellite relies heavily on the use of functional assessment and analysis to identify significant events that may be related to the occurrence of the challenging behavior. In managing challenging behaviors, we place a primary emphasis on antecedent strategies such as teaching alternative responses, altering environmental events, and adapting our teaching methods to support the student's skill acquisition. Consequent strategies are used sparingly and only after full peer review and informed family consent. In addition, prior to their implementation there must be a plan for how to eliminate these interventions.

Secondary Satellite staff complete a comprehensive analysis and develop an intervention plan that allows the student to ultimately control his or her own behavior. Many components of the program contribute to the effectiveness of our methods. For example, the class size is small (seven students); there is a rich staff-to-student ratio; the administration is highly supportive; and the staff is provided with ongoing, comprehensive, performance-based training. Typically, it takes 6 to 8 months to complete an accurate functional assessment and to develop an intervention plan that addresses all functions of the challenging behavior, considers skill acquisition of socially acceptable behavior, and is supported by data analysis.

Following the assessment process, an intensive effort is made to teach alternative responses and to build an adaptive repertoire that will enable students to access reinforcement in a variety of functional ways. Many of the students have had little formal teaching or effective behavioral intervention before coming to the Secondary Satellite. Their lack of success in other placements often has been due to their behaviors serving as either an escape or an avoidance function that kept teachers from making instructional demands, or as an attention-seeking function, by which the student accessed a high level of reinforcement for engaging in challenging behavior. Initially, educational programming is focused on functional assessment of behavior and establishing a positive educational environment where challenging behaviors are minimized and positive skill development is promoted.

Helping students to control their own behavior is not without challenges. One challenge is to demonstrate to staff through documentation that when problem behavior occurs with regularity, the environment is providing cues that reinforcement is available (e.g., escape, avoidance, attention), and that the consequences of engaging in the behavior provide the student with access to that reinforcement. Often, well-meaning staff members who are committed to their jobs do not want to believe that they are playing a part in this learning paradigm—Why would I set up the environment in such a way as to trigger an aggressive episode that might result in injury to others or myself? They may not understand the possible risk of increasing attention by calling for help, or facilitating escape behavior by offering a break in the middle of an instructional session. Learning not to provide these cues initially seems counterintuitive, but with careful planning and the use of less obvious, yet systematic strategies, challenging behavior can usually be reduced, and an emphasis can be placed on the development of replacement skills. We then face the challenge of determining a replacement skill that is of equal, or preferably less, response effort and is as efficient as the behavior targeted for reduction.

Each student is assessed in order to identify those areas of the center's curriculum to target for instruction. Our goals include increasing students' ability to exercise self-control; increasing their rate of production in work-related, recreational, and academic skills; improving their social skills; and decreasing their specific challenging behaviors across a full range of life settings. To achieve the goal of improved work and recreational "productivity," the Secondary Satellite makes extensive use of fluency training (Binder, 1996), in which students are taught to do familiar tasks with increasing speed and smooth integration. Preliminary data indicate that decreasing response effort of a skill is positively correlated with a reduction in challenging behavior. These students have a background of repeated failures in previous educational settings, and the staff members in the Secondary Satellite are committed to ensuring that these young people understand that they are safe, competent, and respected.

The director and assistant director of the Secondary Satellite, who are board-certified behavior analysts, provide daily administrative support to the class, which is staffed with a program coordinator, a teacher, and six assistant teachers. The staff's commitment, persistence, and courage serve as personal and professional assets that are combined with the comprehensive training that is provided by the center's Division of Research and Training. Both the director and the assistant director are available to support the staff (particularly during the first few months a new student is enrolled in our program) by being involved in the implementation of emergency procedures, restoration of the environment, and keeping the door open for discussion of staff concerns. Staff members understand that they are not required to do anything that the administrators are unable or unwilling to do themselves. This support has tremendous impact on staff morale.

The effectiveness of the Secondary Satellite program can currently be assessed in terms of the impact on the quality of life of our students. For example, one student, who once caused serious staff injuries that required medical attention, is now able to go into the community on a regular basis to shop for food, eat at a fast-food restaurant, and use the pool at the campus recreational center. Another student, who smeared feces on school property and on staff members, and who urinated on the floor and on others, is now able to go to the shore for a recreational experience, to take staff and student orders for Chinese food, and to go into the community to purchase the food. The focus of the field of applied behavior analysis is to make a meaningful change in socially significant behavior. We are committed to this philosophy in serving this unique group of students.

In September of 2004, we expanded the Secondary Satellite to serve students with average or better intellectual functioning and a diagnosis of autistic disorder or Asperger syndrome who engage in maladaptive behavior that excludes them from instruction in less restrictive settings. This new high school class is designed to provide intensive services to students who are not thriving in traditional educational settings. The class is staffed with two certified teachers, for up to five students, in order to provide the monitoring and support necessary for the students to pursue educational interests and community experiences. The curriculum is designed to provide the students with the supports that will enable them to succeed in adult life. Goals for the students include achievement of the academic requirements for a high school diploma or a GED, improvement in standardized test-taking skills, successful access of community resources, securing and maintaining a part-time job, and transitioning to a postsecondary education program.

Related Educational Services Provided by Douglass Outreach

Douglass Outreach serves school-age children with autism in three venues: consultation to local school districts regarding individual student programs or entire classes, after-school home-based instruction, and providing psychological and educational planning assessments to the autism community.

School Consultations

As of September 2004, Douglass Outreach was consulting to 60 school programs. While the majority of schools served are primarily public schools, occasionally private programs and agencies will apply. In addition to the director and assistant director, who hold BCBA and BCABA credentials, respectively, there are five other full-time consultants. Currently, one consultant has a PhD in clinical psychology, three are certified teachers of the handicapped, two have a master's degree in special education, one is a BCABA, one is enrolled in a graduate program leading to Learning Disabilities Teacher Consultant certification, and four are enrolled in courses leading to a BCBA or BCABA. One consultant is also a certified trainer in Picture Exchange Communication (Frost & Bondy, 1994).

Consultation to school programs involves a variety of activities that are determined by the needs of a particular school district or school program. For example, one school district may have only one child with autism, whereas another might have one or even numerous classes for children with autism. Representatives from the school will first meet with our staff to assess the need for services and to design a consultation plan, which typically includes an evaluation of the program, training for the staff in the principles of ABA, clinical oversight, curriculum design, IEP and behavioral intervention plan development, and parent training. Table 4.1 presents the range of topics that are typically covered during school consultations.

Each program is assigned one consultant who stays with the program for the school year. A typical consultation schedule begins with weekly, full-day visits for the first 3 to 4 months, then decreases to every other week for the next 4 months, and then to one monthly visit for the remainder of the year. Some 12-month programs also have us consult during the summer months. In addition, during the summer, staff training, workshops, and in-service sessions are provided for returning school programs.

School consultations are carefully monitored. For example, written consultation notes are sent to each program within 1 to 2 weeks of the visit. Copies of the notes are also given to the director. All consultants meet individually with the director each month for individual supervision, as well as meeting in a group. Consultants are also required to attend continuing education courses and are encouraged to present at conferences.

Home-Based Services

Douglass Outreach provides home-based services for children across the age spectrum. Although we are the primary service provider for many preschool-age children, for school-age children home-based services are typically offered after the child's regular school day has ended and are intended to supplement the child's school program. We make every effort to ensure that we do not duplicate or conflict with the services that are being delivered by the child's school, but rather intend the program as one that complements the school's efforts.

Our home-based services include training parents and other teaching staff in the ABA methods needed to work with the child, assessing the child's skills, helping the family develop goals, and providing teaching programs to meet those goals. We offer ongoing consultation to the parents as they and their team work with the child. We aim to make the parents integral to the teaching and supervision effort so that they

Table 4.1

Topics Covered During School Consultations

Academic skill development	Educational programs
Activity schedules	Fluency-based instruction
Behavior support plans	Functional behavioral assessment
Behavioral objectives	Natural environment teaching
Challenging behaviors	Preference assessments
Communication	Schedules of reinforcement
Data collection	Token systems
Discrete trial instruction	Verbal behavior
Educational assessments	

can become proficient in managing their child's ongoing home instruction with backup from our professional staff. Some families hire Douglass Outreach staff to become team members teaching their child; others recruit extended family members and community volunteers, or pay college students to serve as team members. During the initial stages of training, every team member is observed and supervised by a Douglass Outreach staff member each week and then on a monthly basis. When new team members are added following this initial intensive training, outreach staff will again provide that level of intensive supervision if needed.

Several levels of staff are involved in providing home-based services. The outreach coordinator is a senior staff member with extensive experience in working with people with autism. He or she provides the initial training that helps the family and other team members learn the requisite skills in applied behavior analysis. The coordinator provides ongoing assessment of the child's progress, develops training goals, and monitors the child's progress to ensure that the programming is on track and meeting the child's needs. Outreach consultants are individuals with considerable experience who are able to assume a fair amount of independence in their daily activities. The consultants work directly with the child, implementing programs developed by the outreach coordinator. Undergraduate tutors also work directly with the children, carrying out programs created by the outreach coordinator. However, unlike outreach consultants, they are closely supervised by the coordinator.

Assessment Services

Parents of children with autism are often interested in having an initial educational assessment of their child for planning purposes. In some cases, they also wish to establish an ongoing relationship with a team of professionals who can do periodic reevaluations of their child to track progress and identify areas of continuing need. The Outreach Assessment Services serve these families. The members of the team are all experienced in the evaluation of people with autism and have appropriate credentials to document their expertise.

The majority of children seen for evaluation at Douglass Outreach have had a preliminary diagnosis on the autism spectrum. Although we typically confirm that diagnosis, our function is also to move beyond diagnosis to address educational planning, including helping parents find an appropriate placement and making recommendations for the IEP. A typical full assessment includes a psychological evaluation that addresses diagnosis using the *Autism Diagnostic Interview–Revised* (Lord, Rutter, & LeCouteur, 1994), the *Autism Diagnostic Observation Schedule* (Lord, Rutter, DiLavore, & Risi, 2001), cognitive abilities as reflected in performance on the *Stanford–Binet* (Roid, 2003; Thorndike, Hagen, & Sattler, 1986), and an assessment of adaptive functioning on the *Vineland Adaptive Behavior Scales* (Sparrow, Balla, & Cicchetti, 1984). A speech and language evaluation includes the *Preschool Language Scale* (Zimmerman et al., 1992), *Evaluation of Acquired Skills in Communication* (EASIC; Riley, 1991), and the *Test of Pragmatic Language* (TOPL; Phelps-Terasaki & Phelps-Gunn, 1992). The child's educational evaluation, done by a learning consultant, may employ a standardized measure such as the *Autism Screening for Individual Educational Planning* (ASIEP; Krug, Arick, & Almond, 1993) or may rely on observation of the child's performance on a variety of school-related activities that are precursor skills for more advanced school performance. Sometimes that involves observation of the child in his or her current educational setting.

A written report is provided, as well as a conference to discuss the results and consider in detail with the parents and school district the implications of the assessment findings for the child's educational needs. The assessment team makes recommendations concerning appropriate school placement, the kinds of special supports the child needs, and strengths and needs that must be considered in creating the child's IEP. Such questions as the staffing ratio, extent of integration with typical peers, role of the family in the child's home-based learning, and short-term and long-term educational goals are all topics of potential concern at such a meeting.

In addition to these assessments, the outreach staff provide functional behavioral assessment services for families and schools that have concerns about significant behavior problems in children with autism. Center staff members with a background in psychology or special education and extensive experience in conducting functional assessments provide these services, which include an initial in-depth interview and direct observation of the child. The detailed interview with the parents and teacher, and when possible the child, allows the clinician to develop a working definition of the target behavior, discuss potential antecedents and consequences of the behavior from the perspective of the parents and teacher, do an ecological assessment of the settings where the child exhibits the behavior, and generate a working hypothesis about the functions of the behavior.

Following the interview and hypothesis-generating phase, one or more behavioral observation sessions are conducted at the child's home or school, with testing of the hypotheses as necessary to determine what specific factors are related to the child's behavior. A written report summarizing the findings and making recommendations for treatment is provided. If the family or school personnel wish, a Behavior Support Plan can be developed and implemented under our guidance.

Summary

The Douglass Developmental Disabilities Center has been serving school-age children with autism and their families since 1972. Over the course of the last 3 decades, we have developed a range of services, including home-, school-, and center-based programs. Each program type has in common rich resources that include trained and credentialed staff, empirically supported methods, transitional planning, and parent involvement. Although the relative benefits of any particular program type remain unclear, we are just beginning to understand how to match a student's specific learning characteristics with a program option. Regardless of setting, we find that the majority of our students make meaningful progress.

References

American Psychiatric Association. (2000). *Diagnostic and statistical manual of mental disorders* (4th ed., text rev.). Washington, DC: Author.

Baker, B. L., & Brightman, A. J. (1997). *Steps to independence.* Baltimore: Brookes.

Binder, C. (1996). Behavioral fluency: Evolution of a new paradigm. *Behavior Analyst, 19,* 163–197.

Fisher, W., Piazza, C. C., Bowman, L. G., Hagopian, L. P., Owens, J. C., & Slevin, I. (1992). A comparison of two approaches for identifying reinforcers for persons with severe and profound disabilities. *Journal of Applied Behavior Analysis, 25*(2), 491–498.

Frost, L., & Bondy, A. (1994). *The picture exchange communication system.* Cherry Hill, NJ: Pyramid Educational Consultants.

Handleman, J. S., Harris, S. L., Arnold, M. S., & Gordon, R. F. (2001). In J. Handleman & S. Harris (Eds.), *Preschool educational programs for children with autism.* Austin, TX: PRO-ED.

Krug, D., Arick, J., & Almond, M. (1993). *Autism Screening Instrument for Educational Planning–Second Edition* (ASIEP–2). Austin, TX: PRO-ED.

Lord, C., Rutter, M., DiLavore, P. C., & Risi, S. (2001). *Autism Diagnostic Observation Schedule.* Los Angeles: Western Psychological Services.

Lord, C., Rutter, M., & LeCouteur, A. (1994). Autism Diagnostic Interview–Revised: A revised version of a diagnostic interview for caregivers of individuals with possible pervasive developmental disorders. *Journal of Autism and Developmental Disorders, 24,* 659–685.

Maurice, C., Green, G., & Luce, S. C. (Eds.). (1996). *Behavioral intervention for young children with autism.* Austin, TX: PRO-ED.

Pace, G. M., Ivancic, M. T., Edwards, G. L., Iwata, B. A., & Page, T. J. (1985). Stimulus preference and reinforcer value with profound retarded individuals. *Journal of Applied Behavior Analysis, 18*(3), 249–255.

Partington, J. W., & Sundberg, M. L. (1998). *The assessment of basic language and learning skills.* Pleasant Hill, CA: Behavior Analysts.

Phelps-Terasaki, D., & Phelps-Gunn, R. (1992). *Test of Pragmatic Language.* San Antonio, TX: Psychological Corp.

Powers, M. D. (Ed.). (2001). *Children with autism. A parents' guide.* Bethesda, MD: Woodbine House.

Riley, A. M. (1991). *Evaluating Acquired Skills in Communication.* Austin, TX: PRO-ED.

Roid, G. H. (2003). *Stanford–Binet Intelligence Scales–Fifth Edition.* Itasca, IL: Riverside.

Romanczyk, R., & Lockshin, S. (1982). *The Individualized Goal Selection Curriculum.* Vestal, NY: Clinical Behavior Therapy Associates.

Sparrow, S. S., Balla, D. A., & Cicchetti, D. V. (1984). *The Vineland Adaptive Behavior Scales.* Circle Pines, MN: American Guidance Service.

Sundberg, M. L., & Partington, J. W. (1998). *Teaching language to children with autism and other developmental disabilities.* Pleasant Hill, CA: Behavior Analysts.

Thorndike, R. L., Hagen, E. R., & Sattler, J. M. (1986). *The Stanford–Binet Intelligence Scale–Fourth Edition.* Chicago: Riverside.

Zimmerman, I. L., Steiner, V. G., & Pond, R. E. (1992). *Preschool Language Scale–Third Edition.* San Antonio, TX: Psychological Corp.

The Lancaster–Lebanon IU 13 Autistic Support Program

5

Carolyn T. Bruey and Natalie Vorhis

Before we describe the Lancaster–Lebanon Intermediate Unit 13 Autistic Support program, it may be useful to explain how the Commonwealth of Pennsylvania sets up special education classes. The 29 Intermediate Units (IUs) in Pennsylvania are each assigned a number; for example, IU 13 for Lancaster–Lebanon counties. Within the public school system, there are two ways for a specialized classroom to be developed and supervised. The district may create and supervise its own classes; however, if it has only a few children or lacks the expertise to develop a particular kind of special education classroom, the district can opt to contract with the local IU to provide and supervise the special education classroom. If the district wishes to look outside of the public school system or IU, a contract can also be developed with a private school. For children on the autism spectrum, it is common for school districts to rely upon their local IU to develop "Autistic Support" classrooms, due to the highly specialized strategies required, as well as the unique challenges posed by this population.

In addition to Autistic Support classes, the IUs develop and support a wide range of special education programs and services for children with other learning disabilities, mental retardation, and physical or emotional challenges. The Lancaster–Lebanon IU 13 provides special education services to students from Lancaster and Lebanon Counties. The mission of the IU 13 is to assist local school districts to enhance educational opportunities by providing quality, cost-effective services. In total, 2,148 students are served across the 217 IU 13 classes. These classes are all assigned to specific "clusters." Until recently, clusters were geographically defined. Since each support team was expected to provide services to children with a wide range of disabilities who happened to live within the same geographic area, for many years children within the autism spectrum were supported by cluster staff who had varying degrees of expertise in the treatment of this population.

During the 2001–2002 school year, it became increasingly apparent to the IU 13 administration that this model did not optimally match the needs of students with autism spectrum disorders who required staff with highly specialized skills and a specific knowledge base. In the summer of 2002, an Autistic Support cluster was formed, which included a support team that provides services to all children attending Autistic Support classes in Lancaster and Lebanon Counties.

The IU 13 Autistic Support cluster presently provides educational services to approximately 80 students ranging in age from 5 to 21 years, of whom the majority are male (88%). Currently, students in the Autistic Support classes are 76% Caucasian, 13% African American, and 11% Latino. Although there are a few children with Asperger syndrome in the IU 13's Autistic Support classes, most of the students fall within the moderate to severe range of autism, and many have mental retardation, as well. There are 10 elementary school classes, 3 middle-school classes, and 4 high school classes. The maximum number of students assigned to each class is eight, with the actual number ranging from one to eight. The student–staff ratio is very low, ranging from 1:1 to 3:1. Although most of the staff members are IU 13 employees, periodically a therapeutic support staff person employed by an outside mental health agency will be present in the classroom. The classes are generally self-contained, although inclusion opportunities are developed whenever possible. All of the classes are housed in general education public schools, and most classrooms are located next to or near general education classes.

Not all children on the autism spectrum who live in Lancaster or Lebanon County attend Autistic Support classrooms. Many children with autistic spectrum disorders attend less intensive special education classes or regular education classes. For these children, the IU 13 has specially trained staff in addition to the Autistic Support team, who provide consultation and support to facilitate the students' success across a variety of classroom placements. Consultations can involve monthly classroom visits or a single visit with follow-up recommendations. Members of the Autistic Support team are also available to provide consultations regarding students who are challenging or complex in their educational needs but not appropriate for an Autistic Support classroom.

There is fluidity to classroom assignments, in that a student may attend a variety of specialized classrooms. For example, an elementary-age child may be assigned to an Autistic Support classroom but then be transferred to a less intensive IU class as a middle-school student. Decisions regarding classroom changes are based on each student's skills and educational needs. The Autistic Support classrooms are relatively restrictive compared to other types of special education classes, due to the limited opportunities for social interactions with more adept peers, as well as the use of highly intensive teaching techniques. Therefore, transferring a student to a less restrictive classroom setting is almost invariably a high-priority goal.

The creation of an Autistic Support cluster seems to have been an appropriate decision. Feedback from parents of the children with autism, as well as from teachers, indicates that the level of expertise within the Autistic Support team, plus the degree of support that is available, has been much appreciated. The IU 13 found the process to be so successful that it reorganized its system so that all special education services are now clustered according to disability rather than being geographically determined.

Diagnosis and Assessment

The Commonwealth of Pennsylvania uses the federal guidelines provided under the Individuals with Disabilities Education Act of 1990 (IDEA) to determine special education for individual students. Typically, a child is first assessed when applying for the IU 13's Early Intervention services. When a child becomes eligible for school-age programming, the parents and school district meet to decide whether special education is still appropriate. If so, the child is diagnosed with a specific disability, as required by IDEA. As part of the assessment process, an Evaluation Report is developed to answer two basic questions: Does the student (a) have a disability and (b) need specially designed instruction? The evaluation may include observations, interviews, and direct assessments by the school psychologist. Team input from speech–language pathologists, occupational therapists, physical therapists, the former teacher, parents, and community agencies is also included.

While some students enter the school-age program with a formal diagnosis of an autism spectrum disorder provided by a clinical psychologist, developmental psychologist, or physician, most students are given the label of autism via an Evaluation Report and a team decision. As a result, the school psychologist must conduct a detailed evaluation to determine appropriate diagnoses. To determine diagnosis, a variety of assessments may be used. Most commonly used is the *Childhood Autism Rating Scale* (CARS; Schopler, Reichler, & Renner, 1986). If a student is higher functioning, the *Asperger Syndrome Diagnostic Scale* (ASDS; Myles, Bock, & Simpson, 2001) may be used. Other diagnostic instruments that are sometimes used include the *Autism Diagnostic Observation Schedule* (ADOS; Lord, Rutter, DiLavore, & Risi, 1989), the *Autism Behavior Checklist* (Krug, Arick, & Almond, 1993), the *Autism Diagnostic Interview* (Rutter, LeCouteur, & Lord, 2002), or the *Gilliam Autism Rating Scale* (Gilliam, 1995).

Typically an intelligence test or other cognitive measure is also administered to determine whether the student's functioning falls within the mentally retarded range, as well as to assess specific cognitive strengths and deficits. Most commonly used are the *Wechsler Intelligence Scale for Children–Fourth Edition* (WISC–IV; Wechsler, 2003) and the *Stanford–Binet Intelligence Scales–Fifth Edition* (Roid, 2003). The *Vineland Adaptive Behavior Scales* (Sparrow, Balla, & Cicchetti, 1984) and the *Adaptive Behavior Scale–Second Edition* (Lambert, Nihira, & Leland, 1993) may be used to determine the strengths and weaknesses of a student's adaptive behavior compared to that of other students in his or her age range.

Evaluation Reports also provide information about a student's academic skills, behavioral concerns, and background history. To determine academic skills, higher functioning students may be given the *Wechsler Individual Achievement Test–Second Edition* (WIAT; Wechsler, 2002). If a student is less adept, the *Assessment of Basic Language and Learning Skills* (ABLLS; Partington & Sundberg, 1998) is completed to assess the student's abilities across a wide array of areas. If there are behavioral concerns, the *Behavior Assessment System for Children* (BASC; Reynolds & Kamphaus, 1992) or *Child Behavior Checklist* (CBCL; Achenbach, 1991) may be used. These tools measure a child's adaptive and challenging behaviors in community and home settings. Finally, a detailed history of the student's health, educational, and social background helps to form a clear and comprehensive picture of the student.

After the Evaluation Report has been reviewed by all Individualized Educational Program (IEP) team members, the team meets to write the IEP and recommend an appropriate education placement. Each IEP team consists of the parents, special education teacher, specialized therapists, regular education teacher, and home district special education administrator. A member of the Autistic Support team attends any IEP meeting where a student is being considered for placement in the Autistic Support program. The IEP team reviews the recommended instruction strategies within the IEP to determine whether an Autistic Support classroom is the least restrictive environment where the student can be properly educated.

Staffing and Administration

The Lancaster–Lebanon IU 13 consists of the Office of the Executive Director and five departments. The Department of Exceptional Children's Services supports the Autistic Support program, as well as other school-age exceptionality-specific classrooms. Currently, the Autistic Support program consists of 17 classes that are all assisted by the Autism Support team. Teachers may call upon the support team anytime to assist with class-wide concerns or assist with an individual student. While teachers are encouraged to implement the suggestions of the support team, ultimately the teacher is accountable for the structure and effectiveness of the classroom.

Members of the Autism Support Team

The support team for the Autistic Support cluster consists of a program supervisor, a school psychologist, a social worker, the special education consultant (SEC), a speech–language pathologist, a program assistant, and a consulting psychologist. The program supervisor is responsible for the overall functioning of all Autistic Support classrooms, including hiring, training, and retaining staff, finding appropriate classroom space, clinically supervising and evaluating teachers and support staff, resolving conflicts that may arise among teams, supporting families, identifying the needs of the program and making projections regarding future needs, and coordinating the services requested by the 22 school districts with services available within the Autistic Support program. The program supervisor also evaluates teachers and support staff regularly using the Professional Performance Evaluation System, to ensure best-practice service delivery. Evaluations cover the core competency areas of Planning and Preparation, Environment, Instructional–Technical, and Professional Responsibility. Evaluations are shared with the teacher or support staff team member and placed in his or her personnel file. If an evaluation reflects an unsatisfactory outcome, the staff member will be placed in the

Intensive Assistance Program, where a team will be identified to help develop and support the staff member through a written improvement plan. Typically, teachers or support staff following an improvement plan make great strides. Less often, the individual may choose to transfer to another teaching position or be terminated.

The Autistic Support special education consultant is a master's-level individual with experience working directly with students. While most SECs have taught in special education classrooms, others may be former speech–language pathologists, school psychologists, or supervisors. The SEC is responsible for working directly with teachers to help them select appropriate curricula for students, create and implement IEPs, develop successful classroom environments, encourage the implementation of new initiatives through training or consultation, and work with parents and districts to find appropriate, specially designed instruction for students.

The Autistic Support school psychologist is required to have a master's degree and usually has experience working with students with disabilities, as well as training in assessment and the creation of behavior support plans. The school psychologist is responsible for completing initial evaluations and reevaluations, encouraging the implementation of new initiatives through training or consultation, providing group or individual counseling as appropriate, designing and helping to implement class-wide behavior plans or individual behavior support plans, and consulting with teachers.

The Autistic Support school social worker is a master's-level individual who is responsible for introducing parents to the various Autistic Support classrooms where their child may be educated, assisting in transitions as the student moves across grade levels, helping families gain social or medical services in the community, and assisting with role clarification when therapeutic support staff (TSS) is involved. The school social worker is also a resource for families as they navigate access to outside agencies. Assisting families to obtain insurance as well as medical assistance or public welfare monies allows them to provide the best possible care for their children. The school social worker is called upon to assist with divorce issues and custody issues and if there is any type of suspected abuse or neglect.

While seven speech–language pathologists serve Autistic Support program students, only one is assigned full-time to the Autistic Support program. This speech–language pathologist consults weekly with the Autistic Support team and participates in problem solving as communication issues arise. This has been a valued resource, and we hope to increase the number of speech–language pathologists assigned solely to the Autistic Support team.

The program assistant provides a wide variety of services for the Autistic Support cluster. These include assisting the teachers in purchasing materials for the classroom, scheduling rooms for meetings and conferences, monitoring staff absences and obtaining substitutes, assessing new referral packages and distributing them to relevant personnel, guiding staff in their technical needs, and coordinating the paperwork involved when students transfer out of the Autistic Support program.

The Autistic Support team also includes a consulting psychologist, who provides additional support and training for 18 hours per week. The consulting psychologist is a doctoral-level licensed and certified school psychologist with over 20 years' experience working with students with autism. She works with all classrooms and staff, focusing on systemic issues such as proper implementation of ABA methodology, training, and progress monitoring.

Classroom and Therapeutic Staff

Classroom teachers in the Autistic Support program may be working toward or already have a degree in education. The teaching experience of the instructors currently employed in the Autistic Support program ranges from less than 1 year to over 20 years. Teachers are responsible for developing and writing IEP goals and objectives, implementing the IEP and Behavior Support Plans, monitoring student progress daily, making adjustments in instruction if IEP goals and objectives are not being met, reporting student progress quarterly, organizing class and staff schedules, working with families, and collaborating with support staff.

Paraprofessionals (also called personal care assistants) may have a high school, associate's-level, or bachelor's degree, and they assist the teacher in the daily functioning of the classroom. Paraprofessionals also receive training in ABA methods, data collection, and appropriate positive behavior supports.

The Autistic Support speech–language pathologists are bachelor's-level or master's-level professionals. Their expertise is greatest in the areas of articulation improvement, pragmatic language, and the use of assistive or augmentative communication devices. Each classroom is assigned a speech–language pathologist who assesses students' communication abilities as part of the evaluation process, selects appropriate IEP goals and objectives, provides one-to-one or group therapy, consults with the teachers and paraprofessional staff to increase effective communication for students, and creates materials students may use at home or school to facilitate communication. Other specialized skills that are often part of a speech–language pathologist's knowledge base include sign language, the Picture Exchange Communication System (PECS; Bondy & Frost, 2002), and assistive devices.

Each classroom is assigned an occupational therapist, who assesses students as part of the evaluation process, selects appropriate IEP goals and objectives, provides one-to-one or group therapy, consults with the teachers and paraprofessional staff to increase effective participation for students, and creates adapted materials that students may use at home or school to participate more successfully. The occupational therapists are bachelor's-level or master's-level professionals with experience working with children in the areas of sensory issues, fine motor skills (e.g., writing and keyboarding), and self-help skills.

Each class is also assigned a physical therapist, who may be called on to assess students, select appropriate IEP goals and objectives regarding the student's physical development, provide one-to-one or group therapy, consult with the teachers as to ways to increase effective movement and participation, and create individual exercise programs. The physical therapists are either bachelor's-level or master's-level professionals.

Other professional staff who may provide services to students within the Autistic Support program include a job trainer, a teacher of the visually impaired, and an orientation and mobility specialist. The degree to which these professionals are involved is based upon each student's needs.

Curriculum

Before the inception of the Autistic Support cluster, there were no set guidelines regarding a curriculum for the Autistic Support classes. Each teacher developed IEPs based on his or her knowledge of the students' strengths and needs, as well as autism in general. At times, this led to differences in emphasis across classes, as well as frustration on the part of the teachers as they tried to establish some type of formatted procedure for developing IEPs.

When the Autistic Support cluster was established, the determination was made that it would be beneficial to students and teachers alike to have a standardized framework from which teachers could develop IEPs.

This format allowed a greater degree of consistency in curriculum across settings, lessened the pressure on teachers to "reinvent the wheel" each year, and ensured that all classes would emphasize certain essential curriculum components. Having a standardized curriculum was especially advantageous when a student moved from one Autistic Support classroom to another, as the new instructor could easily understand and build upon the student's earlier IEPs. Of utmost importance, the students' progress was enhanced because there was an overall understanding of the best practices for teaching children on the autism spectrum. These practices had been incorporated into the educational program from kindergarten classes through graduation.

The two curricula used by the IU 13 Autistic Support program are the *Assessment of Basic Language and Learning Skills* (ABLLS; Partington & Sundberg, 1998) and the *Individualized Goal Selection Curriculum/ Growth–Relationships–Independence–Participation* (IGS/GRIP; Romanczyk, Lockshin, & Matey, 1996). They were chosen because they were comprehensive, developed specifically for children with autism spectrum disorders, and included goals across a broad range of skill areas. For example, the ABLLS includes four general skill areas: basic learning skills (e.g., accepts reinforcers, seeks approval for task completion), basic academic skills, self-help, and motor skills (fine and gross). The IGS/GRIP is an extensive list of potential IEP goals across 19 areas of development, all of which are clustered within the following general skill areas: communication, behavioral or emotional development, social development, preacademic or academic, and life skills. Target skills in both the ABLLS and IGS/GRIP are operationally defined and are written in a developmentally typical sequence.

Although both the ABLLS and IGS/GRIP are useful when developing IEP goals, each curriculum has its specific strengths. While the ABLLS is especially helpful when assessing younger or less adept students with autism, the IGS/GRIP includes a wider list of more sophisticated skills that can apply to the more advanced student. The teachers in the IU 13 Autistic Support classrooms have tended to mix and match the two curricula, as well as identify skills that happen to be missing from both curricula, thereby producing a truly individualized IEP for each student. Figure 5.1 provides an example of an IEP that incorporates items from both the ABLLS and the IGS/GRIP curricula.

Considering that one of the primary concerns for children with autism spectrum disorders is the presence of qualitative impairments in social and interpersonal skills, all IEPs include goals in that area. These

---

GOALS AND OBJECTIVES　　　　　*SKILL AREA: FUNCTIONAL MATH*

Student's Present Levels of Educational Performance

Matt has been working on labeling the numerals 1–100 and has mastered 1–21 thus far. He can rote-count up to 30. Matt can tell time on an analog clock but not a digital one. Matching skills (2D to 2D pictures) has improved over the past year such that he can now match 34 pictures of common objects. He cannot identify any coins or paper bills. He needs ongoing prompting in order to pay for his lunch in the cafeteria.

Quarterly Progress

Measurable Annual Goal	1st	2nd	3rd	4th
Goal 1. Matt will independently pay for his lunch (11 steps), first time asked across three consecutive probe sessions (IGS/GRIP Area 8, Level 6, Stage 4)				
Goal 2. Matt will match pictures of coins, times, and numbers to identical pictures in a field of three by responding first time asked across three consecutive probe sessions (ABLLS B2 & B4)				
Goal 3. Matt will verbally read digital times to 10-minute intervals first time asked across three consecutive probe sessions (ABLLS R11)				

Benchmark Objectives for Each IEP Goal

Goal 1. Matt will independently pay for his lunch across three consecutive probes by completing the following steps: *In classroom:* • Getting wallet from basket • Getting out money jig • Matching up coins and bills • Placing money in zipper part of wallet • Placing wallet in pants pocket *In cafeteria:* • Taking out wallet to pay cashier • Opening wallet and handing money to cashier • Placing change in wallet • Closing zipper in wallet • Putting wallet in pocket • Putting wallet in basket when he returns to the classroom *Steps will be taught using a backward chaining procedure.*				

(continues)

Figure 5.1. Example of IEP goals using ABLLS and IGS/GRIP curricula.

Benchmark Objectives for Each IEP Goal	Quarterly Progress			
	1st	2nd	3rd	4th
Goal 2. Given a picture, Matt will match to identical picture in a field of three, first time asked across three consecutive probes: • Pennies, nickels, dimes, quarters, half dollars, one dollar bills • Digital clock pictures to the hour • Digital clock pictures to the half hour • Numbers 1–60				
Goal 3. Matt will verbally read digital times first time asked across three consecutive probes: • To the hour • To the half hour • To the quarter hour • To 10-minute intervals				

Figure 5.1. *Continued.*

social goals are wide ranging, depending on the particular child's abilities. Although some students focus on very basic social goals such as making eye contact or initiating an interpersonal interaction by tapping an instructor's arm, more socially adept students may be learning how to take others' perspective, identify their own emotions, or participate in a mainstreamed social activity. "Theory of Mind" strategies (Attwood, 1998; Baron-Cohen, Tager-Flusberg, & Cohen, 1993; Bowler, 1994; Frith, 1989; Gray, 1994), including cartoon conversations, social stories, and developing visual cues such as "emotional thermometers," can also be integrated into the child's school day to facilitate improvements in socialization and interpersonal skills (Hodgdon, 1995).

Because difficulties in the area of communication are also invariably apparent in students with autism spectrum disorders, this is another emphasis across all IEPs. In addition to specific IEP goals regarding expanding the child's communication repertoire that will be taught via classroom instruction, the majority of students receive services from a speech–language pathologist.

Each child's IEP includes a list entitled "Specially Designed Instruction" (SDI), which outlines the individualized, specific teaching techniques or educational experiences to be incorporated into the child's educational experiences to meet curriculum-based goals. These could include specific software programs such as Fast ForWord (2001), as well as provision of visual supports, use of an augmentative communication device, specific instructional methods such as *Handwriting Without Tears* (Olsen, 1998) or the *Edmark Reading Program* (Edmark Corp., 2001) and other individualized strategies to increase the student's overall progress. The IEP also delineates specific supports such as transportation, the amount of inclusion to be provided, hiring of a one-to-one staff, and specialized training for the class instructors.

Instructional Methods

The instructional methods used in the Autistic Support classrooms are based on the principles of Applied Behavior Analysis (ABA). As has been shown in the research literature over the past 4 decades, ABA methodologies have led to the most significant progress for children on the autism spectrum (e.g., Harris & Weiss, 1998; Matson, Benavidez, Compton, Paclawskyj, & Baglio, 1996). Each child's ABA-based educational program is individualized according to instructional needs and behavioral challenges.

One of the techniques under the ABA umbrella that is incorporated frequently during instruction in the Autistic Support classrooms is discrete trial instruction (DTI; Lovaas, 1981; Maurice, Green, & Luce, 1996). Most students receive a minimum of 2 hours of one-to-one DTI each school day. The classroom's daily schedule requires strategic planning such that students take turns working independently at their desks, working within small groups, or receiving one-to-one instruction. The degree to which each student receives a high level of one-to-one instruction is based on educational needs. While younger students tend to require the full 2 hours a day, middle-school and high school students are often able to respond successfully in small groups for a greater part of the day.

One of the overall goals of the IU 13 in general and the Autistic Support cluster specifically is to assign students to the least restrictive educational environment. This may entail having the child transferred to a less intensive special education classroom or a regular education setting as the need for intensive ABA-based instruction lessens due to student progress. As a consequence, students who remain in Autistic Support classes into their high school years are individuals with a significant level of disability (usually a dual diagnosis of mental retardation and autism) who continue to benefit from the intensity inherent to DTI. At the same time, it is acknowledged that high school students need to learn how to respond successfully with less one-to-one support because that level of supervision is rarely available in the workplace. Therefore, teachers are constantly balancing the provision of one-to-one instruction with teaching independence.

Many Autistic Support teachers incorporate strategies from TEACCH (Mesibov, Schopler, & Hearsey, 1994). These include the provision of designated "work stations" or cubbies, visual schedules, and three-tiered cabinets housing independent task activities. Although younger students use independent work time to practice recently mastered skills such as matching and counting, the tasks selected for older students attempt to simulate job skills that will be useful to the student in the workplace.

The instructors also employ a variety of prompting procedures. These include traditional prompts, such as gestures, positional prompts, and verbal cues to guide a student to respond correctly. Generally, physical prompts such as hand-over-hand guidance are avoided in order to lessen the possibility of prompt dependence. We also use a wide variety of visual supports as a means of helping a student to learn and maintain a new skill. For example, many students benefit from the use of social stories (Gray, 2000) as a means of visually presenting ways in which they can respond adaptively to potentially stressful situations, better understand other people's perspective, or learn other socially based skills. Activity schedules (McClannahan & Krantz, 1999) are also helpful in providing a student with a visual framework to sequence and engage in activities independently.

Because communication is always a high-priority focus within the IU 13 Autistic Support classes, the teachers are trained in ways to teach effective and functional communication skills. The particular communication system that is identified for each student is chosen according to the child's skills and preferences, following a total communication philosophy. While some students are able to communicate via verbalizations, others rely upon signing, the PECS (Frost & Bondy, 1994), or augmentative devices. Many students are taught a variety of ways of communicating the same message so that they can choose whichever communicative system is easiest at the time.

Teachers in the IU 13 Autistic Support classes also implement natural environment teaching (NET) to promote spontaneous responses within naturally occurring circumstances. Recess, snack time, free play, and other less structured times of the day all present opportunities to teach many IEP goals. Instructional activities are created that on the surface appear to be merely entertaining but in fact are educationally focused. For example, playing the card game Uno can provide opportunities for students to learn a variety of skills, such as color and number identification, taking turns, following instructions, and waiting. NET is also an effective way to teach play and leisure skills.

The success of instructional methods is inherently linked to the training of the staff. To ensure that the Autistic Support staff members are knowledgeable and up to date, the Autistic Support cluster supports numerous training opportunities for new and seasoned staff members. There are four full-day conferences scheduled across the school year that cover a wide variety of topics specific to the effective instruction of students with autism spectrum disorders. Both teachers and paraprofessionals attend the conferences with the assumption that *all* personnel in the classroom should be optimally skilled and proficient. The teachers also attend three after-school workshops each school year that address various topics specific to autism spectrum disorders. Many teachers attend Pennsylvania State University's annual autism conference and participate in their certification programs for applied behavior analysis and autism.

In addition to these training opportunities, the Autistic Support consulting psychologist conducts a monthly, full-day Basic Training workshop that covers essential skills such as behavioral assessments, learning characteristics of students with autism spectrum disorders, implementing ABA methods to teach skills or decrease challenging behaviors, and data collection. The scheduling of the Basic Training ensures that no staff member will be in a classroom more than 1 month before being trained in these fundamental skills.

A final avenue of training and support incorporated into the IU 13 system is mentoring. All newer teachers are assigned more seasoned instructors as mentors. The new instructor often visits the mentor's classroom early in the school year in order to observe how the ABA methods are incorporated into the school day, and the mentor is available for guidance throughout the school year.

Integration

All of the IU 13 Autistic Support classrooms are located in public schools, so opportunities for integration are easily accessible. Almost invariably, lunch and recess are times when Autistic Support students are integrated into the regular education system. Mainstreaming may also involve the student spending part of the school day in other, less restrictive IU 13 classrooms or in general education settings.

It is essential to think proactively prior to the initiation of integration, so that the experience can be as successful as possible. The proactive phase often includes meeting with the teachers and students in the general education classroom to provide information regarding autism. The degree to which mainstreaming takes place, as well as the types of activities into which the student is integrated, is based on a given child's strengths, interests, abilities, and needs. While some students can be mainstreamed for much of the school day, others are integrated for brief intervals within a specific activity (e.g., Circle Time). Although conventional wisdom may imply that mainstreaming children with autism spectrum disorders into "specials" (i.e., music, art, gym, library) would be the first route to follow, we have found that those types of activities are often more difficult for this population. The loud noise, unstructured atmosphere, and increased stimulation inherent to those classes can trigger increased anxiety and challenging behaviors. Rather than concluding that the child is "not ready" for integration, we have realized that we need to be more planful in our integration process. For example, scheduling integration experiences during more structured activities such as academics is often more successful than mainstreaming into specials due to the higher level of structure, clear expectations, and quieter ambience.

If a student is not yet ready for inclusion into regular education, the most common alternative special education classroom that can serve as a mainstreaming opportunity for a child from the Autistic Support classroom is a Learning Support class. The students who attend Learning Support classes generally have relatively minor learning disabilities or mild mental retardation. They tend to have greater skills in the areas of social interaction and communication, therefore serving as effective prosocial models for students with an autism spectrum disorder. Another strategy that is often incorporated into our classrooms is reverse inclusion. Having regular education students participate in activities within the Autistic Support classroom allows the Autistic Support students the opportunity to observe and interact with more adept peers "on their own turf."

Throughout the integration process, ongoing data are collected to assess how well the student is responding. Behaviors that are monitored may include the student's academic progress, as well as the occurrence of challenging behaviors. If the data indicate that the integration experience is less than successful, modifications are made to enhance success.

Strategies that may be considered in this regard include providing additional staff support, using visual cues (e.g., micro schedules, social stories), decreasing the time spent in the other setting, clarifying to the student the behavioral expectations of the regular education classroom, previewing and practicing ahead of time the anticipated activities that will take place in the alternative classroom, and developing a reinforcement system specific to behaviors demonstrated within the integrated setting.

While we value and encourage integration, we believe it is never beneficial to integrate a student merely for the sake of integration. Any integration process should have clear goals that are linked to IEP objectives. When planning a particular child's integration, it is also important to decide whether the goal is to provide an *adapted* or an *alternative* curriculum within the general education setting. Will the student merely need a few adaptations to the general education activity or will he or she be expected to follow a similar, but significantly simplified, version of the curriculum? This decision requires a fine balance between capitalizing on the student's strengths and being attuned to the need to make integration a time when the child feels competent rather than frustrated.

It is important to keep in mind the preferences voiced by the student involved in the mainstreaming process. We ask the student to voice his or her feelings about being in the other classroom, and we modify the integration plan as needed. For example, while some students feel more comfortable when a paraprofessional accompanies them to the classroom, others state that that makes them feel "different" or singled out and specifically request that the staff member either not come or stay in the background.

Typically developing peers can benefit greatly from mainstreaming experiences. Opportunities to become friends with the Autistic Support students allow for a fuller understanding of differences among people as well as increased tolerances regarding those differences.

Behavior Management

It is common for students in the Autistic Support classrooms to demonstrate challenging behaviors. The specific behavioral manifestations seen across the 17 classes range from passive resistance to significant levels of physical aggression or self-injury. Some of our students had been assigned to a less restrictive classroom but were transferred to an Autistic Support classroom due to the intensity of their behavioral challenges. As a consequence, addressing these behavioral issues is frequently a top priority.

The intensity of behavioral intervention varies according to the severity of the behavioral challenges exhibited. Many of the Autistic Support classrooms have classroom-wide behavior management systems that are implemented across all students. For example, the teacher may provide stickers contingent upon following predetermined class rules and allow the students to trade the stickers for preferred items at the "school store." When a student's behavioral challenge is somewhat more significant, the IEP may include a page devoted to the acquisition of alternative, appropriate skills, coupled with the decrease or cessation of maladaptive behaviors. Interventions listed in this section of the IEP, while individualized for the specific child, are not particularly complex or intensive.

When a child's behavioral challenges are more serious or dangerous, a formal Behavior Support Plan (BSP) is developed. The behavior management procedures implemented in the classroom are invariably based on ABA strategies that have proven effective in the research literature. All teachers are instructed in behavioral analysis and are able to collect baseline data in order to assess the circumstances surrounding a child's challenging behaviors. The antecedents and consequences noted during their observations provide information used by the school psychologist to develop a BSP. The school psychologist also conducts a functional analysis of the challenging behavior in order to begin to identify alternative, functionally equivalent skills that need to be taught. At times when the function is more difficult to discern, an Experimental Functional Behavioral Analysis is conducted, whereby the school psychologist deliberately manipulates various factors in order to gain a clearer understanding of the underlying purposes and triggers governing the behavior.

One of the most extensive sections of the BSP is the "preventive techniques" section, as the school psychologist recommends numerous tactics designed to lessen the chance that the behavioral issue will occur. Preventive strategies often focus on ways to change the classroom environment or modify how tasks are presented so that the child will be less likely to display the behavioral challenge.

The BSPs also describe in detail the way the IU 13 staff should respond when the targeted behaviors occur. Most BSPs involve a planned ignoring response or brief verbal reprimand by the teachers rather than any significant negative consequence. If natural, negative consequences (e.g., loss of recess if student refuses to put on her shoes) can be incorporated into the plan, that can also be considered. Of special importance is the use of differential reinforcement programs, whereby the student is rewarded frequently for the display of alternative, positive behaviors.

Occasionally, more intrusive techniques such as a response cost, time-outs, or physical restraints have been implemented; however, these are considered only if data indicate that less restrictive procedures have proven futile or if students are placing themselves or others in significant danger. Data regarding the behavioral challenges are collected on a daily basis and reviewed on a biweekly basis.

See Figure 5.2 for an example of a graph depicting a BSP. Note that changes are made in the intervention if anticipated progress does not occur.

Family Involvement

The IU 13 Autistic Support program encourages the full involvement of families in their child's education. The student's family is his or her strongest advocate, and family opinions and suggestions are taken seriously. A long-term vision of the student, provided by the family, drives the creation of each year's IEP. IEP meetings, along with frequent communication between teachers and parents, are times when parental input is critical. Further communication is fostered between the families and the school through the use of daily communication books, e-mails, and phone calls. In some cases, parents attend parent–teacher conferences or monthly meetings. To facilitate their involvement, parents are updated regarding their child's progress via weekly reports and graphs. On occasion, the teacher or the school social worker may visit a family's home to update the parents on a student's progress.

Many parents of students in the IU 13 Autistic Support classes are active in local parent support groups. IU 13 also sponsors after-school and evening family groups. These groups tend to be focused around a skill a student may be learning or a transition a student may be going through (e.g., transitioning from early intervention services to school-age services). The Autism Advisory Committee was created in 2002 and comprises parents, professionals from the community, teachers, support staff, local university professors, and IU 13 supervisors. The committee focuses on current topics related to autism, as well as helping to develop local resources for families with students with autism spectrum disorders. The IU 13 also created the Jae Davis Scholarship Fund for parents wishing to attend the National Autism Conference and Pennsylvania Autism Institute held at Pennsylvania State University each year.

The IU 13's Parent Resource Center, which is located centrally in Lancaster County, houses videos, books, and software resources, including

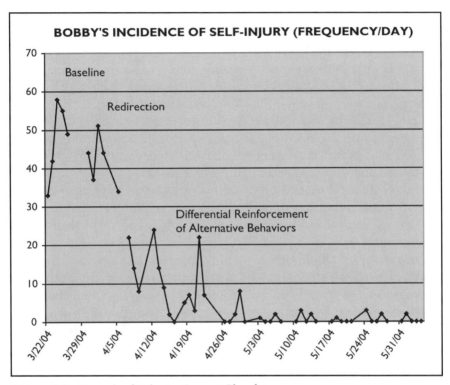

Figure 5.2. Example of Behavior Support Plan data.

Boardmaker (Erinoak of Mississauga, 2001) and Writing with Symbols (Mayer-Johnson, 2002). Computers with related software programs are available for use by parents and professionals at the Resource Center, and there are more than 80 books related to autism spectrum disorders that families can check out.

Transitions

Transitions for students on the autism spectrum require planning and structure to be successful. Students who remain in the Autistic Support program throughout their educational career typically experience a transition from preschool to their primary elementary class, then to a secondary elementary class, a middle-school class, a high school class, and finally to the community upon graduation. Other students transition from an

Autistic Support class to a less restrictive special education classroom, and still other students transition from the Autistic Support class to a general education classroom. To ease these transitions, teachers keep in close contact as a student leaves one class and enters another. Interventions that have helped with behavioral concerns, instructional strategies that have proven effective, and communication techniques are shared. As a result, the new teacher can have the classroom prepared before the student arrives. All transitions follow the student's pace and are monitored closely.

As students with autism enter the middle-school years, parents, teachers, and support staff begin to plan for the student's adult life. Students have the right to access special education services until they turn 21 years old, and nearly all of the students in the Autistic Support classrooms do so. When a student is 14 years old, parents are asked about their future visions for their child. If possible, the student is asked to describe his or her own vision of the future, as well. Areas considered include the kind of employment the student might achieve, anticipated community living arrangements, participation in the community, and leisure and recreation activities. Once a long-term vision is agreed upon, the staff adapts instruction accordingly. The services necessary to meet the vision, as well as how the services will be provided and who will provide them, how they will be coordinated, and other community links that will help the student meet the goals, are delineated in the IEP.

Because the initial planning for the transition to adult living and working begins when the student turns 14 years old, each subsequent IEP meeting brings a new opportunity to revisit the transition plan. Although families often cannot imagine their teenager as an adult when he or she is 14 years old, as the student enters the late teens or early twenties both the family's and the student's needs change. Once a student is 19 years old, a local adult day program usually conducts an assessment of the student's strengths and needs. The IEP team can then make a recommendation as to which work setting is most suitable while the student is still in school-age programming. By the time students begin attending a community-based work setting, they have already visited the location, their parents have visited, and precursor skills have been targeted and improved for greatest success. Students typically attend their future work setting for at least half the week during their final school year.

A job trainer is assigned to students who may be employed in the community in a less sheltered situation. Students are selected according to ability, behavioral self-control, and IEP goals. The job trainer assesses the individual student's interests and tries to match those interests to a job setting to promote optimal success. Initially, students attend a variety of job sites with the trainer one afternoon per week. Common jobs include food preparation and cleaning at local eateries, cleaning furniture and windows at retirement or recreational centers, and vacuuming at video stores. These experiences help the job trainer determine which specific job would be optimal for a given student, and the goal becomes having the student work independently in that setting after graduation.

Outcome Measures

Success within the IU 13's Autistic Support classrooms is determined by assessing two primary factors: the degree to which students' IEP goals are met and the number of students who are transferred to a less restrictive setting for at least part of the school day. Both of these areas have shown notably positive results.

To evaluate students' progress on IEP goals, data are collected in a two-phase system. First, daily data are collected on the acquisition of new IEP skills (this phase is called Active Programming). Once a skill is mastered in the Active Program phase, it is transferred to the Maintenance–Generalization phase. Each student has two data binders: one for data on Active Programs and the second for Maintenance–Generalization data. A skill is not considered fully mastered until it has been mastered both in the Active Program phase and in the Maintenance–Generalization phase.

For many IEP goals, mastery is defined as responding correctly the first time asked across 3 consecutive days ("probe data"). The student's progress is compiled on a Program Sheet, which lists the date each step on a given IEP goal was initiated and the date it was mastered. The number of steps mastered per week for each IEP goal is noted on a graph to monitor the student's overall progress. Aim lines are drawn on the graphs and reflect the anticipated slope of learning. The graphs are evaluated biweekly, and modifications are made in instructional methods if the data are 25% or more below the aim line. See Figures 5.3, 5.4, and 5.5 for examples of a weekly probe data sheet, weekly graph, and Program Sheet.

Evaluating Generalization and Maintenance

The research literature has consistently demonstrated that children with autism spectrum disorders have difficulty maintaining and generalizing

WEEKLY PROBE DATA SHEET

Child's Name: Frances Williams

Week of: 3/22/04   Score "+" if Frances responds correctly the *first time* she is asked each day. Score "−" if she does not respond correctly the first time she is asked. Criteria for mastery is "+" for three consecutive days.

CURRENT IEP GOALS	Prev. Week	Monday 3/22	Tuesday 3/23	Wednesday 3/24	Thursday 3/25	Friday 3/26
OBJECT ID Dog	−	+	+	+ (Mastered)		
Cat					−	
Glasses	+	−	−	−	+	+
Plate	+	+	+ (Mastered)			
Soap	−	−	+	+	+ (Mastered)	
Hat				−	−	
Pencil	+ +	+ (Mastered)				
EMOTIONS Happy	−	−	+	−	+	+
Sad	+ +	+ (Mastered)				
MONEY ID Nickel	−	−	−	−	+	− ˙
Dime	+	−	+	+	+ (Mastered)	
COLORS White	+ +	+ (Mastered)				
Black	−	−	+	+	−	+
Red			−	−	+	+
SURVIVAL SIGNS Exit	−	−	+	+	+ (Mastered)	
Ladies' room						−
TIES SHOES Pulls loops tight	+ +	+ (Mastered)				
Pushes loop through			−	−	+	+

Figure 5.3. Sample Weekly Probe Data Sheet.

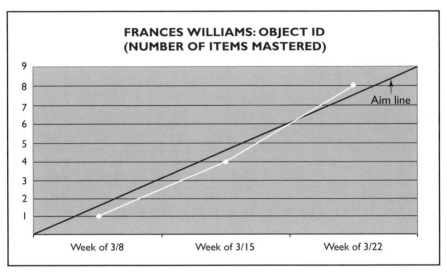

Figure 5.4. Sample weekly graph of IEP goals.

skills (Harris, 1975; Weiss & Harris, 2001). Therefore, 1 day each week, data are collected regarding both maintenance and generalization of newly acquired skills. First, probe data sessions are conducted to assess how well the child has *maintained* new skills. *Generalization* of new skills is then evaluated across people, settings, and novel teaching materials. Similar to the Active Program definition of mastery, a skill is defined as mastered within the Maintenance–Generalization phase if the student responds correctly across three consecutive weekly probes. If the student responds incorrectly during three consecutive Maintenance–Generalization sessions, the skill is returned to the Active Program phase.

Evaluating System-Wide Outcomes

As a means of evaluating outcomes for the IU 13 Autistic Support program overall, data were collected regarding acquisition of IEP goals across the 2003–2004 school year across all 17 Autistic Support classrooms. Data indicated that the students were taught on average a total of 33 IEP goals during the year. On average, the students mastered 15 IEP goals and showed significant progress on 12 goals, thus indicating that they

Student's Name: Frances Williams

Target Skill: Receptive ID of Common Objects

Teaching Method: Discrete Trial Instruction

Criteria for Mastery on Each Step: Frances will independently point to or touch the designated object within 3 seconds following the request when presented with a field of at least four objects

Item	Date Introduced	Date Mastered	Staff Initials
Chair	3/8	3/15	PMB
Desk	3/8	3/12	BTC
Coat	3/1	3/16	PMB
Door	3/3	3/18	WTT
Dog	3/12	3/23	NBT
Cat	3/24		
Glasses	3/14		
Plate	3/14	3/22	MAB
Soap	3/15	3/24	PMB
Hat	3/23		
Pencil	3/15	3/21	WTT

Figure 5.5. Sample Program Sheet.

mastered or showed significant progress on 82% of the IEP goals taught over the school year.

In terms of increased mainstreaming opportunities into less restrictive educational settings across the 2003–2004 school year, data indicate that 29 students (43%) had increased mainstreamed opportunities, 33 (49%) had the same amount of inclusion, and 5 (8%) were mainstreamed less in May compared to the beginning of the school year. In addition, 3 of the Autistic Support students were transferred to a less restrictive classroom placement full time.

Summary

Since its inception in the summer of 2002, the IU 13 Autistic Support cluster has developed a comprehensive, data-based, state-of-the-art program for students with autism spectrum disorders within the public school system. Within the relatively short time that the Autistic Support cluster has existed, we have been able to develop a standardized educational program based on applied behavior analysis. This progress is a reflection of the remarkable efforts of our teachers, paraprofessionals, students, parents, therapists, and support team. Of special note is the support we have received from the IU 13 administration in terms of funding, encouragement, and administrative backup.

Goals for the future include expanding our emphasis on teaching to fluency (Simmons, Derby, & McLaughlin, 2000; West, Young, & Spooner, 1990), building capacity across other IU 13 classrooms, as well as among school district personnel regarding effective instruction for students with autism spectrum disorders, and helping to develop specialized instruction for students with high-functioning autism or Asperger syndrome. It is our mission to continue to grow and provide increasingly successful and comprehensive educational experiences to children with autism spectrum disorders in the Lancaster–Lebanon area.

References

Achenbach, T. M. (1991). *Child Behavior Checklist.* Burlington, VT: University of Vermont Department of Psychiatry.

Attwood, T. (1998). *Asperger's syndrome: A guide for parents and professionals.* London: Jessica Kingsley.

Baron-Cohen, S., Tager-Flusberg, H., & Cohen, D. (Eds.). (1993). *Understanding other minds: Perspective from autism.* New York: Oxford University Press.

Bondy, A., & Frost, L. (2002). *A picture's worth: PECs and other visual communication systems in autism.* Bethesda, MD: Woodbine House.

Bowler, B. (1994). Theory of mind in Asperger's syndrome. *Journal of Child Psychology and Psychiatry, 33,* 877–894.

Edmark Corp. (2001). *Edmark reading program.* Redmond, WA: Author.

Erinoak of Mississauga, Ontario, Canada. (2001). Boardmaker (Version 5.0) [Computer software]. Solana Beach, CA: Mayer-Johnson.

Fast ForWord [Computer software]. (2001). Oakland, CA: Scientific Learning Corp.

Frith, U. (1989). *Autism: Explaining the enigma.* Cambridge, MA: Basil Blackwell.

Frost, L., & Bondy, A. (1994). *The Picture Communication System.* Cherry Hill, NJ: Pyramid Educational Consultants.

Gilliam, J. E. (1995). *Gilliam Autism Rating Scale.* Austin, TX: PRO-ED.

Gray, C. (1994). *Comic Strip Conversations.* Arlington, TX: Future Horizons.

Gray, C. (2000). *The New Social Story Book.* Arlington, TX: Future Horizons.

Harris, S. (1975). Teaching language to nonverbal children with emphasis on problems of generalization. *Psychological Bulletin, 82,* 565–580.

Harris, S., & Weiss, M. (1998). *Right from the start: Behavioral intervention for young children with autism.* Bethesda, MD: Woodbine House.

Hodgdon, L. (1995). *Visual strategies for improving communication. Volume I: Practical supports for school and home.* Troy, MI: Quirk Roberts.

Individuals with Disabilities Education Act. (1990). Public Law 101–476.

Krug, D., Arick, J., & Almond, P. (1993). *Autism Screening Instrument for Educational Planning.* Austin, TX: PRO-ED.

Lambert, N., Nihira, K., & Leland, H. (1993). *Adaptive Behavior Scale–Second Edition.* Austin, TX: PRO-ED.

Lord, C., Rutter, M., DiLavore, P. C., & Risi, S. (1989). *Autism Diagnostic Observation Schedule.* Los Angeles: Western Psychological Services.

Lovaas, O. I. (1981). *Teaching developmentally disabled children: The ME book.* Austin, TX: PRO-ED.

Matson, J., Benavidez, D., Compton, L., Paclawskyj, T., & Baglio, C. (1996). Behavioral treatment of autistic persons: A review of research from 1980 to present. *Research in Developmental Disabilities, 7,* 388–451.

Maurice, C., Green, G., & Luce, S. (1996). *Behavioral intervention for young children with autism.* Austin, TX: PRO-ED.

Mayer-Johnson, Inc. (2002). Writing with Symbols 2000 (Version 2.5) [Computer software]. Solana Beach, CA: Author.

McClannahan, L., & Krantz, P. (1999). *Activity schedules for children with autism: Teaching independent behavior.* Bethesda, MD: Woodbine House.

Mesibov, G., Schopler, E., & Hearsey, K. (1994). Structured teaching. In E. Schopler & G. Mesibov (Eds.), *Behavioral issues in autism* (pp. 195–207). New York: Plenum Press.

Myles, B. S., Bock, S. J., & Simpson, R. L. (2001). *Asperger Syndrome Diagnostic Scale.* Austin, TX: PRO-ED.

Olsen, J. (1998). *Handwriting without tears.* Potomac, MD: Handwriting Without Tears.

Partington, J. W., & Sundberg, M. L. (1998). *The Assessment of Basic Language and Learning Skills.* Pleasant Hill, CA: Behavior Analysts.

Reynolds, C. R., & Kamphaus, R. W. (1992). *Behavior Assessment System for Children.* Circle Pines, MN: American Guidance Service.

Roid, G. H. (2003). *Stanford–Binet Intelligence Scales–Fifth Edition.* Itasca, IL: Riverside.

Romanczyk, R., Lockshin, S., & Matey, L. (1996). *Individualized Goal Selection Curriculum*. Apalachin, NY: Clinical Behavior Therapy Association.

Rutter, M., LeCouteur, A., & Lord, C. (2002). *Autism Diagnostic Interview–Revised*. Los Angeles: Western Psychological Services.

Schopler, E., Reichler, R. J., & Renner, B. R. (1986). *The Childhood Autism Rating Scale*. Los Angeles: Western Psychological Services.

Simmons, E., Derby, K., & McLaughlin, T. (2000). The use of functional analysis and precision teaching to reduce the challenging behavior of a toddler with autism. *Journal of Precision Teaching and Celeration, 15*(2), 20–55.

Sparrow, S. S., Balla, D. A., & Cicchetti, D. V. (1984). *Vineland Adaptive Behavior Scales*. Circle Pines, MN: American Guidance Service.

Wechsler, D. (2002). *Wechsler Individual Achievement Test–Second Edition*. San Antonio, TX: Psychological Corp.

Wechsler, D. (2003). *Wechsler Intelligence Scale for Children–Fourth Edition*. San Antonio, TX: Psychological Corp.

Weiss, M. J., & Harris, S. L. (2001). *Reaching out, joining in: Teaching social skills to young children with autism*. Bethesda, MD: Woodbine House.

West, R., Young, K., & Spooner, F. (1990). Precision teaching: An introduction. *Teaching Exceptional Children, 22*(3), 4–8.

Behavior Analysis and Intervention for School-Age Children at the Princeton Child Development Institute

6

Lynn E. McClannahan and Patricia J. Krantz

T he Princeton Child Development Institute (PCDI), a nonprofit organization, was founded in 1970 by the grandmother and mother of a young boy with autism. When they were unable to locate appropriate, noninstitutional services in New Jersey, they launched a national search that culminated in the selection of a science-based intervention model: applied behavior analysis. PCDI was the first community-based school program in the state that was specifically designed to provide intervention for children with autism.

Students are referred by their local school districts, and tuition is paid by those districts. Tuition covers approximately 84% of educational costs. It does not cover transition services for youngsters who are preparing to enter community settings or follow-up services for those who have already done so. Some school districts agree to pay tuition for children who are participating in a program of gradual transition from PCDI to their local schools, but such payments are not mandatory. Some parents pay PCDI for follow-up services, but because of the importance of these services, they are delivered regardless of ability to pay. Services and programs that are not funded by tuition payments are underwritten by grant-writing and fund-raising activities.

The Institute's mission is to provide effective, science-based education and treatment, to prepare young professionals for leadership roles, and to conduct research on intervention. Research findings are disseminated via journal articles, books, book chapters, and videotapes and are also immediately put into practice to benefit currently enrolled and future students.

The School

In the early years, the Institute occupied leased facilities in churches and then a building no longer used by a local school district. But 1983 marked the beginning of a capital campaign to purchase land and construct a new building at 300 Cold Soil Road in Princeton. The new quarters were especially designed to meet the education and intervention needs of children with autism and to facilitate professional training and research. Members of the board of trustees actively solicited potential donors, enlisted the support of community leaders, and conducted fund-raising activities. In addition, grants were received from The Kresge Foundation, the New Jersey Department of Human Services, and many local foundations. The new building was dedicated in 1985; all necessary funds were raised, and neither long- nor short-term financing was necessary.

In 1994, a second building campaign was inaugurated. This fund-raising endeavor targeted $2.5 million for the addition of approximately 13,000 square feet, more than doubling the existing space. One hundred percent of parents, staff members, and trustees supported the campaign, and many pledges from individual and corporate donors were supplemented by a major grant from The Kresge Foundation, as well as grants from other foundations.

The new facilities were completed in 1997, again with no outstanding debt, and won an architectural award. Architects and intervention professionals often visit the Institute, and the facilities have provided a model for other programs in New Jersey and elsewhere.

All instructional areas of the school are carpeted; this helps to create a quiet environment that promotes ongoing language instruction. Wide hallways not only invite children to use the halls as play areas but also enable groups of visitors to comfortably tour the facilities. Most classrooms provide space for several instructors and students, so that senior teachers can model instructional procedures and assist novice staff members. Perhaps most important, the building is designed to permit easy observation of all areas occupied by students, enabling supervisors, parents, and visitors to view ongoing activities. Further, the offices of senior intervention personnel and program directors are not clustered together in one area but distributed throughout the school, so that supervisors are available to monitor ongoing activities and assist staff members.

Diagnosis and Assessment

Twenty-four of the 26 students who presently attend the Institute's school were previously served in the preschool, and 10 were first seen as toddlers enrolled in PCDI's early intervention program at 21 to 31 months of age. All of the children were diagnosed with an autism spectrum disorder; these diagnoses were conferred by physicians unaffiliated with PCDI. Institute psychologists confirmed the diagnoses, using the *Diagnostic and Statistical Manual of Mental Disorders–Fourth Edition* (American Psychiatric Association, 1994). IQ scores, verbal skills, and presenting repertoires are unrelated to admission criteria.

The progression from early intervention program to preschool to school is virtually seamless. Because school-age youngsters are already well known to Institute personnel, and because of the continuity of their intervention programs, new diagnostic initiatives are of minimal interest. At the request of parents or school district representatives, PCDI professionals conduct formal assessments. But the assessments of choice are the direct observation and measurement procedures that are part of the established practice of applied behavior analysis, such as frequency, rate, and duration measures and time-sampling procedures. Parents and professionals collaborate on the selection of education and intervention goals for each student, and target responses are regularly observed and measured, usually daily or two to three times per week. The resulting data are frequently reviewed, and ineffective programs are revised or replaced.

The Staff

At PCDI, staff members wear many hats. The Institute uses a generalist rather than a specialist model. There is no speech therapy department, occupational therapy department, recreation department, or music or art department. Instead, there is a school program staffed by professionals who use applied behavior analysis technology to teach speech and language, academic skills, daily living skills, leisure pursuits, family and community participation, and other critical repertoires.

Most staff members arrive with a bachelor's or master's degree in education or psychology but with minimal or no academic background or experience with applied behavior analysis or developmental disabilities. Although preservice and in-service workshops are provided, the most important training is hands-on: A trainer–supervisor (also known as a consultant or mentor) accompanies a new staff member to each assignment, models intervention procedures, structures supervised practice opportunities, gives positive and corrective feedback, and offers continuing support. This intensive, in vivo professional preparation is made possible by a trainer–trainee ratio of 1:4. Although it is an expensive ratio, we have not discovered another means to help staffers achieve the sophisticated intervention repertoires that are so important to young people with autism. Major investments in training are essential because, in truth, an intervention program is only as good as staff members' skills.

Year after year, PCDI generates data that make strong statements about training effects. First, the data show that although didactic training changes paper-and-pencil responses, it does not enable most people to achieve criterion intervention performances. Second, the data show that given regular, ongoing, hands-on training, it takes most new staff members 6 to 12 months to acquire basic intervention repertoires.

Each year, after instructors have received 3 or 4 months of hands-on training, they have "practice" evaluations conducted by their primary trainers, who use a protocol developed at the Institute. Then training continues and after 6 to 9 months, a senior professional who is not the staff member's primary mentor conducts an annual performance evaluation. The evaluation protocol is identical to the training protocol—the skills that are evaluated are precisely those skills that are taught. Staff members are successful if they exhibit the repertoires that are the targets of training, *and* if observational data on the children they serve show positive behavior change. Their mentors are successful only if the trainees pass their evaluations *and* the data on child performance show desired behavior change; and school administrators experience success only when data document favorable outcomes for students, teachers, and the teachers' mentors (McClannahan & Krantz, 1993). These group contingencies (Speltz, Shimamura, & McReynolds, 1982) create an intervention system that supports children's progress, and it should be noted that the contingencies are real. There is no tenure system at PCDI; staff members who do not pass their annual evaluations are not reappointed for the following year. However, group reinforcement contingencies promote everyone's success, and most people pass their evaluations.

Program Administration

Baer, Wolf, and Risley (1987) discussed the weak contingencies available to behavior analysts who serve as external program consultants and concluded that it is important for scientists to become program administrators. We concur with that recommendation, but it is noteworthy that our field has done a much more credible job helping young professionals acquire intervention technology than teaching them to apply behavior analysis skills to financial management, public relations, marketing, working with governing boards, contract negotiation, or fund-raising. Some scientist–practitioners acquire these skills from the school of hard knocks, but that is a risky way to do business. Such risks sometimes result in financial disaster, loss of valuable colleagues to our field, failed programs, and adverse publicity for behavior analysis (Krantz, 2003). At PCDI, an important role of program administration is to provide a curriculum for tomorrow's leaders, one that prepares them to become the heads of new autism intervention programs.

Effective intervention programs require precise arrangements of antecedent and consequent variables to achieve desirable, interactive outcomes for service receivers, staff members, staff trainers, and managers. If the CEO is not a behavior analyst, it may be difficult to put relevant measurement systems in place, to introduce new intervention procedures, or to make organizational policy that is based on objective data. We teach the next generation of leaders that autism intervention is most effective when entire systems are designed, managed, and revised on the basis of data.

Administrators must recognize that the intervention business, like other businesses, must achieve an almost-balanced budget in order to survive, especially in an era of reduced expenditures for education and human services. But profit margins that are gained by grossly underpaying intervention personnel or by capriciously altering staff–learner ratios lead to ineffective programs, and sometimes even to the demise of agencies. Typically, the only "profits" that accountable agencies achieve are the result of intervention efforts that defer or preclude larger expenditures. Early intervention often achieves this type of cost effectiveness (Jacobson, Mullick, & Green, 1998); when children make transitions from intensive behavioral treatment to public school classrooms, multimillion-dollar expenditures for long-term treatment are obviated. Similarly, when adolescents acquire skills that later contribute to their success in supported employment, cost savings are achieved through their income tax payments, their reduced or nonexistent SSI and Medicaid benefits, and their contributions to the costs of their training programs.

Although some people with severe developmental disabilities need lifelong services, effective intervention that produces socially significant behavior change can nevertheless result in substantial savings. For example, teaching relevant family- and community-living skills may prevent residential placement, and reduction in the frequency of self-injury or aggression may permit children to continue their intervention programs with less expensive staff–student ratios.

At PCDI, some additional savings are realized because administrative costs (e.g., secretarial, bookkeeping, and business management costs) are distributed across the early intervention program, the preschool and school, the residential programs, and the adult program. This keeps the administrative team very busy, but we have often noted a relationship between a "lean" administration and additional dollars earmarked for intervention.

The Students

At this writing, all 26 students who attend PCDI's school are male; 2 are Asian, and the remainder are Caucasian. They range in age from 5 to 21 years, and they have been enrolled in the Institute's programs for 3 to 18 years. At program entry, none was toilet trained. Most had little or no receptive or expressive language, and they engaged in high-rate stereotypies such as vocal noise, hand-flapping, toe-walking, and other repetitive responses. None of them imitated others or engaged in cooperative play with siblings or peers; none appropriately interacted with caregivers; and none displayed normative visual attending to family members or others. Some were self-injurious, and many engaged in frequent crying episodes or tantrums. Presently, one student lives in a PCDI group home; the others live at home with one or both parents.

Children attend school from 8:30 A.M. to 2:30 P.M., 5 days per week. The overall instructor–student ratio is 1:1.2, but the teacher–learner ratio for the youngest children is 1:1; it gradually changes as students gain skills, so that the ratio for adolescents is 1:2.

Although some writers report that approximately 50% of children with autism do not learn to talk (Spradlin & Brady, 1999), that has not been our experience. The spoken language of currently enrolled students ranges from a few words to *paragraphic* speech (i.e., unprompted verbal productions that include two or more sentences or questions). Presently, 15 children display paragraphic speech. Three students use augmentative communication devices but continue to receive expressive language training.

All of the children use activity schedules throughout the school day (McClannahan & Krantz, 1999), and 17 use written rather than photographic activity schedules. Reading levels range from prekindergarten to fourth grade.

Curriculum and Instructional Methodology

The curriculum is a series of intervention programs developed at the Institute during the last 3 decades. An intervention program is defined as a document that includes, at minimum, (a) a written response definition that describes observable behavior or products of behavior, (b) a specified measurement procedure, and (c) a written description of the teaching procedures. At last count, there were 794 such programs that addressed the following skill areas: arithmetic, art, activity schedules, community living, correspondence and matching skills, direction following, engagement or on-task behavior, expressive language, handwriting, health care, home living, keyboard skills, leisure activities, money, motor imitation, music, physical education, peer interaction, reading, receptive language, science, self-care, social skills, social studies, spelling, time, verbal imitation, and vocational skills.

At the outset of intervention, toddlers' and preschoolers' programs typically include visual attending, matching and picture–object correspondence skills, following photographic activity schedules, following directions, motor imitation, verbal imitation, receptive labeling, social initiations, play skills, and appropriate use of the potty or toilet. Professionals and parents jointly participate in selecting an initial curriculum for a child, based on his or her presenting skills and skill deficits. The curriculum is individualized for each youngster; programs are added or deleted, based on the child's repertoire. For example, one child's instructional plan may include a program that teaches eating a variety of foods and a program that teaches riding a tricycle; another youngster's curriculum may feature fine motor skills such as coloring or using a computer mouse and dressing or undressing.

As children acquire new skills, some programs are discontinued and others are added. The selection of new programs continues to be based on data on the student's current skills. Matching skills are prerequisites for learning picture–object correspondence; imitating phonemes is a necessary prerequisite for learning to imitate longer utterances.

Not only is curriculum content individualized, but teaching procedures are also individualized for each youngster. The manner in which instructional stimuli are presented, prompting and error correction procedures, and types of rewards are tailored to each child's existing skills and learning style. Of course, children learn at different rates, have unique preferences, and display faster progress in some areas and slower progress in others. As a result, when they make the transition from preschool to school, each child's curriculum may be quite different from his peers'.

Programs may be implemented at school, in children's homes, and in community settings. Many programs begin at school, and when the relevant skills are mastered in that setting, generalization is programmed to home. For example, a student may learn to read, take pills, make a bed, or make a sandwich at school, but when the goals are met in that setting, the program is introduced at home; this accelerates young people's progress and promotes parents' success in delivering instruction and intervention at home.

Other programs begin at school and are later implemented in the community. It is important to teach youngsters to behave appropriately in barber shops and in dentists', pediatricians', and optometrists' offices but impractical to teach all of the requisite skills in those settings; therefore, relevant events are first simulated at school, and basic repertoires are established before the children visit such shops and offices. Likewise, youngsters may initially practice making purchases in the classroom "store," and when that skill set is acquired, they next practice making purchases at fast-food restaurants, ice cream parlors, convenience stores, grocery stores, and other establishments. Many skills require community programming; for example, most schools do not offer the variety of toilets, stalls, urinals, faucets, hand dryers, and paper towel dispensers that are necessary to program generalized use of public restrooms.

The PCDI curriculum does not feature one or a few intervention procedures; rather, it includes a plethora of empirically based procedures that are represented in the research literature of behavior analysis. Young people with autism, like all of us, must learn to learn in a variety of ways; from discrete trial teaching and incidental teaching; from stimulus shaping and fading procedures; from pictorial, auditory, and textual cues; from television, videotapes, and computers; and from parents, teachers, peers, and employers (Krantz, 2000).

Integration

When students develop the requisite skills, it is important to program social interaction opportunities with siblings, peers, and community members. For example, young PCDI students learn to play board games, engage in exercise routines, and participate in sports such as swimming, biking, skiing, and skating with their brothers and sisters.

Based on the data on students' skills, staff members help arrange interaction opportunities with peers without disabilities. When attending "play dates," gymnastics lessons, after-school programs, day camps, and religious education classes, children are initially accompanied by staff members, whose presence is gradually faded when data show that youngsters are displaying appropriate social repertoires. Special programs also help young people participate in family and community events such as birthdays, weddings, funerals, bar and bat mitzvahs, confirmation ceremonies, church choirs, holiday celebrations, and local sports events.

In addition, when children meet certain readiness criteria, they begin gradual transitions from PCDI to general or special education classrooms in their local communities. Variables that appear to be predictors of children's success in public school classrooms include displaying sustained engagement with teacher-directed activities and class assignments, consistently following individual and group directions, responding to temporally delayed consequences delivered via behavioral contracts or school notes, using novel or generative language, displaying skill generalization across settings, and exhibiting low rates of inappropriate behavior such as stereotypy or tantrums (Krantz & McClannahan, 1999).

At this writing, two youngsters, ages 7 and 8 years, are making gradual transitions from PCDI to public schools. They are accompanied by Institute professionals whose presence is gradually faded, based on the data on children's performance in the receiving classrooms.

Although some people need lifelong support, ever expanding community participation is actively programmed. Students of varying abilities learn to make grocery lists and do grocery shopping; use ATMs; place orders in restaurants; use recreation facilities such as tennis courts, driving ranges, and gyms; and use public laundromats. Presently, six young people, ages 18 to 21 years, participate in a work-study program designed to smooth their transitions to adult employment. PCDI personnel accompany them to their part-time jobs and to after-work activities in the community.

When discussing integration, a cautionary note is in order. Although "social integration" is widely touted, it too often means that children with autism attend public school classrooms where they engage in parallel activities that only vaguely resemble those of their classmates and receive noncontingent attention and ineffective prompts from aides who have no training in behavioral intervention. This type of programming is very expensive because there is often no return on the dollars invested.

Integration is also irrelevant if children have not yet learned to visually attend to interaction partners, imitate others' behavior, or participate in nonverbal social exchanges such as showing or turn taking. When children are beginning to acquire social repertoires, adults are often better interaction partners than peers, because adults can provide clear models, control the pace of interaction, and pause and wait for children to respond. Donald M. Baer, a founder of applied behavior analysis, noted:

> The political value of keeping autistic children in mainstreamed society is not to their benefit if they're failing to learn the skills necessary for mainstreamed life in adulthood. If a relatively independent and happy life as an adult is our goal, then I think the literature, indirectly, but I think fairly consistently, supports the notion that you're going to have to have a fairly restrictive environment, a very closely structured program when the individual is younger. And in the long run that will turn out to be the least restrictive programming you could have had that will accomplish the desired outcome. (Heward & Wood, 2003, p. 299)

Transitions from Childhood to Adulthood

Expectations for typical children change radically when they cease to be preschoolers and attain school age, and expectations continue to change as they move from elementary school to middle school to secondary school. It is the same for young people with autism. Parents, siblings, relatives, neighbors, and community members have increased performance expectations as children with autism get older. If programming emphases do not change to reflect changes in expectations, students with disabilities are vulnerable to public disapproval and discrimination.

As a case in point, after preschoolers learn to use words and phrases, we teach "please" and "thank you," and when they arrive at school age, we begin to teach other polite responses, such as "no, thank you," "you're welcome," and "excuse me." Not long after that, we teach them to introduce themselves, to give and accept compliments, and to offer assistance to others. A repertoire of "please" and "thank you" may be adequate for a preschooler, but it is an impoverished repertoire for a 10-year-old or an adolescent with autism.

Likewise, we are happy if preschoolers independently wash their hands and follow parents' directions at bath time, but elementary-age youngsters must learn to bathe or shower with less assistance, and teenagers must acquire self-care repertoires that include acne prevention, shaving, feminine hygiene, nail care, use of deodorant, and other grooming skills that are typical of adolescents and adults without disabilities. Each skill set serves as a foundation for the next accomplishments. Young children make simple snacks and set the table; later, they learn to make sandwiches and use the microwave; adolescents make their own breakfasts and lunches, and adults prepare complete meals. Smooth transitions from childhood to adulthood require that, at each age level, we identify the next repertoires that enable people to achieve optimum independence in adulthood.

Almost 20 years of experience providing services to adults with autism has a continuing impact on the curriculum for school-age children. Data on adults' skills and skill deficits often suggest skill areas that should be taught earlier, or repertoires that should be elaborated before students arrive at adulthood (McClannahan, MacDuff, & Krantz, 2002). Learning to wait is an example of a repertoire that must expand throughout childhood and adolescence. Preschoolers learn to wait for 1 or 2 minutes, long enough for a parent to pay a store clerk, put an infant in a car seat, or turn off the bathwater. Elementary-age children wait for somewhat longer intervals while parents answer the telephone or the door, put a casserole in the oven, or listen to a sibling's account of the school day. Teenagers learn to wait in designated locations at shopping malls, restaurants, or other community settings, because it is no longer appropriate for them to go into public restrooms with parents of the opposite gender. Before they enter supported employment programs, adolescents and young adults must be capable of waiting for more extended periods of time when parents, instructors, job coaches, or employers are out of sight.

Family Participation

Parents are welcomed to PCDI for school visits, and a home programmer (a member of the professional staff who has daily contact with a student) regularly visits the home. After parents give consent for a new intervention program, the program begins at school, and the parents are invited to observe, to collect data on their child's performance, and, later, to implement the program at school with the assistance of the home programmer. When the student acquires the target skills at school, the home programmer and parents introduce the program at home; and when the young person dependably displays those skills at home, the home programmer's assistance and presence are gradually faded from that activity, leaving the parents to maintain or extend it. These events represent a continuing cycle; when a boy or girl masters one skill set, a new program is initiated. During the past year, home programmers delivered 1,915 hours of home programming services (the equivalent of 48 forty-hour workweeks), made 1,049 visits to 25 families (a mean of 42 visits per family), and helped parents implement 198 intervention programs in their own homes.

Parents' involvement with their children with autism appears to follow much the same pattern as their involvement with their sons and daughters without disabilities. That is, they expect to spend a great deal of time with toddlers, preschoolers, and young elementary-age children, but when children arrive at puberty, expectations often shift toward greater independence; and when children become adults, those expectations are further magnified.

PCDI professionals help parents select intervention goals that are consistent with their changing expectations. Upon returning home from school, a 9-year-old learns to remain independently engaged in leisure activities for longer time periods. A 10-year-old helps by unloading the dishwasher, setting the table, and folding towels. A 12-year-old completes homework assignments with minimal assistance. A young teenager independently follows an activity schedule to complete a workout that includes doing calisthenics and walking on a treadmill. An older adolescent independently arises when his alarm clock rings, makes his bed, showers, and shaves with minimal supervision. Other intervention programs help youths learn to take responsibility for their own belongings. Behavioral contracts help them arrive at school with completed homework assignments; school lunches they made the previous evening; wristwatches (important for time-telling and appointment-keeping skills); wallets (necessary for acquisition of purchasing repertoires); gym bags; and notes from parents that verify that they completed a home activity schedule, prepared a target food, practiced piano, or vacuumed and dusted a room. Learning to respond to delayed contingencies—for example, responding to positive or corrective feedback delivered at school for behavior at home on the preceding day—promotes independent performances that are valued by parents and that also expand students' opportunities to hold jobs and to participate in community activities.

Outcome

Approximately 42% of children who arrive at PCDI before 60 months of age later make successful transitions to public schools, and the majority of them participate in general education rather than special education. Some have completed college and are now pursuing careers; some finished high school and found jobs in business and industry; and some are attending elementary schools, middle schools, and high schools in their own school districts and neighborhoods. The outcomes and accomplishments of some of these young people are described in greater detail in McClannahan and Krantz (2001).

The data on outcome have remained quite stable for more than a decade, and because about 58% of enrolled children will need lifelong services, there is no defined age for program exit. Useful data are derived from providing a continuum of services for toddlers, preschoolers, school-age children, and adults with autism. As noted earlier, data on intervention for young children often enhance outcomes for tomorrow's adults, and data on adults' skills and skill deficits suggest improvements in the curriculum for young children (McClannahan et al., 2002).

Special measures are needed to assess outcomes for students who remain at PCDI; therefore, once a year, an outside evaluator—a professional with expertise in autism intervention—reviews as many programs as possible during a 3-day visit to PCDI, using a protocol that was developed and validated at the Institute. During the past year, 723 behavior-increase programs, 198 home programs, and 44 behavior-decrease programs were delivered to 29 children—a total of 965 programs. Because of the large number of programs implemented during a 12-month period, it is impossible to review all of them; therefore, the evaluator is asked to devise a sampling procedure.

The evaluator scores a program as completely documented if it includes a written response definition, a specified measurement procedure, a description of intervention procedures, and a graph or other form of data summary that displays the target responses over time. Programs are also scored as producing desired behavior change, producing no behavior change, or producing unfavorable behavior change. Further, evaluators are asked to determine whether a program is consistent with professional ethics and the published literature of the field. If the answer is affirmative, the program is rated "may continue"; programs that are not viewed as consistent with professional ethics or the literature of behavior analysis are scored "stop immediately"; and programs that are not fully documented are rated "can't ascertain."

The evaluator also notes the presence or absence of written parent consent, obtained within the prior 365 days or since the last program revision, and determines whether four or more interobserver agreement measures were obtained for that program during the past year. Of course, documentation of parents' or guardians' consent is important for reasons of rights protection and professional ethics. And assessment of inter-observer agreement is relevant because decisions about intervention are only as good as the data upon which they are based. Table 6.1 displays the results of the most recent evaluation by an outside expert.

Table 6.1 shows that, on the last external evaluation of intervention programs, 100% of school behavior-increase programs, 98% of school behavior-decrease programs, and 99% of programs implemented at home by students' parents were scored as completely documented. Thus, most programs contained the information necessary to the assessment of students' progress.

The table also shows that 98% of school behavior-increase programs, 80% of school behavior-decrease programs, and 95% of home programs were scored as producing desired behavior change. The lowest score shown in Table 6.1 is the percentage of school behavior-decrease programs rated as producing desired behavior change. Behavior-decrease programs often address repertoires that are difficult to alter, such as vocal noise, motor stereotypy, noncontextual laughter, aggression, and self-injury. Typical intervention procedures include reinforcement of incompatible responses, token loss, behavioral rehearsal, and graduated guidance. For some years, we have examined "opt out" procedures—procedures that teach people to appropriately exempt themselves from settings and activities that evoke stereotypy, aggression, or self-injury—and the data indicate that students with severe disabilities and long histories of disruptive behavior can learn to appropriately excuse themselves, depart to the privacy of an unoccupied classroom at school or a bedroom at home, and return to ongoing

Table 6.1

Results of an Annual External Evaluation of Intervention Programs

Measure	School Behavior-Increase Program $N = 66$ of 723 (9%)	School Behavior-Decrease Program $N = 44$ of 44 (100%)	Home Program $N = 198$ of 198 (100%)
Programs scored as completely documented	100%	98%	99%
Programs scored as producing favorable behavior change	98%	80%	95%
Programs rated as appropriate (i.e., "may continue")	100%	98%	98%
Programs for which parents' or guardians' consent was obtained	98%	93%	90%
Programs for which four or more interobserver agreement assessments were obtained	94%	91%	90%

activities after a period of time that they select. But behavior change is often gradual, and treatment may continue over months or years before intervention goals are achieved. Nevertheless, most years, at least 80% of behavior-decrease programs are scored as producing favorable behavior change.

On the last evaluation, 98% to 100% of programs were scored appropriate or "may continue"; one school behavior-decrease program and four home programs were rated "can't ascertain" because documentation (e.g., information about the target response, measurement procedures, or intervention procedures) was unclear. Ninety percent to 98% of the sampled programs included signed consent given by parents or guardians within the past year or since the last program revision.

Of the 308 programs evaluated, 90% to 94% included four or more interobserver agreement measures that were obtained during the year prior to the evaluation. Many of these programs exceeded the criterion, but if they had merely met the criterion of four measures per year, that would represent 1,232 interobserver agreement assessments. Of course, there were actually many more interobserver agreement measures, but the total number is not known because not all school programs were drawn into the sample and evaluated.

Using the same protocol as the external evaluator, PCDI co-observers scored a subsample of programs selected by the evaluator. Mean interobserver agreement between the outside evaluator and PCDI co-observers, across all evaluation dimensions, was 98% for school behavior-increase programs, 95% for school behavior-decrease programs, and 93% for home programs.

These evaluation data, obtained annually for nearly 2 decades, led to the establishment of benchmarks; a score of 80% or better on an evaluation dimension is regarded as a positive outcome; scores below that benchmark indicate that major corrective action is necessary. Of course, every evaluation produces data that generate program revisions and lead to improvements in the curriculum. In addition to scoring the dimensions noted in Table 6.1, evaluators provide verbal and written feedback that enhances intervention.

The 767 school behavior-increase and behavior-decrease programs delivered to 29 students last year represent a mean of 26 programs per student, and the 198 home programs represent an average of 8 programs per student. Over the course of the year, some programs were discontinued because the target skills were acquired, a few were discontinued because they did not achieve the desired outcomes, and new programs were introduced.

A very different assessment of students' progress is a measure of their engagement with activities and other persons. A substantial research literature documents relationships between engagement and the acquisition of new academic, language, social, and self-care skills (Greenwood, 1999). At PCDI, engagement is defined as scrutinizing, manipulating, or otherwise appropriately using instructional or leisure materials; visually attending to an instructor or a peer interaction partner, or following directions (McClannahan, Krantz, MacDuff, & Fenske, 1988). Children are not scored as engaged if they are exhibiting stereotypic, disruptive, or other inappropriate behavior.

Every minute on the minute mark, observers first count (from left to right) and record the number of students present in a classroom or activity area and then count the number of students who are engaged. Repeated observations are summed and converted to mean percentage of students scored as engaged. At PCDI, engagement measures are used in several ways. Data collected during staff training sessions and performance evaluations provide feedback on instructors' skills. Data on a single student's engagement over a period of time or in different activities show the extent to which he or she exhibits sustained attention to assigned tasks. And periodically, supervisors walk through the school and collect a time sample in each classroom or activity area; this produces a programmatic measure of engagement. Eight recent measures of school-wide student engagement ranged from 83% to 97% (mean = 92%).

After more than 25 years of assessing the engagement of young people with autism, it is evident that, given an effective intervention system, one can expect engagement to be 80% or higher across students, instructors, settings, and time. It is noteworthy that in many day care centers, public school classrooms, and after-school programs for children with and without developmental disabilities, engagement falls far below this benchmark (Favell & McGimsey, 1993; Fishbein & Wasik, 1981; Harris, 1986; Pfiffner & O'Leary, 1987).

The most important outcomes are related to the quality of life of the young people who receive services. Ted lives in one of PCDI's group homes and attends the Institute's adult program. He is not in supported employment because he has frequent seizures that are not well controlled by medication. He is paid for his participation in contract work, and he makes many choices—choices about how to sequence his own activities, choices of meals at the group home, choices of restaurants, and choices of leisure activities. He completes self-care tasks with minimal supervision and contributes to his household by assisting with meal preparation and housekeeping tasks. Although his vocabulary is not large, he enjoys talking about his family members, amusement parks, and favorite restaurants.

Charles also lives in one of the Institute's group homes. His PCDI job coaches take him to his full-time grounds maintenance job at a local college and to after-work activities in the community. He pays his own bills and balances his checkbook. He enjoys movies, videos, and going to baseball games.

Adam lives with his parents. He independently takes a commuter train to his data-entry job in an insurance company. He works quickly, and his error rate is very low; he receives on-the-job assistance when he is given new assignments or when he encounters unexpected situations.

Clark earned a bachelor's degree and is engaged to be married. Alan is attending an out-of-state university, pursuing a degree in special education. George finished high school in his home town and is employed in a warehouse; Juan is earning good grades in a middle school in his community; and Roger attends a general education elementary school classroom and receives some assistance in a resource room. We are proud of the accomplishments of these young people and appreciative of the ways in which applied behavior analysis has contributed to their futures, but the clock is always ticking. In a teleconference in 2002, Baer noted,

> The essence of treatment for autism, in my opinion, is a race against time. We have a great number of behavior changes to make, and we don't have a lot of time in which to make them because once the autistic child becomes an adult—although the laws of behavior don't change just because that has happened—the probability that we can get social programs running for them, aimed at their inclusion in everyday society, becomes much lower. I think the notion of programming an adult back into society is harder to sell than the notion of programming a child's acceptability to society. Therefore, I think we have to make a lot of behavior changes during childhood and not in adulthood if we can possibly avoid it. (Heward & Wood, 2003, p. 297)

Programs for school-age children with autism have a mandate to win this race.

Summary

The Princeton Child Development Institute uses the science of applied behavior analysis in all areas of operation, including administration, staff training and evaluation, intervention strategies, work with families, and program evaluation. The data that are produced in these arenas support integration of all program components, permit rapid error correction, contribute to program fidelity, and foster positive outcomes for students.

References

American Psychiatric Association. (1994). *Diagnostic and statistical manual of mental disorders* (4th ed.). Washington, DC: Author.

Baer, D. M., Wolf, M. M., & Risley, T. R. (1987). Some still-current dimensions of applied behavior analysis. *Journal of Applied Behavior Analysis, 20,* 313–327.

Favell, J. E., & McGimsey, J. F. (1993). Defining an acceptable treatment environment. In R. Van Houten & S. Axelrod (Eds.), *Behavior analysis and treatment* (pp. 27–29). New York: Plenum Press.

Fishbein, J. E., & Wasik, B. H. (1981). Effect of the good behavior game on disruptive library behavior. *Journal of Applied Behavior Analysis, 14,* 89–93.

Greenwood, C. R. (1999). Reflections on a research career: Perspective on 35 years of research at the Juniper Gardens Children's Project. *Exceptional Children, 66,* 7–21.

Harris, K. R. (1986). Self-monitoring of attentional behavior versus self-monitoring of productivity: Effects on on-task behavior and academic response rate among learning disabled children. *Journal of Applied Behavior Analysis, 19,* 417–423.

Heward, W. L., & Wood, C. L. (2003). Thursday afternoons with Don: Selections from three teleconference seminars on applied behavior analysis. In K. S. Budd & T. Stokes (Eds.), *A small matter of proof: The legacy of Donald M. Baer* (pp. 293–310). Reno, NV: Context Press.

Jacobson, J. W., Mullick, J. A., & Green, G. (1998). Cost-benefit estimates for early intensive behavioral intervention for young children with autism—General model and single state case. *Behavioral Interventions, 13,* 201–226.

Krantz, P. J. (2000). Commentary: Interventions to facilitate socialization. *Journal of Autism and Developmental Disorders, 30,* 411–413.

Krantz, P. J. (2003, May). *Autism, science, and politics.* Address given at the meeting of the Association for Behavior Analysis, San Francisco, CA.

Krantz, P. J., & McClannahan, L. E. (1999). Strategies for integration: Building repertoires that support transitions to public schools. In P. M. Ghezzi, W. L. Williams, & J. E. Carr (Eds.), *Autism: Behavior analytic perspectives* (pp. 221–231). Reno, NV: Context Press.

McClannahan, L. E., & Krantz, P. J. (1993). On systems analysis in autism intervention programs. *Journal of Applied Behavior Analysis, 26,* 589–596.

McClannahan, L. E., & Krantz, P. J. (1999). *Activity schedules for children with autism: Teaching independent behavior.* Bethesda, MD: Woodbine House.

McClannahan, L. E., & Krantz, P. J. (2001). Behavior analysis and intervention for preschoolers at the Princeton Child Development Institute. In J. S. Handleman & S. L. Harris (Eds.), *Preschool education programs for children with autism* (2nd ed., pp. 191–213). Austin, TX: PRO-ED.

McClannahan, L. E., Krantz, P. J., MacDuff, G. S., & Fenske, E. C. (1988). *Staff training and evaluation protocol.* Unpublished manuscript, Princeton Child Development Institute, Princeton, NJ.

McClannahan, L. E., MacDuff, G. S., & Krantz, P. J. (2002). Behavior analysis and intervention for adults with autism. *Behavior Modification, 26,* 9–26.

Pfiffner, L. J., & O'Leary, S. G. (1987). The efficacy of all-positive management as a function of the prior use of negative consequences. *Journal of Applied Behavior Analysis, 20,* 265–271.

Speltz, M. L., Shimamura, J. W., & McReynolds, W. T. (1982). Procedural variations in group contingencies: Effects on children's academic and social behaviors. *Journal of Applied Behavior Analysis, 15,* 533–544.

Spradlin, J. E., & Brady, N. C. (1999). Early childhood autism and stimulus control. In P. M. Ghezzi, W. L. Williams, & J. E. Carr (Eds.), *Autism: Behavior analytic perspectives* (pp. 49–65). Reno, NV: Context Press.

Application of the Pyramid Approach to Education Model in a Public School Setting

7

Andy Bondy and Kris Battaglini

E ffective teaching involves many intricate factors. Within a school system, professionals and paraprofessionals arrive with a variety of educational and theoretical backgrounds. For the students to benefit from everyone's educational efforts, teachers, speech–language pathologists (SLPs), psychologists, and other professionals must coordinate their actions. Over the years, we have put together an approach to organizing the complexities that constitute the key elements of designing effective lessons for students with autism in multiple environments. This model is the Pyramid Approach to Education (Bondy & Battaglini, 1992; Bondy & Sulzer-Azaroff, 2002).

The Pyramid Approach uses a three-dimensional structure to represent the highly interactive nature of teaching elements while simultaneously implying that we need to start at the base of a building before constructing the main body (see Figure 7.1). The foundation of the model involves the principles of learning (and thus teaching) derived from the large compendium of literature that makes up the field of applied behavior analysis. We refer to this aspect of the model as related to the "why" of behavior. Next, we consider the "what" of teaching, as in, "What should we teach?" We begin this review by looking at the long-term goal of an education: helping each person become a contributing member of society, primarily by ultimately getting a job in the real world and living somewhere other than the home of one's parents. The four elements here include (a) functional objectives associated with activities and materials, (b) the use of powerful reinforcement systems, (c) development of functional communication and social skills, and (d) addressing contextually inappropriate behaviors.

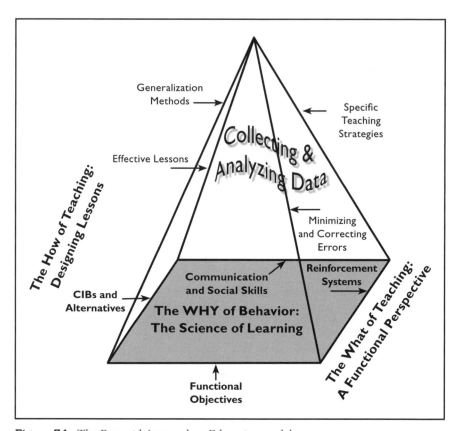

Figure 7.1. The Pyramid Approach to Education model.

The body of the pyramid deals with issues concerning the "how" of teaching. These issues are organized around (a) generalization, including issues related to stimulus as well as response factors (including fluency); (b) designing effective lessons, including discrete trials and sequential lessons led by either the teacher or the student; (c) specific lesson strategies, including using and eliminating prompts, as well as using shaping to teach new skills; and (d) minimizing and correcting errors with strategies associated with the type of lesson in which a student is engaged.

Of course, the entire model is underscored by the systematic collection and analysis of data. This last issue aligns federal (and often state) mandates for evaluation with the core feature of behavior analysis: basing educational decisions on data collection and review.

The order in which we describe this model is the order in which we teach staff to implement the model. All staff members, independent of their professional background, experience a common training sequence. This sequence also forms the basis for parent training. In this manner, the Pyramid Approach is viewed as a problem-solving strategy that promotes communication and collaboration between team members. When lessons are constructed, a common language is used, so that all team members can understand (and implement when appropriate) the teaching strategies selected for particular goals. When problems arise, as when students do not make anticipated progress, the pyramid model serves as an anchor around which further discussion and problem solving can arise.

The use of this approach was noted previously for preschool programs (Bondy & Frost, 1994a). This chapter outlines how this approach has been used for school-age students with autism. This approach was developed within a statewide public school system and has since been successfully implemented in private programs, as well as residential settings, vocational settings, and in-home programs. We will showcase the implementation of this model in one public school program, the Sussex Consortium (SC), which is part of the statewide Delaware Autism Program (and is under the direction of the second author). This program received the 2002 Wendy F. Miller Autism Program of the Year Award in recognition of its excellence by the Autism Society of America (ASA).

The SC designs educational opportunities in accordance with its mandate to provide services within a continuum of placement options. That is, no one setting makes up the SC. It consists of self-contained classes where there are appropriate and partial mainstream opportunities, as well as full placement with part-time support in general educational settings. The statewide program provides year-round educational services and includes a residential component where appropriate. The program serves over 400 students from under 2 years to age 21 years.

We will provide operational details regarding the SC as an example of how the Pyramid Approach model can be implemented across grades for children with autism displaying varying functioning levels and placed in a variety of school and community settings.

Introduction to the SC Program

The SC currently serves a population totaling over 100 students with an educational classification of autism. Students range in age from preschool to young adults, as the state code calls for provision of educational services commencing at any point from birth to age 21 years. The preschool program makes up the single largest age group within the SC program components and appears to be disproportionately large, given the relatively small population base of southern Delaware. This is likely the result of several factors, including the continuing pattern of growth of the local community, the continuing development of early intervention screening programs and thus referral sources, the increased awareness of autism (in general and, in particular, among clinicians such as pediatricians), and the overall increase in the incidence of the disorder. The success of the SC program as perceived by parent consumers also has apparently influenced the growth of the program. Over the past several years, parents have reported that the primary impetus for their relocation to the Lewes area has been to access services for their child identified with autism. The receipt of ASA's award also has likely influenced this phenomenon.

Diagnosis and Assessment

The process of identification of student eligibility for services has been an evolutionary one as a result of the several general circumstances related to the manner in which students come to SC. Some students have been referred with a relatively thorough medical diagnostic file identifying autism, while others have been referred for assessment by program staff. A third scenario has involved transfers from other school systems or programs. In each of these instances, and consistent with state and federal requirements, the ultimate determination of eligibility (as well as educational placement) remains with the child's Individualized Education Program (IEP) team. Specialists within the program, including school psychologists and SLPs, typically participate in the assessment and IEP team processes. Upon receipt, a referral is reviewed with respect to the breadth of the information available. Given one of the three circumstances or scenarios mentioned, a determination is made with respect to what if any additional information is needed or recommended. Delaware code requires that eligibility be supported by an assessment generated by a school psychologist, psychologist, or physician.

When the school performs the initial assessment, a multidisciplinary team, including a psychologist, an SLP, and a classroom teacher, complete the assessment. The team teacher typically holds a master's degree in special education, has several years of experience within the program, and is familiar with a number of observation protocols and specific instruments. The assessment includes standardized instruments and adaptive social–behavioral measures, as well as protocols selected at the discretion of the respective specialists as a result of the review of the intake information. Features of autism are considered in the context of various scales or criteria designed for that purpose, such as the *Autism Diagnostic Observation Schedule* (Lord, Rutter, DiLavore, & Risi, 1999), the *Childhood Autism Rating Scale* (Schopler, Reichler, & Renner, 1988), or the criteria of the *Diagnostic and Statistical Manual of Mental Disorders–Fourth Edition–Revised* (DSM–IV–R; American Psychiatric Association, 2000).

Observations across multiple environments as well as input from multiple sources are collected and reviewed. If the team is not fully convinced of eligibility, a temporary placement can be used for the specific purpose of completing the identification process. Scrutiny also is applied to cases involving transfers to the program, given the concern relative to differential diagnosis. For example, occasionally, referred students present with significant behavioral difficulties but not necessarily atypical social or communicative characteristics.

The distinction of educational classification versus diagnosis has been important, as occasionally a child presents with unique characteristics or a less than clearly defined profile, even after the opportunity for extended observation following a temporary placement. In such instances, the discretion of the IEP team regarding eligibility prevails, allowing for the application of the "best-fitting descriptor" with respect to educational classification. This denotation is critical given the importance of developing an appropriate educational plan rather than concerns regarding identification of a "narrow band group" for purposes such as pure research. Thus, the initial responsibility of the IEP team is to determine educational classification, not medical diagnosis, and on occasion this emphasis may result in some degree of incongruence with the conclusions of medical practitioners.

Staffing and Administrative Structure

Staffing ratios within Delaware are largely a function of the state's unit-count system, which specifies all levels of educational service. The state provides a significant portion of funding for key direct service staff regarding the classification of autism, with the remainder coming from local funds. Four students delineate one autism unit, which is supported by funding for one teacher and one paraprofessional, as well as one SLP for every three units, and one psychologist for every six units. From this core support, provisions can be designed to support adaptive physical education or other specialists. In general, this system leads to typical class sizes of four to six students when self-contained classrooms are viewed as appropriate.

There is a unique statewide certification process to support additional training for teachers. Teachers with a general background in special education can be hired, provided they complete the certification process within 3 years. This process calls for five graduate-level courses to obtain certification in Autism/Severely Handicapped. These courses include Introduction to Autism, Methods and Curriculum Development in Autism, Functional Communication, and two electives related specifically to autism (e.g., applied behavior analysis, vocational or community-based instruction). Psychologists and SLPs typically work with more than the number identified by the unit system. In general, SLPs work with 4 to 5 classes of varying ages and abilities, while a psychologist (typically a school psychologist) usually works with 8 to 10 classes of students. Services are provided within a collaborative model, meaning that SLPs (and other specialists) work within the classroom or community setting when appropriate. Students may be pulled out of the classroom if special equipment is deemed necessary.

Related services, including occupational and physical therapy, as well as residential placement, are decided upon on a student-by-student basis. Delaware directly operates three group homes, which is unique to public schools, though students in these homes attend the program in the northern part of the state. Currently, none of the 105 students who attend the SC receives such residential services, though in the past, part-time and, in rare instances, full-time services have been provided via the northern facility.

Another residential option involves part-time placement within the local community, typically in homes of program staff, who receive additional salaries for such responsibilities. Such services are provided within the context of the IEP process and are evaluated for appropriateness, as are any other objectives and services.

An emphasis is placed upon ongoing training by requiring all staff (including paraprofessionals) to complete training (reading, watching demonstrations, showing direct skills, etc.) in all elements of the Pyramid Approach to Education, as well as the Picture Exchange Communication System (PECS; Frost & Bondy, 2002). Although not every student uses PECS, key teaching elements as well as an overall approach to expanding functional communication opportunities is beneficial to all staff and students. All staff members are trained by on-site instructors certified in an independent safety restraint protocol (Devereux Institute of Training and Research, 2002a, 2002b). When feasible, new staff members are assigned a mentor to help them learn the practical issues associated with the position, as well as the required educational materials. Staff members also are encouraged to participate in broad training opportunities by attending and participating in various state and national conferences related to autism, education, communication training, and applied behavior analysis.

There are three committees included within the organization of the statewide program that serve quality assurance functions. The Monitoring Review Board, which includes the statewide director, provides an annual review of the general programming needs of all students within the Autism Program. The role of this group also includes the communication of effective strategies across the three statewide program centers. The Peer Review Committee, which consists of three experts in the field of applied behavior analysis who have no other affiliation with the program, is charged with reviewing all highly intrusive behavior management plans for appropriateness with regard to professional and community standards. The Human Rights Committee is charged with providing input relative to community standards on the more general aspects of the program.

Curriculum, Instructional Management, and Skill Acquisition

The SC follows no single curriculum guide. Rather, each student's IEP content is based on an individual needs assessment within the overall functional orientation offered by the Pyramid Approach to Education. The contents of the IEP objectives are organized around functional domains, including domestic skills, social skills, community skills, vocational skills, recreation and leisure skills, contextually inappropriate behavior, communication skills, and school-based skills. Some students have school-based objectives that are purely academic, while others may work on reading or math within a functional context; thus, academics are thought of as being within the context of school-based skills.

These domains are used across age level and overall functioning level of the student. While a 3-year-old and a 13-year-old may have the same general objective (e.g., going shopping in a supermarket, requesting help), the specifics would reflect the current skills of the child. That is, it may be reasonable to expect a 3-year-old to hand over a toy that does not work, but we may expect a 13-year-old with strong language skills to use someone's name and ask for help with a description of the specific type of help that is needed. Each teacher and specialist uses the elements of the Pyramid Approach to guide lesson plan development (see Bondy & Battaglini, 1992, for an example of the lesson plan format).

Teachers describe the functional context for each lesson and describe generalization issues in terms of both stimulus (i.e., who, where, when, materials, etc.) and response (i.e., number, rate, accuracy, intensity, duration, etc.) factors. They indicate whether the lesson involves a primary discrete trial format or is a sequential lesson. For each of these types of lessons, they also describe whether the skill is initiated by the student or by the teacher. For all lessons, teachers describe the current stimulus control (including type of prompt) and the long-term stimulus control (or natural cue). For lessons involving prompts, teachers describe the strategy they will use to eliminate (or alter) the prompt, as well as the specific error-correction strategy they anticipate needing (given the nature of the lesson format). If they are using shaping or an errorless strategy, they describe the size of each step or change. A description of the type of reinforcement system, the schedule, and the plan for thinning the schedule of reinforcement over time also is noted. Finally, teachers specify the plan for data collection and analysis, in terms of how often data will be taken and by whom, when reviews are planned, and related issues (e.g., planning to reduce frequency of data collection over time). Typically, each lesson form includes an area for data collection, depending on the nature of the lesson (e.g., percent correct, prompt level, duration, intensity, accuracy). If the lesson involves a sequential task, the task analysis is included on the form.

It is important for each lesson to contain all of this information because there are no perfect lessons, nor can we expect a single lesson to be effective for all learners. There are many types of prompts, including verbal, gestural, and physical (Foxx, 1982b). While it often seems difficult to find an effective prompt, the key feature of a lesson is the plan to eliminate that prompt. Teachers are taught to use an array of prompt strategies, including hierarchies (most-to-least and least-to-most), delayed prompting (both fixed and increasing), fading, and graduated guidance. Modeling is an effective prompt for some children but not for those who are acquiring imitation skills. We suggest that teachers select a single prompt and try to eliminate that prompt rather than using multiple prompts, such as using both physical and verbal prompts simultaneously. In this latter case, the lesson would not be completed until both prompts were eliminated, a task that is generally more difficult than removing just one prompt. Therefore, when staff must use a physical or gestural prompt within a lesson, they would not add a verbal prompt. Once the child has engaged in the step or skill, the teacher is free to verbally acknowledge the step or simply name what has occurred (e.g., "Nice job tying your laces!").

Shaping is another teaching strategy that is stressed. Most teachers know in theory about how to use reinforcement to shape successive approximations toward a goal, but our experience has indicated that few use this strategy. In a true shaping lesson, no prompts are used—we note that we can "teach without touching." However, this strategy takes great patience and a degree of flexibility, and many teachers are attracted to the immediate power of using a prompt to ensure response production. Combining prompting and shaping still requires the elimination of the prompt, while in shaping there is no prompt to eliminate. The use of shaping also promotes lessons that are dynamic in nature—that is, what the student is doing at the end of the session is not the same as what was done at the start.

Of course, there are times when repetition within a lesson is warranted. Many skills improve over time only with successful practice. However, the knowledge that practice is important can lead to ritualistic strategies on the part of the teacher. Many teachers set up blocks of 10 trials for various skills, not because a block of 10 trials has been shown to be the most effective grouping of trials but rather because we all can figure out the percent correct easily, given 10 trials. We ask teachers to consider the issue of repetition in terms of each activity. If repetition is warranted, they make a determination of how many trials leads to the best acquisition and generalization of the skill. Ease of data collection should not be a criterion on which educational decisions are made.

Instructional Management

For each IEP objective, teachers take at least one data point per week. Of course, many objectives are associated with far more data collection. Therefore, the team decides how often, and by whom, data will be collected. Teachers typically keep a student's data form in a three-ring binder, although they may create separate binders associated with objectives in other parts of the school or for community-based objectives. Teams review all data forms on a weekly basis, and teachers submit progress summaries to the administrators and parents. These reports contain general narratives as well as detailed data-based statements and are scheduled in a manner consistent with the general education reports of grades (report cards).

If a student engages in contextually inappropriate behaviors, a behavior management plan must be in place. These targets include actions that are harmful to the child (self-injury), to other people (aggression), or to the environment (tantrums, property destruction, etc.); that interfere with traditional educational approaches (self-stimulation, disruptive noise, etc.), either for the child or for other students; or that may bring social sanctions against the child or caretakers (e.g., disrobing in public, speaking in a weird or bizarre manner, certain lengthy rituals).

A statewide Peer Review Committee (PRC), along with a Human Rights Committee, has established a guideline regarding the level of intrusiveness of various interventions. Some interventions (differential reinforcement schedule, verbal reprimand, token response cost, etc.) do not require review by the PRC. Other strategies (isolated time-out, etc.) require periodic data reporting, while yet another set of strategies (certain types of restraint) can be implemented only with prior committee approval. Staff routinely meet with the PRC regarding use of the most intrusive strategies.

Skill Acquisition

The rapidity with which a student acquires a skill is, in part, a function of the type of lesson being taught, the type of teaching strategy selected, the type of error-correction strategy used, and, of course, the system of reinforcement in place to support the skill. For all lessons, staff members describe the current source of stimulus control, including the type of prompt used (i.e., the type of help that will be removed across the lesson), as well as the long-term cue (i.e., the controlling stimulus that will not be removed) for that skill. Staff members decide whether the skill will be under instructional control or environmental control. For example, when teaching a child to wash his hands, we could begin the lesson with the teacher saying, "Go wash your hands." However, this tactic would severely limit the functionality of the skill. Ultimately, the student must learn to wash his hands under many cues, including when his hands are dirty, when someone announces that it is lunchtime, or after he has finished using the toilet.

For some lessons that focus on initiation, we have found it helpful to separate the source of reinforcement from the source of the prompt. Thus, some lessons will involve two teachers—one to entice (or create a problem) and another to provide the prompt that eventually will be eliminated. For example, we could try to teach a child to exchange a picture in order to request an offered desired item by having the teacher say, "What do you want? Give me the picture!" However, this would not readily lead to spontaneous communication. Instead, one teacher silently offers the item, and a second teacher uses physical prompts from behind the student to help with the exchange. Once the physical prompts are removed, the student can request without prompts or questions from the communicative partner. This same analysis can help children who speak or sign (or use any other modality). Blending the reinforcer with the prompt often leads to prompt dependency, while separating these two factors reduces that type of outcome (Sailor & Guess, 1983).

As noted earlier, teachers are encouraged to use verbal prompts only when such prompts are used in isolation and are highly effective. While adding verbal prompts to other types of prompts is easy, it is our observation that few teachers systematically plan to remove both sources of prompting, and thus the verbal prompts linger. If teachers do not add them into the lesson, they subsequently will not need to eliminate them.

How teachers arrange for lessons, especially the initial trials, has a great impact on generalization. Traditionally, teachers have arranged lessons in order to meet the goals noted in an IEP. If there is an objective such as, "Mary will learn to identify colors," many teachers will create a color lesson for that goal. The teacher then may select materials that are easy to present in a well-controlled situation. Only after the student has mastered the lesson within this ideal situation will generalization training occur. However, another approach to generalization focuses on planning for generalization from the start (Stokes & Baer, 1977). Within this viewpoint, rather than trying to create a "color" lesson at 10 A.M. because that is the next lesson on the list, teachers at the SC consider designing lessons within functional activities. For example, a teacher working with a 6-year-old student would consider what activities are occurring at 10 A.M. in which colors might be important to the child. During an art activity, if the teacher observes the child reaching for a red crayon, that would become the focus of the lesson. Or, after telling a student it's time to write, the teacher could "encourage" the selection of the red pencil by arranging for all the other pencils to have no nibs. Of course, the teacher plans for how many repetitions should be arranged for within the lesson to maximize acquisition while avoiding unnecessary (and potentially confusing) iterations.

Integration

The SC operates within the parameters of the least restrictive environment (LRE) as a guiding principle with respect to the integration of students with autism and typical peers. As noted by Bondy (1995), it may be more appropriate to consider LREE (least restrictive *effective* environment) because if educational effectiveness cannot be demonstrated, the placement is not appropriate (see VanHouten et al., 1988, for a more extended discussion on this issue). While it is beyond the scope and purpose of this chapter to address the many philosophical issues associated with inclusion models, our approach is consistent with that suggested by Mesibov and Shea (1996). Efforts to integrate these students are based on individualized decisions and are focused on the development of specific skills and their generalization. For students participating in the general education curriculum, modifications and accommodations are typically made in the context of individual needs and the strategies described above.

The SC program maintains a continuum of placement options consistent with the requirements of the Individuals with Disabilities Education Act (IDEA) Amendments of 1997. As mentioned previously, in addition to the center-based program, SC classrooms are currently established for students ranging in age from pre-K to high school levels. The pre-K unit includes six preschool groups of students with autism, a group of students with varied educational classifications (including autism), and two typical peer pre-K classrooms, for 3- and 4-year-olds, respectively. The typical peer classrooms are maintained by a local, privately operated pre-K and day care center and work directly with the SC groups throughout the course of the school day. During the 2.5-hour pre-K period of the school day, students throughout the complex are cross grouped for selected activities. Activity centers are scheduled in both the SC and private pre-K classrooms simultaneously, and students are grouped to participate in respective centers contingent on the objectives to be addressed for the particular student. These might include social or communication objectives, pre-academic skills, or combinations thereof. Students from any given classroom within the complex may participate in any of the various other classrooms within the complex, based on the activities.

SC also has program classrooms in two elementary schools, one middle school, and the high school of the hosting school district, Cape Henlopen Schools. In each of these public school settings, SC classrooms are operated with SC administrative and specialist support. Students are served by way of individually determined placement options ranging from self-contained to full-day integration into the respective mainstream classrooms. Support during the integrated time ranges from consultative to small group or, in some limited instances, one-to-one support by a paraprofessional or teacher-credentialed staff. In all instances, the emphasis is on specific objectives, as well as range and level of independent functioning on the part of the student. The decision regarding the integrated activities is made by the IEP team and typically includes consideration of specific objectives, issues related to content area, level of capacity for comprehension of abstract concepts, and range and level of social and behavior requirements associated with the placement.

Decisions regarding integrated activities are made by the IEP team and include consideration of specific objectives, issues related to content area, level of capacity for comprehension of abstract concepts, and range and level of social and behavior requirements associated with the placement. Data to assess placement and assist in planning and adjustments are typically generated using a formal observation protocol. The protocol consists of interval recording of specific skills of the identified student as well as simultaneous observations of one or more comparison students. For example, given a science class activity in which an SC student is participating, the observation would focus on the identified SC student as well as at least one typical peer in the class. This co-observation permits a comparison of responses within the same context to provide a data-based measure of expected levels of performance on social as well as academic grounds. Group scans of task-related behavior also are typically noted. Targeted behaviors include responses to group directions, initiations to other students or adults (tracked individually), and responses to peer initiations (Battaglini, 1999). Prompt levels and types by staff are recorded, as are staff responses to contextually inappropriate behaviors. These data provide an informative picture not only of the student but also of the classroom environments in which the student is expected to perform.

The IEPs of SC students are developed using a domain-based approach, which, in addition to school-based skills, includes consideration of various domains of adaptive functioning. One of the best predictors of adult functioning of individuals with autism is the range of community environments in which these individuals have been successful over time (White, 1999). Community environments provide the ultimate integration experience, given the possibility of random events within selected locations.

Community-based objectives are identified for almost all children in SC programs beginning with parent report and formal adaptive measures. This emphasis results in nearly all students participating in community environments as a component of their respective weekly schedules. That is, community objectives are incorporated into the IEP, as opposed to being viewed as occasional "field trips." Exceptions to this are typically limited to the youngest of the pre-K students and to those students participating in a relatively full academic course of study. In the case of the latter, if community skills are noted as being a relative deficit, they are usually addressed during the summer program.

Objectives for students may be as basic as walking through or tolerating a line at a fast-food restaurant or department store (e.g., K-Mart). For older students, targets may be relatively complex and involve problem-solving tasks, including dialogue with store employees or other customers. Lessons involving various situations are often systematically controlled to a point, such as allowing for crowd size contingent on time of day or day of week, but also take advantage of the incidental opportunities that are always part of the experience. In addition to addressing specific skill deficits, this approach often contributes to an expanded tolerance for changes in routine. These teaching opportunities in the real world also provide families with support in addressing specific problems. In some instances, parents are invited to join staff and students in the community to address such problems. The SC parent training program, which includes an emphasis on the use of differential reinforcement procedures (Foxx, 1982a, 1982b) may serve as a precursor to parent–staff teaming. Differential reinforcement procedures (especially of alternative responses) typically are a key element for success in community activities. Thus, the community activity serves as a follow-up to parent training and supports generalization of parent skills, as well as those of the child.

Community-based activities provide a natural segue to vocational training experiences. Student visits to community environments serve as a preview to potential employment-related environments. In addition, the gradual expansion of community-based activities over time into vocational settings and activities is consistent with the process of shaping.

Range of Methods

Central to the education of all students at the SC are skills related to functional communication. Upon entry, and throughout their education, students are assessed regarding a set of critical communication skills (see Frost & Bondy, 2002). Additional assessment employing standardized protocols as well as direct observation is employed as individual case issues necessitate, as identified by the team SLP. Some are related to expressive skills, while others relate to receptive skills. For each skill, modality is assessed independently from the function.

Critical expressive skills include requesting powerful reinforcers, help, and breaks, as well as responding to "Do you want …?" with yes or no. On the receptive side, we view responding to "wait" as critical, as well as following functional directions, using visual aids to follow schedules, and calmly handling transitions between activities (or locations). The assessment for these skills involves naturalistic situations rather than simply using a checklist to note if a skill is possible. That is, students may be able to ask for help, but if they can do so only in response to prompts, they are not viewed as using that skill at a sufficient level.

All students use visual aids to bolster their skills associated with following a schedule. These systems initially involve pictures or concrete materials and become increasingly based on print as academic skills progress. The younger students may find their schedule posted in a common area of the classroom, but once integration and movement around the school (or community) comes into play, personal systems are introduced. Similarly, all students use a visually mediated reinforcement system. These systems frequently are token-like to begin with but progress to point systems and others commonly used within school settings. These systems are in place wherever the student goes, including other school building rooms or into the community. Some students have an additional visual system tied into their particular contextually inappropriate behaviors. These systems typically involve some type of response-cost system but are independent of reinforcers (including tokens or points) earned for appropriate academic and interpersonal behaviors.

All students are initially taught to wait using visual support. Although teachers often only consider this lesson after a student has failed to adequately wait, all SC students are taught this critical lesson. The key to effectively teaching students to wait involves controlling the reinforcer for waiting. Thus, the lesson is arranged rather than being a surprise for both teacher and student. Teachers design a situation in which they anticipate what the child wants—either by manipulating motivational operations or upon a request by the student for a specific controlled reinforcer. For example, if the child requests a toy, the teacher immediately provides a large card with "wait" written on it, pauses for just 1 second, and then immediately says, "Good job waiting" while providing the toy. This lesson can be so short only in situations when the teacher can provide the reward following the designated wait period. Gradually, the wait interval is increased (and occasionally decreased following an unsuccessful trial). Furthermore, as the interval grows past a minute or so, students are taught to engage in explicit activities during the wait interval. It is not sufficient merely to expect children to stay out of trouble while they are waiting—teaching and reinforcing specific wait-time activities is essential and is consistent with the emphasis on teaching alternative responses. The length of the wait interval is adjusted according to age and other general factors.

Contextually Inappropriate Behaviors and Differential Reinforcement

With regard to contextually inappropriate behaviors (CIBs), the prime strategy is to determine the function of the behavior and then identify feasible functionally equivalent alternative responses, some of which may involve communication skills. For example, students engaging in CIBs to gain attention or some material reinforcers will be supported for requesting those types of rewards directly. Actions that serve to escape or avoid particular events or activities would be replaced by skills designed to more appropriately result in seeking a break, or help, or some other form of relief. Finally, since some CIBs are elicited by situational factors, including the loss or reduction of reinforcement or the presentation of aversive (from the student's perspective) stimuli, students would be taught to improve their waiting skills, since no one can ensure the timely delivery of all anticipated reinforcers.

To help ensure a high rate of reinforcement for these alternatives, teachers not only monitor their use but also use a variety of differential reinforcement schedules to help maintain their rate. Especially for the elementary-age students, teachers often use a system involving tape-recorded tones (or other sounds) presented on a variable-interval basis that serve to remind all staff to "catch the students being good." These systems may start at 1-minute average intervals but gradually are stretched to 15 or more minutes. A substantial, and sustained, increase in the overall rate of reinforcement, as well as a reduction in negative or corrective feedback from staff, has been observed when such systems are put into place (McCleery & Whitlow, 2000). For some students, use of such overt systems may lead to self-monitoring and eventually self-reinforcement systems, thus improving the possibility of generalized self-control skills.

The Picture Exchange Communication System

Many of the students, especially the young ones, use the PECS as an alternative or augmentative system (Bondy & Frost, 1994b; Frost & Bondy, 2002). Although PECS is often introduced to preschoolers, several students continue to use the system if they have not become proficient in oral communication or if a transition to an electronic augmentative system has not been successful (or deemed necessary). The PECS protocol begins with requesting (e.g., manding) reinforcers, ensures discrimination of icons, builds simple sentence structure, and encourages the use of various attributes, as well as responding to simple questions (e.g., intraverbals) and commenting (e.g., tacts). The system promotes spontaneous communication and teaches students to be responsible for their communication binder. In this manner, students commonly use PECS with their peers and take their own binders to other classrooms or areas of the school, as well as into the community. Rarely do the binders contain more than 100 or so pictures, as our observation (Bondy & Frost, 1994b) has been that most of the young children with autism who begin before age 5 years and use the system for more than a full year are competently using speech. Research supporting the effectiveness of PECS as well as its positive impact on speech development and reductions in behavior management issues for children and adults continues to grow (see Charlop-Christy, Carpenter, Le, LeBlanc, & Kelley, 2002; Ganz & Simpson, 2004; Kravits, Kamps, & Kemmerer, 2002).

The PECS protocol also has been an effective base on which to build more sophisticated communication skills. In addition to its primary function as an expressive tool, for some students it serves as a framework on which to expand descriptive and relational concepts, as well as positively affecting receptive skills, such as in responding to the daily schedules previously described. For students who can read brief scripted social phrases such as greetings or other conversational starters, the use of the two-person prompting strategy has been effective in helping expand repertoires of social interactions, variations of functionally equivalent response, and the environments in which these are employed.

Other visual support systems designed to augment expressive communication are used with students, including those who do not use PECS. For example, students frequently are taught to ask for "help" as well as a "break" using visual cards (to be used directly or as ongoing reminders regarding other modalities). When students request a "break," they typically move to an area of the classroom (including inclusion settings) in which no demands are placed on the student for a short time. Teachers provide a number of "break" cards in accordance with the rate of CIB associated with an escape or avoidance function.

Family Involvement

Since its inception, the SC has placed significant emphasis on working with families of its students. The SC employs a team approach to the intake process out of its recognition of the importance of the first point of contact with families. The process begins with a parent interview, followed by a series of observations, including one or more in the home. These contacts provide the opportunity to develop a positive working relationship between parents and school. The initial IEP meeting, often a new experience for the parents, follows the completion of this process. Given the state format for IEPs (*Administrative Manual for Special Education Services,* 2001), the complexities associated with the disorder, and the domain-based approach employed by SC, these meetings typically involve several hours or more and are often extended to two or more sessions. In addition to discussing the child's needs and subsequent program, we take advantage of the opportunity to provide parents with a rationale for the focal points and methodology of the SC. In addition to the interactions associated with the intake and IEP processes, the SC provides an extensive menu of services to families, including those described below.

Communication between the parents and the school is a continuous process. A home–school communication notebook is completed on a daily basis by the classroom staff and is delivered from school to home and back via the student's backpack. Entries will vary with case specifics but may include a review of the day, notations regarding any specific events, and questions related to important events. Although the format may vary, checklists and data summaries centered on objectives may be included. The parents are encouraged to make daily entries, reporting on events at home and responding to questions from staff, as well as noting any questions of their own.

The SC, guided and supported by state mandates, provides respite services for as many as 24 hours per month. Most of the funding for this service is provided by the state, with limited parental copay. Respite care is provided by qualified program staff who voluntarily participate and are compensated for the time on an hourly or per diem basis, depending on the time involved. Staffing is managed by a coordinator, and while first preference with parent input is given to available staff most familiar with the student, respite care can be performed by any willing staff members available from across the entire program. The training of staff members in methodologies employed by SC (e.g., PECS protocol, differential reinforcement of alternatives [DRA] procedures, scheduling) is a key factor with respect to the breadth of the pool of staff from which a potential provider can be drawn. Respite care can be used for any purpose deemed necessary at the discretion of the parents.

Parent information and support groups are scheduled across the school year and are usually conducted twice a month. These groups serve several purposes, including the establishment of a parent support network, discussion of autism-related issues, and sharing parent specific experiences. Staff psychologists lead the groups and review program procedures and guidelines, such as the peer review process and the manner in which classroom groups are developed. Guest speakers are periodically scheduled and are invited on the basis of topics of interest identified by the groups. Typically, each meeting includes both an informational component and an opportunity for parent-to-parent discussion and support.

A sibling support group is offered on a monthly basis. The group is led by a school psychologist trained in the SibShops model (Meyer & Vadas, 1994). Hands-on activities are used as a basis for group discussions of various aspects of life with a sibling who has autism. Participation is offered to siblings of program students age 5 years and older, and siblings may be divided into two groups (younger and older children) when age distribution necessitates. Students from a community service club of the local high school also participate as volunteers. This element has led to the establishment of a peer-mentoring program at the high school for students from the program.

A parent training program has been developed as a means of assisting parents in effectively managing challenges they encounter in day-to-day life with their children. Parent participation in these sessions is often held out as a precursor to home visits by the staff. This program is scheduled as a series of four 2-hour sessions followed by a classroom observation. The group is "advertised" as an exercise in "perspective taking," as the primary objective is to shift parent focus away from the behavior of their child and onto their own actions. The initial discussions are designed to provide the parents with a fundamental understanding of behavior concepts using their own day-to-day and life experiences rather than their child's maladaptive behaviors as the center of discussion. For example, reinforcement schedules are discussed using examples such as a slot machine; "extinction burst" is explained by noting how adults respond with the light switch to a burnt-out light bulb or responses that follow a failed attempt to obtain a soda after placing coins in a machine. Subsequent topics include review of the common antecedent–behavior–consequence three-term contingency, stimulus control, and their relationship to prompt dependence.

The importance of developing routines and understanding the value of consistent "sequences" is reviewed. Specific methodologies such as various differential reinforcement procedures are then addressed, as are communication training strategies, including a basic review of PECS and the rationale for two-person prompting strategies. As a supplementary opportunity, the parents are then invited to observe the application of the course content in an SC classroom.

In addition to access to the group homes operated by the program in the northernmost county of the state, residential services are provided directly by SC. Unique intervention formats have been developed in response to case-specific variables. One such case included a combination of an initial pullout of the student from the home to a school-operated facility with the capacity for overnight accommodations. The pullout was based on the occurrence of one or more targeted behaviors, such as aggression, and the child was immediately removed by on-call staff at the time. Return to the home setting was contingent on a prespecified behavior performance with a maximum for any given episode defined as a component of the intervention plan. The child's school schedule remained intact. On days for which the child successfully remained at home, a schedule was maintained on a 24-hour on-call schedule by staff visits to the home during nonschool hours (evenings and weekends). These staff members responded to any reported behavior targets that warranted initiation of the pullout process. The purpose of the staff visits included direct application of skill building and behavior management methods (e.g., alternative response and communication training, DRA), as well as parent training and the eventual shift of stimulus control to the parents.

The key element of this approach involved establishing a discrimination via controlling child access to the parents and the home environment in contrast with the pullout experience.

In order to evaluate the impact of this array of services, feedback is collected via several processes. A parent satisfaction survey is distributed biannually and includes a review of all major components of the SC program. Staff members also work within clusters to complete various forms of program review such as the *Autism Program Quality Indicators* (New York State Education Department, 2001). This information is used in concert to make adjustments to respective program services.

Transitions

All transitions for students between grades and schools are predicated on achieving the long-term functional goals of assisting them to improve their chances of getting a job in the community and living as independently as possible away from their parents' home. We believe this goal to be valid for all students, with and without disabilities. Thus, our goal is to teach reading, writing, and other academic skills not simply to achieve some test score but to ensure that improvements in these areas contribute in practical ways to achieving the broader goals. Our commitment to these goals includes the introduction of community-based training for very young students, including preschoolers. It has been our experience that the more experience students have in community settings, the better the probability of community-based vocational success.

There are two broad tracks for our students. In one track, students are placed in general education classes to work on the curriculum guidelines established by the state and local district; these students use academic materials selected by general education educators. One variation of this approach involves providing students with alternative or supplemented curriculum materials, but the overall goal remains completion of the traditional academic curriculum set. For these students, community-based instruction will coincide with after-school and home-based activities, because the school time is completely filled with assigned classes. The other major track is associated with teaching students skills that will result in the greatest degree of vocational and domestic success without addressing traditional academic domain skills. On this track, the state requires the development of a personal portfolio that reflects the overall skills acquired by the students. For these students, time in the community will likely increase with age, aiming toward maximum community involvement prior to graduation at age 21 years.

As we have noted, the Pyramid Approach model views successful job placement and reasonably independent residential placement as critical long-term goals for students with autism. These far-reaching goals are incorporated into the IEP process at every grade level. Thus, students have a "vocational" domain within their IEP from a relatively early age. Issues broadly thought of as involving response generalization can be conceptualized as part of vocational objectives. That is, improvements in the number of responses, rate, accuracy, durability and duration, complexity, and fluency, as well as variations in intensity are all necessary for high levels of job performance. Teachers target these areas but use materials that are age appropriate. In this manner, students may be working within the vocational domain without necessarily working with what would be considered vocational materials.

For example, elementary-age students may work on putting away art materials following a group lesson. Skill targets viewed as "vocational" would include increasing the number of pieces to be put away, increasing the complexity of the pieces to be accurately sorted, decreasing the time required to complete this task, and decreasing the supervision (and thus prompt level) needed to complete the task. As the student continues to move through higher grades, these factors would be modified according to the task materials relevant to specific classes, but teachers would be able to track via the IEP process whether general work skills continue to improve.

In middle school or high school, tasks involving functional use of current academic skills would be targeted so that students may spend some time working on office-related skills. These targets would include such tasks as delivering messages and materials to teachers throughout the school and using office equipment, including copiers, fax machines, and computers (when keyboard skills are present). Skills related to the cleaning up noted earlier may be expanded in high school to include cleaning the cafeteria or other common areas within the school. For students displaying aptitude in this area, efforts will be made to find comparable work skills in community settings. Often, the initial settings involve nonprofit (and thus nonpaying) locales such as churches or charity organizations, but efforts will increasingly become focused on salaried positions.

In middle school, and continuing in high school, some students will spend increasing amounts of time on various assembly and disassembly tasks (though not consecutively). The activities use real materials, such as nuts and bolts, as opposed to a set of arbitrary items, to practice on. Thus, a teacher may use small sewing kits, tools kits, complex pens, or materials from actual job sites and teach students to assemble them. In addition to how well the student learns to complete the task, the teacher will evaluate other indicators of whether the student seems to enjoy or dislike the task. For example, it may be noted that a student does not like to stand for long periods of time; thus, work that permits the student to sit will be a better long-term match. Another student may be highly distracted by certain types of materials according to their appearance or feel, and that may interfere with maximizing production rates. Over time, the teacher, as well as transition and vocational specialists, will seek to match not only a student's specific job skills but also nonspecific factors that may influence on-the-job success.

An auxiliary skill that may be taught involves use of public transportation, such as bus systems. The early targets will include calmly sitting on the bus, surrounded by strangers, often people who will talk directly to the student. Over time, skills related to managing money and interacting with the bus driver, as well as learning what do while riding on the bus, will be taught. Finally, an assessment will be made to determine whether the student will be able to perform this task without assistance. Such skills will significantly expand the long-term job options for a student.

Another aspect of vocational skill development focuses on the communication and social skills needed for successful community-based job placement. Communication skills will include asking for help, requesting more material, asking for a break, and responding to spoken and visual directions. Social skills may include greeting people, taking turns, and responding to direct questions and will involve job-related skills as well as nonspecific skills, such as those involved with taking a break in a communal area and eating lunch. While individuals with autism may not initiate many social interactions with new people, they will have to learn how to calmly respond to those making friendly, and sometimes assertive, approaches. In some work situations, the student will need to learn to interact not only with co-workers but also with consumers of the particular service. For example, while the student may be learning to clean in a fast-food restaurant, it is highly likely that he or she will have to interact with customers in some manner. It is often these seemingly less critical work skills that determine long-term job placement success. That is, students (and subsequently, workers) lose their jobs more often for interpersonal issues than for deficits in the specific job skill.

For students who are unlikely to obtain academic diplomas, the goal is to find a job site that calls for up to 20 hours of work per week. The SC uses a job coach model to promote job skill acquisition in community-based sites. Most of the community locales have the potential for becoming the site of a true job for the student upon graduation. The SC does not look for training sites that students can practice at; rather, each site is developed with the hope that it can become a real postgraduate work site for the student.

One way to examine the program's impact on its students is to review their general functioning over the course of their SC involvement. The fact that SC functions as a public school rather than a clinic or research facility prevents it from controlling many factors related to the broad impact of the overall intervention. Instead, we review clusters of students and present reliable information pertaining to long-term outcome issues. The following includes several descriptions of outcomes that have been selected to illustrate the effectiveness of the consistent application of the Pyramid Approach model in a public school setting.

Placement

We will examine placement from two different perspectives, the first being a snapshot of the distribution of current SC students and their respective placement history, and the second being a review of the current placements based on a specific entry date.

Current Distribution

As discussed previously, SC maintains a continuum of options with respect to educational placement for students with an educational classification of autism. While consideration of the least restrictive (and effective) environment is always involved with respect to placement, "inclusion" per se is not a driving issue. As a result, one placement option for students presenting more severe behavioral challenges is at the center-based program. The current distribution of the 81 SC students with autism includes 33 students served at the center-based program, 14 at the elementary level, 12 at the middle-school level, and 7 at the high school level. Of these students, only 6 (18%) began and continued their education at the SC from preschool. Twenty-one of these students have had part-time mainstream experience, some have increased this type of involvement over time, whereas others have had relatively fixed schedules. As noted earlier, all students also participate in community-based activities on at least a weekly basis.

Currently, 48 students are placed in various mainstream settings, ranging from part-time placement with several activities per day to full-time academic participation. The distribution includes 26 students within elementary schools, 11 within middle schools, and 11 at the local high school. Of these students, 22 (46%) began their education at the SC preschool and remained within the overall program. This group includes 16 elementary students, 2 middle-school students, and 5 high school students. It should be noted that a much higher percentage of students who started their education within the SC preschool and had continuous contact with the program have been successfully mainstreamed than students whose education at the SC began after the preschool level. An additional 24 preschoolers with autism are currently served at the SC preschool site.

We will use a group of 11 students who entered the SC's preschool program in 1994 to illustrate functional outcomes in greater detail. Of this group, 6 have returned to local district programming, 2 are included among the SC full-time mainstream placements previously noted, 1 continues at the SC center-based program, 1 has withdrawn, and 1 transferred to the northern county state program. Of the 6 students who returned to local districts, 2 have been declassified, 3 were reclassified (2 as MR and 1 as LD), and the outcome for 1 is unknown. With regard to the 5 students within the SC, 1 is currently placed within general education without any related services, although his educational classification has not changed.

Favorable Shift in Cognitive Functioning

As part of the intake assessment of individuals entering SC, formal assessment of cognitive ability is attempted. Table 7.1 provides information for 8 of the 11 students for whom intake and follow-up data are available. In most instances, the intake data of the students include information from the *Battelle Developmental Inventory* (Newborg, 2004). In Table 7.1, we convert the typical score into a developmental quotient (DQ) equivalent only for comparison purposes relative to subsequent IQ types of tests (e.g., the *Kaufman Assessment Battery for Children* [1983] and the *Wechsler Intelligence Scale for Children–III*). The dates of the subsequent

Table 7.1

Intake and Follow-Up Measures for Eight Students Entering the SC in 1994

Student	Initial DQ (Battelle)	Initial Post IQ (Kaufman)	Initial Post Measure (ABC/CARS)	Post Measure (ABC/CARS)
1	70	73 MPC	94 ABC	20 ABC
2	75	102 MPC	60 ABC	22.5 CARS
3	60	88 MPC	32.5 CARS	25 CARS
4	57	66 W (81 PS)	95 ABC	27 ABC
5	45	76 MPC	39.5 CARS	22 CARS
6	56	88 MPC	33 CARS	28 CARS
7	"Significant delay"	97 MPC	39 CARS	33.5 CARS
8	50	75 MPC	35 CARS	38 CARS

Note. SC = Sussex Consortium; DQ = developmental quotient; ABC = *Autism Behavior Checklist* (Krug, Arick, & Almond, 1980); CARS = *Childhood Autism Rating Scale* (Schopler, Reichler, & Renner, 1988); MPC = mental processing composite; W = *Wechsler Intelligence Scale for Children–Third Edition* (Wechsler, 1991); PS = performance scale.

reevaluations vary, ranging from 2 to 3 years after intake. For measures regarding the severity of autistic features, the *Childhood Autism Rating Scale* (CARS; Schopler et al., 1988) and the *Autism Behavior Checklist* (ABC; Krug, Arick, & Almond, 1980) are provided.

As can be seen from the profiles in the table, functional performance improved across time for all students, sometimes substantially. On the other hand, although ABC scores drop significantly for a few students, CARS scores remain relatively stable.

Changes in Communicative Functioning and Modality

Eight of the 11 students began to use PECS virtually immediately following entry into the SC. By the time these students reached elementary school age, none continued to use PECS (or any other augmentative system) as their primary mode of communication. This transition happened anywhere from 6 months to 3 years after entry and when picture repertoire size was between 50 and 80, a pattern noted by Bondy and Frost (1994a). As with students who displayed functional speech from the start, other visual supports were used to bolster other communicative functions.

Vocational Placements: Post-21 Placements

The SC program was initiated in 1980 with three students; by 1990, the student population had grown to 26. As a result, and in combination with the number of students who move to other placements before completing their education, the actual number of students graduating or leaving as a function of age has been relatively low. The SC is just now beginning to have groups rather than individual students graduate or leave as a result of age. Of the 18 who have completed the educational process at SC to date (commencing in 1990), 2 have completed full academic diplomas, and both also were working in competitive employment placements at the time of graduation. Of the remaining 16, all but 1 exited the program with supported work experience in community settings for 2 to 9 hours per week. Two of the earliest graduates (1990 and 1991) remain employed in the full-time placements they had at the time of exit. That is also the case for an additional 3 individuals who maintain at least 20 hours of work per week. The range of vocational placements include factory assembly work, clerical support, data entry, fast-food services, hospital support services, retail, and tourism industry occupations.

Unfortunately, of the students who had previously been in competitive employment placements with supports, 5 have been placed in sheltered workshops by the state adult services agency and either remain there or are not working at all. This outcome has reportedly been the result of limited funding for job coaching services in most instances. Two individuals, including the one who did not have a school-supported community work placement, currently do not have any form of work-related placement as adults.

Parent Satisfaction

To obtain feedback from parents regarding specific components of the program, a parent survey is conducted biennially. The results of the most recent administration (December 2003) again reflected a generally high degree of satisfaction with programming at SC by those responding ($N = 36$). Responses to the 37-item Likert scale questionnaire indicated very strong support for the program. For example, under the section of questions addressing programming, in response to the item "Behavior Support and Management," 26 responses were *very satisfied,* 5 were *satisfied,* 3 were *neutral,* 1 was *somewhat dissatisfied,* 0 were *very dissatisfied,* and 1 was *not applicable.* In response to the item "Communication," 21 responses were *very satisfied,* and 7 were *satisfied.* Similar distributions were realized for the questions relative to processes. For example, with respect to IEPs, 25 responses were *very satisfied,* and 7 were *satisfied.* For the remaining sections on issues such as training (staff and parents), interactions, and configuration, responses also reflect a generally high degree of satisfaction.

Two indirect signs of overall parent satisfaction with the SC can be reported. One involves the formation of the parent-initiated Lower Delaware Autism Foundation (LDAF) in 2002. A board of directors was established including parents, community business leaders, and two representatives of SC (the SC program director and an SLP). The overall mission of LDAF is to contribute to the lifelong support of individuals with autism in Sussex County via public awareness events, support for individuals and families by way of specialized recreational activities during nonschool hours (e.g., a swimming program and a specialized bicycle training camp), and fund-raising activities. These funds have been used to support the activities of the group on numerous fronts, one of which has been a scholarship program for SC staff. Over the course of the 3 years since its inception, LDAF has provided substantial financial support to current SC staff opting to continue their autism-related studies. Additional funds have been awarded to several local graduating high school seniors and full-time college students. These have been awarded based on a competitive process involving submission of a scholarly paper with autism as the core topic. LDAF also has other initiatives geared directly to supporting the school, including financial support for staff publications or professionally presented papers, several annual staff appreciation events, and a grant-like process to support specific classroom-based initiatives.

A second indirect indicator involves a review of due process cases experienced by SC. Although such cases may reflect the continuous appeasement of parental requests, the overall strategies of the program have remained consistent with the Pyramid Approach. Since the inception of the program in 1980, the SC has provided services for approximately 450 students, and a total of three student cases have resulted in external re-view. Two of these were resolved via the mediation process, while the third was addressed via a due process hearing. Given the often conten-tious climate permeating public school services for students with autism, we believe this outcome reflects the SC's ability to provide high-quality services in a manner that is recognized and appreciated by the parents.

Summary

We hope that this chapter has demonstrated how the complex issues associated with providing comprehensive and behaviorally oriented edu-cational services to school-age students with autism can be managed within a public school setting. While it is beyond the scope of this chap-ter to discuss, the Pyramid Approach has been successfully implemented in other settings, including private programs, programs for the severely disabled, and residential programs, as well as vocational settings. The use of the Pyramid Approach at the SC is only possible via an ongoing com-mitment to staff development and training, as well as an emphasis on par-ent training and involvement. With everyone working to provide quality services to students with autism, their long-term outcomes can be mark-edly improved.

References

Administrative manual for special education services. (2001). Dover: Delaware Depart-ment of Education.

American Psychiatric Association. (2000). *Diagnostic and statistical manual of mental disorders* (4th ed., rev.). Washington, DC: Author.

Battaglini, K. O. (1999). *Integrating children with autism, or, what is this thing called stimulus control?* Paper presented to the National Association of School Psycholo-gists Convention, Las Vegas, NV.

Bondy, A. (1995). What parents can expect from public school programs. In C. Maurice, S. Luce, & G. Green (Eds.), *Behavioral intervention for children with autism.* Austin, TX: PRO-ED.

Bondy, A., & Battaglini, K. O. (1992). A public school for children with autism and se-vere handicaps. In S. Christenson & J. Conoley (Eds.), *Home school collaboration.* Silver Spring, MD: National Association of School Psychologists.

Bondy, A., & Frost, L. (1994a). The Delaware Autistic Program. In S. Harris & J. Handleman (Eds.), *Preschool programs for children with autism* (pp. 37–54). Austin, TX: PRO-ED.

Bondy, A., & Frost, L. (1994b). The Picture Exchange Communication System. *Focus on Autistic Behavior, 9,* 1–19.

Bondy, A., & Sulzer-Azaroff, B. (2002). *The Pyramid Approach to Education* (2nd ed.). Newark, DE: Pyramid Products.

Charlop-Christy, M. H., Carpenter, M., Le, L., LeBlanc, L., & Kelley, K. (2002). Using the Picture Exchange Communication System (PECS) with children with autism: Assessment of PECS acquisition, speech, social-communicative behavior, and problem behaviors. *Journal of Applied Behavior Analysis, 35,* 213–231.

Devereux Institute of Training and Research. (2002a). *Devereux personal restraints training manual.* Villanova, PA: Author.

Devereux Institute of Training and Research. (2002b). *Devereux safety techniques training manual.* Villanova, PA: Author.

Foxx, R. M. (1982a). *Decreasing behaviors of severely retarded and autistic persons.* Champagne, IL: Research Press.

Foxx, R. M. (1982b). *Increasing behaviors of severely retarded and autistic persons.* Champagne, IL: Research Press.

Frost, L., & Bondy, A. (2002). *The Picture Exchange Communication System* (2nd ed.). Newark, DE: Pyramid Products.

Ganz, J., & Simpson, R. (2004). Effects on communicative requesting and speech development of the Picture Exchange Communication System in children with characteristics of autism. *Journal of Autism and Developmental Disabilities, 34,* 395–409.

Individuals with Disabilities Education Act Amendments. (1997). 20 U.S.C. § 1401.

Kaufman Assessment Battery for Children. (1983). Circle Pines, MN: American Guidance Service.

Kravits, T. R., Kamps, D. M., & Kemmerer, K. (2002). Brief report: Increasing communication skills for an elementary-aged student with autism using the Picture Exchange Communication System. *Journal of Autism and Developmental Disorders, 32,* 225–230.

Krug, D. A., Arick, J. R., & Almond, P. J. (1980). *Autism screening instrument for education planning.* Portland, OR: ASIEP Educational Co.

Lord, C., Rutter, M., DiLavore, P., & Risi, S. (1999). *Autism Diagnostic Observation Schedule.* Los Angeles: Western Psychological Services.

McCleery, J. P., & Whitlow, J. W. (May, 2000). *An evaluation of a procedure for increasing praise and decreasing correctives by teachers of children with autism.* Poster presented at the Association for Behavior Analysis Annual Convention, Washington, DC.

Mesibov, G. B., & Shea, V. (1996). Full inclusion and students with autism. *Journal of Autism and Developmental Disorders, 26,* 337–346.

Meyer, D., & Vadas, P. (1994). *SibShops: Workshops for siblings of children with special needs.* Baltimore: Brookes.

New York State Education Department. (2001). *Autism program quality indicators.* Albany, NY: Author.

Newborg, J. (2004). *Battelle Developmental Inventory–Second Edition.* Itasca, IL: Riverside.

Sailor, W., & Guess, D. (1983). *Severely handicapped students: An instructional design.* Boston: Houghton Mifflin.

Schopler, E., Reichler, R. J., & Renner, B. R. (1988). *The Childhood Autism Rating Scale.* Los Angeles: Western Psychological Services.

Stokes, T. F., & Baer, D. M. (1977). An implicit technology of generalization. *Journal of Applied Behavior Analysis, 10,* 349–367.

VanHouten, R., Axelrod, S., Bailey, J., Favell, J. E., Foxx, R., Iwata, B., et al. (1988). The right to effective behavior treatment. *Journal of Applied Behavior Analysis, 21,* 381–384.

Wechsler, D. (1991). *Wechsler Intelligence Scale for Children–Third Edition.* San Antonio, TX: Psychological Corp.

White, J. (1999). Components of successful school-to-work transition programs for 19–21 year old students with mental retardation. *Dissertation Abstracts International, 1–97.* (UMI No. 9932115).

Summit Academy: Implementing a System-Wide Intervention

8

Stephen R. Anderson, Marcus L. Thomeer, and Douglas C. King

· ·

S
ummit Academy is a program of Summit Educational Resources, originally incorporated in 1978 to serve preschool children with developmental disabilities. During its earliest years, the program focused primarily on the needs of children with speech and hearing disorders and delays. Since 1996, most new admissions have fallen within the autism spectrum.

The program was founded on several key beliefs, principles, and assumptions. The first was a core belief that children learn best by experiencing their physical and social environment through touching, hearing, and seeing. Second was the belief that the primary job of the teacher is to provide highly stimulating materials and activities that encourage children's play. Third was an assumption that given access to stimulating materials and activities, children with disabilities will play for extended periods of time and many opportunities for instruction will result—the concept of "teachable moments."

This model appeared to work well for very young children who presented speech and hearing delays without significant social or cognitive issues, but it was less effective when applied to children with autism. Anecdotally, it seemed as if the children with autism were less inclined to play consistently or appropriately (possibly lacking the necessary skills); thus, few opportunities for instruction occurred. Beginning in 1996, Summit modified its approach to include instructional methods empirically proven

Thank you to Ann Orlando-Parker and Deborah Carroll for their many helpful comments on this chapter and to Ellen Spangenthal, who provided editorial advice. We also wish to thank the dedicated and committed staff at Summit Academy, who make it such a wonderful place to work and learn.

to help children with autism. These methods are largely derived from behavioral psychology and special education research under the rubric of applied behavior analysis, which has consistently produced outcomes that are described in precise terms, are reproducible, and are tied to extensive experimental support. The goal was not to generally dismiss the language-based methods that existed prior to programmatic reorganization. The plan has always been to build better systems of accountability to determine which methods are most effective and to overlay methods already empirically shown to work for most children with autism.

Important Elements of the Approach

Summit's approach includes a strong emphasis on the importance of ongoing measurement and analysis of individual progress; the use of a functional assessment approach to identify skills for learning and to address problem behaviors; a highly individualized curriculum for each child based on formal and functional assessments; the selection of intervention techniques with documented effectiveness; and the proactive planning of generalization. In addition, Summit believes that the best educational outcomes are achieved through a partnership with parents; thus, a broad range of home-based, after-school, and Saturday programs are available for children and families.

Applying evidenced-based practices across the agency has not been quick or easy, and the model is still evolving. First, Summit had to overcome a philosophical schism between proponents of a "natural approach" and those who emphasized the importance of scientific accountability—not necessarily incompatible approaches. In short, it was important to effect a culture change that emphasized the importance of clearly defined goals for each learner and ongoing ways to measure individual outcomes. Second, change involved a large-scale application of behavioral treatment and educational methods across 395 preschool and school-age students, 44 classrooms, 6 sites, and 285 school-based staff and faculty members.

Several practice manuals have been developed to guide staff members and to create more consistent practices within and across classrooms. The goal of these manuals is to clearly communicate philosophy and provide a common standard of service delivery while, at the same time, allowing staff members the flexibility to exercise clinical judgment and develop specific interventions for particular children. Some of the common service standards are as follows:

- establish goals for learning that are based on a functional assessment of the child's and family's needs;
- use a broad array of systematic teaching methods to build skills (e.g., discrete trials, one-to-one and small-group instruction, positive reinforcement, task analysis);
- use other methods, such as activity-embedded learning, when appropriate and capitalize on naturalistic teaching opportunities across a variety of settings (incidental teaching);
- plan for generalization from the outset;
- emphasize the importance of building the child's independence by teaching functional life skills, particularly among the adolescent and young adult group;
- use a comprehensive individualized curriculum that is developmentally sequenced (at least for the younger children), providing teaching in all areas, including social, play, academic, communication, self-help, domestic, and vocational;
- focus, in particular, on the development of communication skills using a wide variety of techniques and modalities, including speech, picture–symbol systems, sign, and gestures;
- individualize the objectives and the approach to reflect the child's developmental level, strengths and needs, likes and dislikes;
- continually monitor progress using direct observation methods;
- conduct functional assessments of behavioral concerns and develop treatment strategies consistent with the results;
- deliver services using well-trained staff who are monitored and evaluated regularly;
- involve each child's parents or other caregivers; and
- include careful planning and support to help each child progress toward a less restrictive setting.

Population Served

Summit Educational Resources (our parent agency) serves more than 1,600 students each year, including children who participate in clinical evaluations and consults, home- and community-based programs, and after-school and Saturday programs. About 395 students, ages 3 to 21 years, are served in specialized schools that we collectively call Summit Academy. The school-age portion serves 217 students with developmental disabilities (5–21 years old) in 31 classrooms and at three sites.

Thirty-nine percent of the students have a primary diagnosis of autism, and another 58% are classified as having multiple disabilities. Many of the students who are classified as having multiple disabilities have a primary or secondary diagnosis of autism. A small number of students have a primary diagnosis of speech impairment. Table 8.1 provides a brief summary of the population served by Summit.

Diagnosis and Assessment

The New York State Education Department has approved Summit to serve children who are classified as having autism, speech impairment, or multiple disabilities. Summit administers no diagnostic instruments as part of the admissions process, although most children are evaluated at unaffiliated clinics prior to referral and are classified into one of these three groups. Commonly, children are seen by a neurologist or a developmental pediatrician, who interviews the parents and briefly observes the child in his or her office on one or two occasions. Typically, the professional accepts or rejects a diagnosis of autism based on criteria from the *Diagnostic and Statistical Manual of Mental Disorders–Fourth Edition* (DSM–IV; American Psychiatric Association, 1994). Summit also operates a clinic that conducts diagnostic evaluations for young children suspected to be within the autism spectrum. A psychologist-and-pediatrician team completes a medical examination, conducts a semistructured observation of the child using the *Autism Diagnostic Observation Schedule* (ADOS; Lord et al., 1989), and performs a detailed interview of the parents using the *Autism Diagnostic Interview–Revised* (ADI–R; LeCouteur

Table 8.1
Summary of Summit's Student Population by Age, Disability, and Gender

Student Age (in yrs)	Autism (males/females)	Multiple Disabilities (males/females)	Speech Impairment (males/females)	Totals
5–10	53 (42/11)	58 (44/14)	4 (4/0)	115
11–14	23 (21/2)	40 (31/9)	3 (3/0)	66
15–21	8 (7/1)	28 (18/10)	0	36
Subtotals	84 (39%)	126 (58%)	7 (3%)	217

et al., 1989). These evaluations most often are conducted at the request of the child's parents to clarify diagnostic questions, determine eligibility for services under the laws and regulations of New York State, and assist the parents and funders in placement decisions. Although Summit may refer to these evaluation results as part of its admission process, a diagnosis of autism is not required for admission.

Prior to admission, formal testing results and a current Individualized Education Program (IEP) are requested and received from the child's school district. After admission, the teacher and other professionals (e.g., speech–language pathologists, occupational and physical therapists) conduct criterion referenced and standardized testing to help identify objectives for learning and to serve as a baseline against which progress can be measured. No additional testing is done unless there is a specific concern about a developmental or behavioral area (e.g., augmentative communication). Thereafter, academic and behavioral assessments are often used as part of an annual review process to measure any changes in the deficit areas and identify individualized objectives for the coming year.

Faculty and Staff

Summit Academy is a private school approved by the New York State Education Department to serve children with developmental disabilities. It is loosely organized into three programs, consisting of elementary school (students age 5–10 years), middle school (students age 11–13 years), and secondary school (students age 14–21 years). Each level provides a highly individualized program in a specialized classroom. Summit Academy is located in Amherst, New York, and serves children from communities throughout western New York, particularly the Greater Buffalo area. It is an alternative education program for children whose needs cannot be met in a local public school.

Summit Academy provides a 12-month school experience (210 days) for all students. Small groups of 6 to 12 students work in classrooms with a team that includes a special education teacher, classroom aide, and speech–language pathologist. Each classroom may include one or more one-to-one aides that further enrich the staff-to-student ratios. A variety of related service staff (e.g., occupational and physical therapists, psychologists, audiologists) address IEP mandates by integrating services into the classroom curriculum with the active involvement of teachers and aides. While children enter and leave the school-age program at various ages based on individual progress, Summit Academy strives to provide intensive intervention that enables each child to return to his or her local school district program or a community work experience.

A division director, a master's-level speech–language pathologist, oversees the educational programming for students. The division director reports to the executive director of Summit Educational Resources, a licensed psychologist. Directly supporting the division director are two program directors; one assists in the day-to-day oversight of the educational programs, and the other oversees the development and implementation of behavioral assessments, behavioral treatments, and treatment fidelity. Directly supervising the elementary, middle, and secondary programs are four master's-level coordinators. Each coordinator oversees the staff and activities of 10 or 11 classrooms within a program. (This model is being revised so that coordinators individually supervise only 5 to 7 classrooms. This change has been initiated to give coordinators more time to train, support, and supervise faculty.)

The staffing pattern for each classroom is linked to the age, academic abilities, and behavioral needs of the students served. The elementary school classrooms typically consist of a certified teacher, a speech–language pathologist, and a classroom aide for each group of six students. Additionally, many students (72 children, or 33% of all students) have a one-to-one aide because they exhibit a high rate of challenging behaviors or have significant medical needs. Collectively, the adult-to-student ratios at the elementary school level are nearly one adult to every one student.

Most of the middle-school classrooms employ a teacher and a classroom aide with six students. There are two exceptions to this model: one classroom with 9 students and a second classroom that has 13 students to a teacher and a classroom aide. Additionally, seven speech–language pathologists work across 16 classrooms to provide individual and group instruction, as mandated by each student's IEP. As with the elementary classrooms, several middle-school students have one-to-one aides because of behavioral and health concerns. Thus, the adult-to-student ratio at the middle school is slightly less than one adult to one student.

The secondary school classrooms consist of groups of 6 or 12 students, depending on the age and severity of the children's disabilities. Each of these classrooms has a teacher and a classroom aide. There is one speech–language pathologist, who works across the classrooms to deliver individual and group instruction for speech, as mandated by each student's IEP. Fewer students have one-to-one aides at this level, but there are some who do. The ratio of adults to students in the secondary classrooms is slightly less than one adult to every two students. The larger class sizes for the older population is a planned approach designed to prepare adolescents for transition to competitive or supported employment.

Nine additional staff members assist middle- and secondary school students (ages 11–21 years) to acquire and apply functional academic and vocational skills in a variety of settings, including the classroom, an on-site analogue work center, and the general community. One job developer oversees Summit's transition-to-work program by creating relationships with local businesses and agencies to provide students with cooperative work experiences.

At all levels (elementary, middle, secondary), classroom teachers are certified in special education (59% hold a master's degree) and are the identified leader of the classroom team. Their responsibilities include establishing the classroom schedule, supervising classroom and one-to-one aides, conducting individual assessments, developing goals and objectives for learning, ensuring that IEP mandates are achieved, and assessing and reporting individual progress.

Classroom aides and one-to-one aides have at least a high school diploma, and many have a bachelor's degree in psychology or a related field. The primary duties of the aides are to assist classroom teachers to implement individual student lesson plans, collect and graph data, develop and organize curriculum materials, and assist teachers to conduct general classroom activities (e.g., lunch). Additionally, one-to-one aides are responsible for implementing specific behavioral intervention plans for the student they are assigned and ensuring that any medical precautions are followed.

Speech–language pathologists are master's-level certified and licensed speech–language pathologists (45%) or certified teachers of the speech and hearing handicapped (New York State certification). The speech–language pathologists work with children individually and in small groups to meet IEP mandates. In addition, they work cooperatively with teachers to develop classroom activities and lesson plans, and spend some of their time providing direct support in the classroom. As much as possible, the speech–language pathologist works as an integrated member of the classroom team and organizes integrated language-based activities into the daily schedule.

Other professionals providing services to the students in the classrooms are occupational therapists (11), physical therapists (5), teachers of the deaf (2), and audiologists (1.5). These professionals work across programs to provide IEP-related services mandated by each child's school district. Summit's philosophy is that these professionals work collabora-tively with the classroom team to develop specific goals for learning for each child and to ensure that goals are achieved. That is, the team, not just the physical therapist, is responsible for ensuring that gross motor goals are met. The model also assumes that, all things being equal, the best place for learning is the classroom or a similar natural environment. Thus, to the degree possible, speech, motor, social, and behavioral goals are integrated into the classroom or other natural settings with the active involvement of the teacher and other classroom support staff. Although some pullout sessions may occur, the professional understands that he or she must communicate and model recommended practices, so that the entire team participates in the learner's efforts to achieve goals defined by the IEP.

Finally, there are four educational consultants assisted by four edu-cational technicians who provide behavioral consultation and support to classroom teams. These individuals come from various professional dis-ciplines, including psychology, education, social work, and related fields. A significant portion of their time is devoted to addressing the needs of students with behavior problems. General duties include conducting be-havior assessments, writing behavior support plans, training the class-room teams in the recommended instructional and behavioral practices, assessing student progress, and monitoring the staff implementation of prescribed procedures (treatment integrity). Two of the educational con-sultants are board-certified behavior analysts.

Staff Training

Summit has a comprehensive preservice and inservice training program for its staff, which begins with a basic orientation to the agency. Employ-ees must also complete a series of training modules (Table 8.2 provides a list of topic areas). Basic information about Summit is available on DVD and can be reviewed individually or in a group. This allows new staff to receive critical and consistent information before the first days of employ-ment. More detailed information is provided through a traditional format of lectures, hands-on activities, role playing, and discussion. In addition to the basic orientation package, Summit provides in-service training and workshops throughout the year. Checklists have been developed to iden-tify some key performance competencies, and supervisors use these task

Table 8.2
Summary of Topic Areas for Staff Training

General Orientation	Serving Students
Overview of Summit	Developmental disabilities and autism
General policies and procedures	Working with families
Basic office procedures	Orientation and advanced SCIP–R
Health and safety	Data collection
Roles and responsibilities	Teaching methods
Quality assurance	Curriculum planning
Customer service	Teaching communication
Incident reporting and investigation	Using reinforcement
Students' rights and HRC activities	Generalization planning
Basic and advanced computer	Functional assessment
Integrated services and team building	Positive behavioral support

lists to ensure that critical skills are demonstrated on the job. The results of these direct observations form one part of each individual's annual performance appraisal.

Curriculum

The student curriculum addresses each of the major skill areas of attention, communication, social, motor, self-help, domestic, play and leisure, health and safety, vocational, community, academic, and appropriate behavior. General classroom schedules are determined by the teacher and approved by one of the educational coordinators. Because Summit Academy serves such a broad age range, the schedules vary according to age and other developmental considerations. Table 8.3 provides examples of classroom schedules for three age groups. Throughout the day, related service staff (e.g., speech–language pathologists) work with children individually or in small groups.

A broad range of materials is used to identify skills for learning, but no single instructional curriculum is used exclusively. The curriculum

(*text continues on p. 206*)

Table 8.3

Examples of Typical Daily Schedules for Three Age Groups

5-Year-Old Group		12-Year-Old Group		18-Year-Old Group	
Time	Activity	Time	Activity	Time	Activity
9:00–9:20	Arrival/structured play	9:00–9:15	Homeroom: Arrival and greetings	9:00–10:00	Homeroom: Group speech
9:20–10:00	Small-group and individual instruction	9:15–10:00	Homeroom: Independent work or speech	10:00–11:00	Rotation 1: Academics
10:00–10:30	Morning circle	10:00–10:30	Physical education	11:00–12:00	Rotation 2: Vocational
10:30–11:30	Small-group and individual instruction	10:30–11:15	Rotation 1: Academics	12:00–12:45	Lunch
11:30–12:00	Lunch	11:15–12:00	Rotation 2: Vocational	12:45–1:30	Homeroom: Language arts
12:00–12:30	Adaptive physical education	12:00–12:30	Lunch	1:30–2:30	Rotation 3: Activities of daily living
12:30–1:00	Small-group or individual speech	12:30–1:00	Homeroom: Self-help	2:30–3:00	Independent chores and preparation for dismissal
1:00–1:40	Small-group or individual instruction	1:00–1:45	Homeroom: Reading or other core curriculum area	3:00	Dismissal

(continues)

Table 8.3 *Continued.*
Examples of Typical Daily Schedules for Three Age Groups

5-Year-Old Group		12-Year-Old Group		18-Year-Old Group	
Time	Activity	Time	Activity	Time	Activity
1:40–2:00	Afternoon circle (speech focus)	1:45–2:30	Rotation 3: Activities of daily living/occupational therapy		
2:00–2:20	Curriculum extensions (e.g., art and music)	2:30–3:00	Snack and preparation for dismissal		
2:20–2:45	Snack	3:00	Dismissal		
2:45–3:00	Closing activities and preparation for dismissal				
3:00	Dismissal				

for each child is developed based on the results of formal and informal testing and reference to commercially available materials such as *The Individualized Goal Selection Curriculum* (Romanczyk, Lockshin, & Matey, 1996); *A Work in Progress* (Leaf & McEachin, 1999); *Behavioral Intervention for Young Children with Autism* (Maurice, Green, & Luce, 1995); *Making a Difference* (Maurice, Green, & Foxx, 2001); *Teaching Language to Children with Autism or Other Developmental Disabilities* (Sundberg & Partington, 1998); *The Syracuse Community-Referenced Guide for Students with Moderate and Severe Disabilities* (Ford et al., 1989); *The Picture Exchange Communication System* (Bondy & Frost, 1994); *Edmark Reading Program* (Holmes, Seiler, & Randolph, 2001); *Handwriting Without Tears* (Olsen, 1998); *HELP Strands: Curriculum-Based Developmental Assessment* (Parks, 1996); *Early Literacy Guidance* (New York State Education Department, 2004); *KeyMath: Diagnostic Arithmetic Test* (Connolly, Nachtman, & Pritchett, 1976); and *Soar to Success: The Reading Intervention Program* (Cooper, Boschken, McWilliams, & Pistochini, 2001).

The secondary school classrooms provide a comprehensive educational and vocational program that fosters the development of functional academics, leisure, domestic, and self-care skills that enable each individual to live most independently. Students participate in a unique program that allows them to transition between several classrooms, each team focusing on a different area of instruction (e.g., vocational, academic, activities of daily living). This model simulates a typical middle- and high school environment and is designed to keep the students focused and engaged. The young adult program also strives to provide training and cooperative work experiences that will ultimately allow each individual to achieve work, preferably in the community alongside people without developmental disabilities. Summit builds relationships with local community centers, churches, and businesses that provide opportunities for training in a variety of skill areas, including housekeeping, product assembly, and product packaging. Contracts for goods and services are procured from the local community so that the work is truly meaningful. To train students for these community placements, Summit operates an analogue work site on school grounds that attempts to match conditions in the typical work environment. Prior to being placed in community work sites, students must pass training sessions in the analogue setting to ensure that they have the requisite skills to be successful in the community settings.

Instructional Methods

Summit's model establishes a priori that the selection of assessment and educational approaches should be based on scientific evidence of effectiveness. Much of the research literature that guides its activities comes from the area of applied behavior analysis. Its roots are strongly research oriented and have been applied to the area of autism for many decades. Systematic research investigations have demonstrated that specific components of behavior analysis (e.g., reinforcement, task analysis, shaping) can be used to teach new skills (e.g., language, self-help, academics) and effectively assess and treat behavioral challenges (e.g., aggression and self-injury). In addition, several group studies have demonstrated promising outcomes for children with autism after a period of intensive intervention (Anderson, Avery, DiPietro, Edwards, & Christian, 1987; Birnbrauer & Leach, 1993; Green, 1996; Lovaas, 1987; Sheinkopf & Siegel, 1998; Smith, Eikeseth, Klevstrand, & Lovaas, 1997). These studies provide detailed descriptions of successful multiyear behavioral interventions for young children with autism.

Summit teachers and related service staff begin by completing any needed academic or behavioral assessments for an individual child. The team then identifies 20 to 25 goals for learning. Per New York State Education Department (1998) directives, these goals must fall within four content areas: learning characteristics, social development, physical development, and management needs. (The four areas for students 15–21 years old are learning characteristics, vocational achievement, physical development, and social–management.) Within each area, students must achieve specific statewide standards for learning. While the majority of students served by Summit are exempt from required statewide testing, teachers are required to submit a portfolio of each student's work at the equivalent age of students in 4th, 8th, and 11th grades.

In Summit's model, each classroom faculty member is assigned as a "case manager" for one to three children. The case manager organizes a three-ring notebook ("casebook") for each student that includes a list of the student's educational goals, an individualized data collection system, a copy of the IEP, data sheets, and lesson plans for each goal. In addition, a graph shows the child's progress on each lesson plan, and there is a historical summary of all objectives targeted and achieved. It is the case manager's responsibility to maintain the casebook, monitor progress, initiate changes to programs as needed, and report at least quarterly on progress at mandated intervals.

A lesson plan is a written document that details the team's approach to teaching the specific goals identified for learning (i.e., an instructional program). Thus, if 25 goals have been identified for learning, then at least 25 lesson plans will be developed. The lesson plan provides the context in which the targeted skill should be exhibited, a definition of the skill, and established criteria to demonstrate acquisition and maintenance of the skill. The lesson plan indicates instructional methods and steps, identifies a plan of evaluation, and suggests ways to promote generalization. Summit has developed a library of lesson plans for over 450 skills that teachers can select and reuse with more than one student. However, it is common to find that plans that have been used successfully with many students may have to be modified to meet the individual needs of one particular student. Lesson plans are intended to be dynamic documents that change according to the individual and collective needs of students, rather than a fixed curricular or instructional approach. An example of a lesson plan used to teach a child to sequence letters and numbers is provided in Figure 8.1.

Lesson plans are placed in an individual student notebook with tabs labeled with a word or short phrase (e.g., receptive labeling). Throughout each day, the staff may tab through the notebook to remind themselves of the current instructional step and other key components of a lesson plan (e.g., correction procedure). The case manager typically records the child's progress on a data sheet throughout the day, then summarizes and transfers that data to a graph at the end of the day. Each student's case-book and related instructional materials are placed in a portable storage container for easy access.

Direct observation data are collected on each lesson plan at least weekly (often daily) to measure progress and to help determine educational and clinical decisions. Often, a data sheet is designed on a single sheet of paper to capture data on all of the lesson plans. When the instructor conducts repeated trials on a particular concept (e.g., labeling common objects), a small sample of trials (e.g., 5–10) is typically scored. Additional trials are often conducted without record keeping, and they provide informal and incidental opportunities for the student to practice the desired concept. This format also gives the instructor the opportunity to skip among several objectives (interspersed trials format), making the instructional session more varied and presumably more interesting to the child.

Summit's model uses a variety of naturalistic (e.g., incidental teaching) and directive approaches (e.g., discrete trials) to teach simple and complex skills (Anderson & Romanczyk, 1999). At any given point in time, each method may have benefits and limitations. Within a single session or activity, a teacher may use a more directive method to obtain the child's attention, decrease distractibility, and ensure sufficient practice but at the same time seize upon natural opportunities to actively program the generalization of skills being taught. In short, Summit uses the full range of evidence-based techniques available to us (i.e., natural, embedded, and directive).

Behavior Management

In western New York, the number of children with disabilities served in general education classrooms with typically developing peers has increased significantly. The children who are placed in more restrictive out-of-district agencies, like Summit, are generally the children with significant learning and behavioral needs (e.g., aggression, self-injury, noncompliance).

Summit has developed an extensive behavior support policy and treatment protocol that includes tools for identifying needs, assessing function, evaluating and monitoring progress, and developing formal behavioral plans. The policy also includes safeguards to ensure that interventions are safe and effective. As noted, staff members participate in several training modules related to conducting functional assessments, measuring behaviors, and using behavioral strategies to resolve disruptive behaviors. In addition, every staff member is required to complete *Strategies for Crisis Intervention and Prevention–Revised* (SCIP–R; New York State Office of Mental Retardation and Developmental Disabilities, 1998).

Soon after a child's admission to Summit, he or she is assessed using an internally developed instrument called the Needs Assessment Tool (NAT). The NAT consists of a list of problem behaviors, social and self-help deficits, and communication delays that may prevent or interfere with learning. The NAT enables the classroom team to pinpoint specific skill deficits and behavior excesses and rank and prioritize each student's needs. From this rank ordering, the classroom team selects three to four behaviors for remediation and decides if these behavioral targets can be addressed via a classroom plan, an instructional lesson plan, or an individualized behavior plan. If an individually tailored behavior plan is

(*text continues on p. 212*)

LESSON PLAN

Name: Gary Patterson

Objective Name: Sequencing Letters and Numbers

Start Date: July 7, 2004

Objective #: A-104

Materials: Letters (uppercase) and numbers (1–20) individually printed on cards, approximately 2 × 2 in. Optional: Place Velcro on the back of each card and use an alphabet and numbers strip.

Objective: When given the instruction "Count" or "Show me the alphabet," child will correctly sequence 1–20 or A–Z (cards) with two or fewer prompts in each of three of four consecutive sessions or two consecutive sessions with one or no prompts in each session.

Step	Materials Display or Instructional Display	Discriminative Stimulus (instruction and preresponse cues or physical prompts)	Child's Target Response	Correction Procedure	Scoring Procedures and Step Criterion	Generalization Methods
Baseline	Cards with numbers or letters are randomly sorted into a stack and placed in front of child.	Adult instructs child to "Count" or "Show me the alphabet." Conduct task with numbers; break for a few minutes, then conduct task with letters.	Child will correctly sequence cards, placing them linearly from left to right in order.	If the child fails to respond, ask him or her to watch as you do the first few cards, then place the cards back into the stack and repeat the instruction.	Score as a prompt any verbal, gestural, or physical help.	N/A

(continues)

Figure 8.1. An abbreviated example of a lesson plan used to teach adaptive skills (sequencing of letters and numbers).

1	LETTERS (matching step): Place letter strip in front of child and the letter cards A–D randomly sorted into a stack. Gradually, add one or more letters as the child demonstrates competency.	Adult instructs child to "Show me the alphabet," then physically prompts child to match each letter along the strip with the matching letter card (A–D). Fade prompts.	Child matches letter card to corresponding letter on the number strip.	If child fails to respond, provide a hand-over-hand prompt, using only the amount of help needed to correctly match the card to the corresponding letter.	Same as Baseline	Whenever natural situations arise, recite the alphabet in order; bring the child's attention to situation when the alphabet is represented—books, toys, etc.
2	LETTERS (fading match): Same as above, but omit every fourth letter on the alphabet strip. Continue removing letters until all 26 letters have been removed from the strip.	Adult instructs child to "Show me the alphabet," then pauses. Adult labels each letter as child places it on alphabet strip.	Child places card in order on letter strip.	Same as Step 1	Same as Baseline	Same as Step 1
3	LETTERS: Remove letter strip and place cards in front of child in random order. NUMBERS: Repeat steps 1–3 with numbers.	Same as Step 2	Child places cards in order without letter strip.	Same as Step 1	Same as Baseline	Ensure that child is able to generalize task to other materials and other contexts.

Figure 8.1. *Continued.*

warranted, the team, under the direction of an educational consultant, conducts a functional behavioral assessment using survey and direct observation methods. Based on this assessment, a behavior intervention plan is developed, implemented, and monitored.

Target behaviors are monitored daily, and data are graphed for ease of inspection—demonstrating progress or showing the need to make plan modifications. To ensure the fidelity of treatment, the educational consultant monitors team members for their proper implementation of treatment protocols. In addition, a Human Rights Committee (consisting of parents, community members, and staff members) regularly reviews and monitors behavior plans to ensure that they are effective, safe, and appropriate.

Integration

As Summit is a private special education school, daily opportunities for inclusion with typically developing peers is impractical. However, Summit provides programs, training, and consultation at all age levels that promote integration with peers without disabilities to the greatest extent possible. For the youngest children, Summit Academy operates an integrated nursery school program called Discovery Kids Learning Center. Although the program primarily serves 3- and 4-year-olds, some 5- and 6-year-old children with disabilities are included each year. Summit also collaborates with a local school district to provide a kindergarten-through-second-grade program for children with autism in a general education school building. The children receive one-to-one and small-group instruction in a highly specialized classroom and are supported in general education classrooms throughout the day for some academic instruction and curriculum extension activities (e.g., music, art, computers).

At the adolescent and young adult level, Summit operates a vocational training program that places many students in supported jobs in the community. Individual students and teams work in a variety of community settings, gaining valuable employment skills and interacting with individuals without disabilities.

Summit also operates a highly structured summer program for children with Asperger syndrome. The Connections program provides children with intensive training, experience, and practice in social functioning and making friends.

Parental and Family Involvement

Summit begins with the philosophical tenet that the best outcomes for each child are likely to be achieved when the parent feels adequately informed and competent to participate in the education of their son or daughter. Summit offers a variety of informational, training, and support services to families and children. Included in our continuum are a variety of outreach services funded through the New York State Office of Mental Retardation. These services provide respite, home-based instruction to teach daily living skills, and parent training. Our unique Saturday Life Skills program provides parents with skills needed to effectively teach activities of daily living and address challenging behaviors at home and in the community. These services extend educational opportunities beyond the traditional classroom and help ensure that parents remain engaged in their child's education.

Transition Planning

Summit engages in a variety of activities designed to return students to district-based placements as soon as possible. First, we identify the specific skill deficits and behavior excesses that prevent the child from full participation in a district-based classroom. These deficit areas become a major focus of our educational programming, along with other district and state prescribed areas for instruction. Second, we provide in-service training and ongoing consulting services to school districts to help build their capacity to serve children with autism. For example, Summit conducts a summer institute to prepare district-based teams to support returning students. It also sponsors conferences for professionals and parents throughout the year, featuring leading national experts.

For the youngest elementary students, particularly children transitioning into kindergarten, we have developed materials and action steps to help districts plan for transition to a general education classroom. In this model, Summit first provides some general background on the characteristics of autism and offers specific information on the strengths and weaknesses of the child who is transitioning. The classroom team conducts a "contrast analysis" to isolate differences between classroom expectations and the target child's abilities at entry. Based on this information, we assist the team to identify specific learning goals, ascertain needed program accommodations, and specify the responsibilities of each team member. Summit also provides ongoing technical assistance to develop instructional methods and design classroom management strategies.

The transition model for older elementary, middle, and secondary students follows a similar course that includes observation of the child at Summit, preservice training to the school district, and in-service and ongoing consulting after the transition occurs. Training and consulting are often requested each year as the child progresses through each subsequent grade level.

The transition of students from school to work presents a different set of challenges. Summit's young adult program (for those 17–21 years old) was developed just 4 years ago; thus, only six students have "graduated." Transition planning for every child begins at 14 years, when the team completes a summary of the individual's strengths, weaknesses, interests, and expectations. Based on these findings, the team develops objectives for learning that reflect its best estimates of the child's future work and home environments. For most of our children, functional academics, leisure, vocational skills, and daily life skills dominate the focus of instruction.

Based on our limited findings with the first graduates, it appears that increasing each student's ability to work in increasingly larger groups is also important for successful transition. Between ages 14 and 22 years, most students at Summit progress from participating in a group of 6 students to 9 students to 12 students over a period of several years. This approach was developed after observing that students were often unprepared for the significantly larger groups (20 or more consumers) and reduced staff-to-consumer ratios that exist in most adult-supported and sheltered work settings. Of course, this step assumes that each student continues to acquire skills and behaviors that will lead to greater independence and increased personal choice as adults.

Student Achievement

One of Summit's core values is "accountability." We strive to be accountable by first demonstrating that identified goals for learning are achieved. Summit accomplishes this by continually measuring progress, regularly reviewing the results, and making program modifications as needed. It is not a retrospective approach but rather an ongoing approach of instruction and continuous analysis.

Annual reports summarize the number of objectives in progress or mastered compared with the total number of objectives targeted for all students served at Summit Academy. For each of three reporting years, 70%–75% of the objectives targeted were either showing good progress or achieved on the date they were sampled. Our goal is to continually improve this outcome through a combination of better goal selection and more effective instruction.

Plans have been finalized to regularly measure other areas of student performance, including academic engagement, compliance with instructions, outcomes on formal assessments, changes in core autistic symptoms, outcomes on key areas of performance (e.g., toileting, communication), and placement. We have also introduced ways to measure procedural outcomes, such as the correct application of effective teaching and behavior management methods. These targets will be regularly sampled by coordinator-level professionals to determine the progress of individual children, as well as the general effectiveness of teams, departments, and the agency as a whole.

Twice a year we mail a survey to parents and to school districts served by Summit to measure their satisfaction with our programs and services. The Parent Satisfaction Survey includes 13 items concerned with services (e.g., Are you satisfied with the progress your child is making?) and staff (e.g., Are you satisfied with the cooperation and pleasantness of Summit staff?). Each item is rated on a seven-point scale (1 = *completely satisfied*; 7 = *completely dissatisfied*). Each year, 90%–95% of parents report significant satisfaction with our program. The school district satisfaction survey also included 13 items concerned with services (e.g., Are you satisfied with progress reports?) and staff (e.g., Are you satisfied with the level of cooperation you receive?). Overall, 92% of the responses were rated as *completely satisfied* or *satisfied*.

Summary

Implementing a large, system-wide intervention has been a challenging and lengthy project. Although a general goal of "increasing effectiveness" has been accepted by various stakeholders, the methods used to achieve that goal often have been debated. In addition, broad organizational objectives needed to be achieved first—or at least simultaneously—such as improved agency financial health and a variety of human resource enhancements (e.g., pay equity and staff training). Clearly, reorganizing a well-established agency required changing many long-term (and, sometimes, highly valued) practices. For example, one of the first necessary organizational changes was to move classroom staff from a 10-month work calendar, with a voluntary option to work in the summer, to a 12-month work calendar. This had to be achieved with no demonstrable change in personnel expense.

Reorganization also required a change in the culture of the agency. Although the agency was highly regarded for its early childhood practices, many of the most valued methods appeared less effective as they were applied to children with greater behavioral and learning challenges, including children with autism. Early methods were built on philosophical or conceptual tenets (e.g., the belief that children learned best when the context was most natural) but lacked rigorous scientific analysis. Initially, our approach was to emphasize the importance of accountability and best outcomes for children without dwelling too much on systematic explanations of how desired results were achieved (Baer, Wolf, & Risley, 1987). Thus, there was, and continues to be, a strong emphasis on (a) establishing measurable goals and (b) engaging in continuous measurement and analysis. These canons were fixed, whether the desired changes were agency related (e.g., improved financial performance) or child centered (e.g., number of goals achieved by students).

Looking to the future, our focus is on several key areas: (a) systemic implementation of best educational practice methods across all school and outreach services, (b) improving immediate and long-term individual student and general agency outcomes, (c) training qualified professionals and paraprofessionals, and (d) increased applied research.

Recently, Summit has developed and implemented written operational policies and procedures for the classrooms. A *Best Practice Manual* provides a general agency overview, describes students and families, outlines student assessment methods and timelines, explains the development of goals for learning, illustrates various instructional methods, and so on. A second manual, *Behavioral Support Policy*, provides specific instructions on functional assessment and treatment of severe behavior disorders, including detailed methods for tracking student progress. Although still in the early phases of implementation, these standards and desired practices will be tied to job descriptions, staff training, and performance appraisal systems. A variety of "treatment fidelity" measures also have been developed to monitor whether recommended and required practices are evident in daily engagement with students and whether these result in improved student outcomes. These systems will help ensure that there are standardized methods for curriculum planning, effective instruction, and monitoring of student process. This broad systematic approach is particularly important given the large number of faculty and staff required for the 217 school-age students and 180 preschool students served by Summit each day. We also believe these systems are important given the more than 100 practicum and intern students who pass through Summit each year. Our goal is to ensure that these individuals witness and participate in best-practice activities and that this exposure will lead to improved regional capacity to serve children with autism.

Summit values its related service staff (e.g., psychologists, speech–language pathologists, occupational and physical therapists, adaptive physical education teachers). This multidisciplinary approach historically has been a major underpinning of the agency's approach to education. Nevertheless, the professional training and philosophical orientation of some of these professionals is sometimes inconsistent with the general direction of the agency, particularly the current emphasis on empirically based practice. Summit has approached this contradiction by communicating some basic expectations: (a) clearly defined goals for student learning that identify objective and measurable behaviors, (b) the need for continuous measurement of student progress, and (c) the integration of service delivery into the classroom with active team collaboration. Although some clinical methods are grounded more in common-practice methods than empirical practice, there is considerable interest in subjecting practice to rigorous objective study so that the most effective methods are identified, preserved, and replicated with other learners. A goal over the next several years is to continue this line of investigation.

We also want to improve our ability to evaluate outcomes, not just on an individual child level but also on a broad systems level and over longer periods of time. What are the longitudinal outcomes for a child who transitions from Summit into a kindergarten classroom in a neighborhood public school? What about those young adults who transition from Summit at age 21 years into adult life? Is there a way to adequately measure their improved quality of life because of their placement at Summit? In short, we are motivated and committed to long-term follow-up on our students and to using that information to improve our current and future operations.

Summit Academy has made great strides in improving its services to children with autism and related disabilities. It has been a challenging task that may never be complete, as we continuously identify and evaluate promising intervention strategies and implement them across a large organization. Fostering the growth and development of children with autism and witnessing their individual progress toward personal independence inspire our continued commitment to improvement.

References

American Psychiatric Association. (1994). *Diagnostic and statistical manual of mental disorders* (4th ed.). Washington, DC: Author.

Anderson, S. R., Avery, D. L., DiPietro, E. K., Edwards, G. L., & Christian, W. P. (1987). Intensive home-based early intervention with autistic children. *Education and Treatment of Children, 10,* 352–366.

Anderson, S. R., & Romanczyk, R. (1999). Early intervention for young children with autism: Continuum-based behavioral models. *The Journal of the Association for Persons with Severe Handicaps, 24,* 162–173.

Baer, D. M., Wolf, M. M., & Risley, T. R. (1987). Some still-current dimensions of applied behavior analysis. *Journal of Applied Behavior Analysis, 20,* 313–327.

Birnbrauer, J. S., & Leach, D. J. (1993). The Murdock Early Intervention Program after 2 years. *Behaviour Change, 10,* 63–74.

Bondy, A., & Frost, L. (2002). *A picture's worth: PECS and other visual communication strategies in autism.* Bethesda, MD: Woodbine House.

Bondy, A., & Frost, L. (1994). *The Picture Exchange Communication System.* Cherry Hill, NJ: Pyramid Educational Consultants, Inc.

Connolly, A. J., Nachtman, W., & Pritchett, E. M. (1976). *KeyMath: Diagnostic arithmetic test.* Circle Pines, MN: American Guidance Service.

Cooper, J. D., Boschken, L., McWilliams, J., & Pistochini, L. (2001). *Soar to success: The reading intervention program.* Boston: Houghton Mifflin.

Ford, A., Schnorr, R., Meyer, L., Davern, L., Black, J., & Dempsey, P. (1989). *The Syracuse community-referenced curriculum guide for students with moderate and severe disabilities.* Baltimore: Brookes.

Green, G. (1996). Early behavioral intervention for autism: What does research tell us? In C. Maurice, G. Green, & S. Luce (Eds.), *Behavioral intervention for young children with autism: A manual for parents and professionals* (pp. 29–44). Austin, TX: PRO-ED.

Holmes, T., Seiler, B., & Randolph, P. (2001). *Edmark Reading Program.* Austin, TX: PRO-ED.

Leaf, R., & McEachin, J. (1999). *A work in progress.* New York: DRL Books.

LeCouteur, A., Rutter, J. L., Lord, C., Rios, P., Robertson, S., Holdgrafer, M., et al.

(1989). Autism Diagnostic Interview: A standardized investigator-based instrument. *Journal of Autism and Developmental Disorders, 19,* 363–387.

Lord, C., Rutter, M. L., Goode, S., Heemsbergen, J., Jordan, H., Mawhood, L., et al. (1989). Autism Diagnostic Observation Schedule: A standardized observation of communicative and social behavior. *Journal of Autism and Developmental Disorders, 19,* 185–212.

Lovaas, O. I. (1987). Behavioral treatment and normal educational and intellectual functioning in young autistic children. *Journal of Clinical and Consulting Psychology, 55,* 3–9.

Maurice, C., Green, G., & Foxx, R. M. (2001). *Making a difference: Behavioral intervention for autism.* Austin, TX: PRO-ED.

Maurice, C., Green, G., & Luce, S. C. (1995). *Behavioral intervention for young children with autism: A manual for parents and professionals.* Austin, TX: PRO-ED.

New York State Education Department. (1998). *The learning standards and alternative performance indicators for students with severe disabilities.* Albany, NY: Author.

New York State Education Department. (2004). *Early literacy guidance: Prekindergarten–Grade 3.* Albany, NY: Author.

New York State Office of Mental Retardation and Developmental Disabilities. (1998). *Strategies for crisis intervention and prevention–revised.* Albany, NY: Author.

Olsen, J. Z. (1998). *Handwriting without tears.* Potomac, MD: Handwriting Without Tears.

Parks, S. (1996). *HELP Strands: Curriculum-based developmental assessment.* Palo Alto, CA: VORT Corp.

Romanczyk, R. G., Lockshin, S., & Matey, L. (1996). *The Individualized Goal Selection Curriculum.* Apalachin, NY: Clinical Behavior Therapy Associates.

Sanford, A. R., & Zelman, J. G. (1981). *Learning accomplishments profile.* Winston-Salem, NC: Kaplan Press.

Sheinkopf, S. J., & Siegel, B. (1998). Home-based behavioral treatment of young children with autism. *Journal of Autism and Developmental Disorders, 28,* 15–23.

Smith, T., Eikeseth, S., Klevstrand, M., & Lovaas, O. I. (1997). Intensive behavioral treatment for preschoolers with severe mental retardation and pervasive developmental disorder. *American Journal on Mental Retardation, 102,* 238–249.

Sundberg, M. L., & Partington, J. W. (1998). *Teaching language to children with autism or other developmental disabilities.* Pleasant Hill, CA: Behavior Analysts.

The TEACCH Approach to School-Age Education

9

Victoria Shea and Gary B. Mesibov

reatment and Education of Autistic and Related Communication Handicapped Children (TEACCH) is a division of the Department of Psychiatry in the School of Medicine at the University of North Carolina–Chapel Hill (UNC-CH). As such, TEACCH is a service, training, and research program. The administrative headquarters of the TEACCH program are in Chapel Hill, and there are also nine regional TEACCH centers around the state of North Carolina. Clinical services in those centers include diagnostic evaluations, parent and family training, social groups, individual counseling for high-functioning clients, and consultation and training for other service providers. Clinical services from the TEACCH centers are free to citizens of North Carolina.

TEACCH is partially funded by an allocation from the North Carolina General Assembly. Other significant sources of funds are training and research grants from the federal government, support from Vocational Rehabilitation and Medicaid for vocational and residential services for adults, private donations, and fees for in-state, national, and international training.

TEACCH and Educational Programs

The TEACCH program began in 1972 as a continuation and expansion of a federally funded research grant (1966–1971) to Eric Schopler, PhD, at UNC-CH for clinical work with children with autism and their families. At the time, the federal law mandating a free, appropriate public education for students with disabilities had not yet been passed, and not all of the youngsters with autism who were seen in Dr. Schopler's program were even permitted to attend public schools. Those who were in school were generally in special education classes for students with emotional disturbance (Mesibov, Shea, & Schopler, 2005).

Because of Dr. Schopler's belief in the importance of specialized education for children with autism, the original legislative funding and mandate for the TEACCH program included direct operation by TEACCH of 11 public school classrooms for students with autism. The teachers and assistants were hired, trained, and supervised by TEACCH, and students were referred to those classes by TEACCH.

After P.L. 94-142 (Education for All Handicapped Children) was adopted in 1975 by Congress, all states, including North Carolina, began to develop special education services in all local school districts. In 1985, direct operation by TEACCH of classes for students with autism ceased, and the education of students with autism in North Carolina became the responsibility of local school districts ("local education agencies," or LEAs), of which there were 115 as of July 2004. An agreement was made between TEACCH and the North Carolina Department of Public Instruction (DPI) for TEACCH to provide consultation and training for interested school districts in the state. There are no longer public school classrooms over which TEACCH has programmatic or administrative control.

In 1997, the DPI Procedures Governing Programs and Services for Children with Special Needs were clarified to define *autism* as including PDD-NOS, Asperger syndrome, and other forms of pervasive developmental disorders, further increasing the number of students with autism eligible for public special education services, supports, and modifications. The number of students in North Carolina public schools identified with a primary handicap of autism reached 5,006 in 2003–2004, and undoubtedly there are students with clinically diagnosed autism who have other primary educational labels.

TEACCH's current role with respect to educational programs for students with autism spectrum disorders (ASD) varies widely. Some students are taught by teachers who have extensive training and experience in the TEACCH approach, and who collaborate closely with their local TEACCH center. Similarly, some LEAs employ itinerant autism resource specialists with strong TEACCH backgrounds and working relationships with their local TEACCH center. Other LEAs have formal agreements with TEACCH for consultation in specific autism-focused classrooms, and TEACCH center staff visit those classrooms when requested. There are also North Carolina LEAs (and private schools) that serve students with autism without involving TEACCH in their educational programs. However, if those students are seen at TEACCH centers and if their families request TEACCH involvement, an individual consultation with a teacher can be arranged at the school's request.

Since 1985, TEACCH centers around the state have conducted intensive, week-long teacher-training sessions during the summer, combining lectures and readings with hands-on practice in a model classroom under the direction of TEACCH staff (Mesibov et al., 2005). In the summer of 2004, 18 weeks of training were provided to approximately 475 teachers and other school professionals. In addition to summer training, TEACCH centers offer 2- and 3-day Fundamentals training sessions throughout the year. This training model does not involve actual work with students but includes simulated application of TEACCH principles to scenarios of actual students and school situations. In both training models, work with high- and lower functioning students of various ages is included.

In summary, TEACCH is a state-funded, university-based, statewide program for individuals with autism of all ages, which does not provide education services directly. Nevertheless, the educational techniques developed by TEACCH play a major role in the public education system in North Carolina. Further, because of the training, research, and dissemination activities of TEACCH, these educational methods are influential nationally and internationally (e.g., Schopler, 2000). The remainder of this chapter will describe the application of TEACCH methods in educational programs for students with ASD.

Diagnosis and Assessment

When the TEACCH program began, few child development professionals (e.g., pediatricians, child psychiatrists, psychologists, speech–language pathologists) were familiar with autism or comfortable or skilled in making such a diagnosis. Dr. Schopler and colleagues developed some of the first objective measures for identifying youngsters with autism (Mesibov et al., 2005; Schopler & Reichler, 1979; Schopler, Reichler, DeVellis, & Daly, 1980). Since that time, dramatic advances in professional awareness and assessment techniques (e.g., Filipek et al., 1999) mean that increasing numbers of children with ASD are diagnosed by a variety of professionals and referred to their LEAs for educational services. Once the primary conduit to public education, the TEACCH program now is one of many agencies that can provide the initial assessment and diagnosis of ASD.

Diagnostic evaluations by TEACCH typically include the following components: (a) review of previous evaluations, which have usually included a medical evaluation and standardized developmental testing; (b) review of parent questionnaires that describe current behaviors and a typical day at home, parents' estimates of the youngster's developmental levels in various areas, and parents' major concerns and questions; (c) observation of the child in both structured and relatively unstructured situations throughout the evaluation day; (d) administration of an autism-specific assessment tool, usually either the *Psychoeducational Profile* (PEP), which was developed at TEACCH and first published in 1979 and was revised in 1990 as the PEP–R and revised again as the PEP–3 (Schopler, Lansing, & Marcus, 2005), or the *Autism Diagnostic Observation Schedule* (Lord, Rutter, DiLavore, & Risi, 2002); (e) administration of an adaptive behavior scale; and (f) completion of the *Childhood Autism Rating Scale* (Schopler et al., 1980) by the TEACCH center director. These evaluation procedures are modified as appropriate on an individual basis.

This information is gathered by the TEACCH center staff ("psycho-educational therapists"), who come from a variety of professional backgrounds. Most have advanced degrees in special education, but other related fields are also represented among the staff, including speech–language pathology, social work, early childhood education, and psychology. The TEACCH center directors are all doctoral-level, licensed psychologists. The directors lead the diagnostic teams, integrate the information, and establish the diagnosis of an autism spectrum disorder if appropriate.

Curriculum, Instructional Management, and Skill Acquisition

A fundamental principle of the TEACCH approach to serving people with ASD of all ages is individualization. This principle has several manifestations in educational settings.

First, individualization means that each student's plan is developed based on that individual's unique pattern of skills and deficits. Learning is most efficient when it is based on a foundation of current skills (Klinger & Dawson, 1992). This is particularly relevant in ASD because skills are typically widely scattered, so that abilities in one area often are not highly correlated with skill levels in other areas of development. For example, most students are much more skilled in visual perception and rote auditory memory than they are in language comprehension, spontaneous and pragmatic language, and social skills (Gray, 1998; Hodgdon, 1995; Janzen, 2003; Quill, 1997). Educational goals cannot be based on chronological age, an overall "developmental age," or other broad or standardized guidelines. Instead, each student's unique profile of knowledge, talents, cognitive and communication difficulties, sensory issues, motor skills and deficits, personality traits, and special interests must be the foundation for educational planning.

A related implication of the principle of individualization is that the education of students with ASD, although influenced by standard curricula of educational goals and materials, is not based solely on them. Instead, within the TEACCH model, the goals and strategies for each student are individually crafted, based on a particular student's and family's needs and preferences. The eventual goal of TEACCH educational programs is the highest degree of independent adult functioning possible. For students without mental retardation, this can mean typical academic attainments (such as a high school diploma and perhaps college-level or technical school education) leading to economic self-sufficiency and independent community living (including rewarding social relationships). For these students, the content of educational programs from year to year would likely incorporate the regular education curriculum, taught using specialized strategies and supports (to be described in subsequent sections). For students with both autism and mental retardation, educational goals would typically focus on developing the highest possible degree of spontaneous, effective communication; productive engagement in work and leisure tasks; self-care and daily living skills; community living skills; and meaningful, enjoyable social relationships.

A third implication of individualization is that there is no model of service delivery that is appropriate for all students. This means that sociopolitical goals such as "normalization" or "full inclusion" are not considered as meaningful as individualized educational goals (Mesibov, 1976; Mesibov & Shea, 1996). Within TEACCH, we believe that some students are best served in autism-specific, self-contained classes, while others can thrive in general education settings with adequate modifications and supports.

The Culture of Autism

A second fundamental principle of the TEACCH approach is our concept of the culture of autism (Mesibov et al., 2005). This concept suggests that, like cultures, ASD yields characteristic patterns of thinking, communicating, understanding the world, and behaving. Some of these characteristic patterns are focusing on details rather than on the underlying, integrated meaning of the details (that is, limited central coherence; Frith, 1989); concrete rather than abstract thinking; distractibility and disorganization; difficulties with generalizing from one situation to another; difficulties with time concepts and sequencing in time; strong interests and impulses; excessive anxiety; and sensory and perceptual differences. The role of the teacher should be that of a cross-cultural interpreter, who understands both the culture of autism and the "neurotypical" culture, and who translates information and expectations from the nonautistic environment to the student with autism so that he or she can function more easily and successfully. The techniques through which this is done are called Structured Teaching.

Structured Teaching

Structured Teaching is the name used within TEACCH for the principles and strategies we have developed both for teaching new skills and for organizing settings so that they are understandable and meaningful for individuals with ASD (Mesibov et al., 2005). Structured Teaching is based on an understanding of the culture of autism and on the recognition that each individual with ASD functions better with some amount of visual or written information to supplement auditory input and with some degree of external organizational support. Structured Teaching involves both increasing the individual's skills and adapting the environment so that it is more comprehensible and more suited to the individual's needs. Structured Teaching is not limited to schools; it is useful in all settings, including home and community activities, job sites, and specialized therapy sessions, and is adaptable for individuals of all ages and skill levels.

The elements of Structured Teaching are

- organization of the physical environment;
- a predictable sequence of activities, with flexibility incorporated;
- visual schedules;
- work–activity systems; and
- visually structured activities.

Organization of the Physical Environment. Organization of the physical environment is particularly important for younger students and concrete learners with ASD, who might otherwise wander (or run) throughout classrooms or other school environments instead of remaining in the appropriate places for learning activities. We recommend using existing architectural features (such as walls and pillars) along with furniture to help these students know where to be and where to focus their attention. Examples of this are (a) defining areas through the use of bookcases, rugs, walls, and room dividers (e.g., group area, snack area, free play area, individual work space); (b) minimizing distractions by having students work away from doors, windows, or other idiosyncratic sources of distraction or sensory discomfort; and (c) simplifying and reducing the physical transitions that very impulsive or disorganized students must make in going from one activity to the next. Even for more developmentally advanced students, it is useful to provide clear guidance (or options) about where to sit, where to put their possessions, and what routes to take from place to place in the school.

A Predictable Sequence of Activities. A predictable sequence of activities helps students learn that the school day is not a set of random events and disconnected materials, but an organized series of activities that they can understand and master. For young students and concrete learners, predictability is the foundation for learning the routines of daily living; the language for meaningful materials, events, and people; and the power of communication to get their needs met. For older or more capable students, predictable situations help to make new activities and expectations understandable and less stressful.

Predictability does not mean that each day is exactly the same, because that is not possible in the real world, and because many students with ASD tend to become overly attached to routines and rituals, and then become upset when they are changed, a pattern we do not want to encourage. We emphasize the importance of flexibility within routines, varying small details and encouraging students to rely on up-to-date visual schedules rather than their memory for routines to understand upcoming events (see the next section). However, we also believe that it is important for students' cognitive understanding and emotional security to have predictable rhythms and expectations for the school day. For example, their schedules are always in the same place, all transitions take place in the same way (by first going to or looking at the schedule), and they can be certain that physical needs such as hunger and a need to use the bathroom will be taken care of before they become problems.

Visual Schedules. Visual schedules of upcoming activities have been demonstrated to be important and effective for students with autism, in terms of increasing independence, reducing behavior problems, and improving skill levels (Mesibov, Browder, & Kirkland, 2002). Schedules also serve the function of letting students know where they are supposed to be, since the activities on the schedule take place in consistent, logical locations (i.e., lunch is in the cafeteria, math is always in a particular room or at a particular work space, etc.).

Visual schedules take many forms, depending on the skill levels of the students. For the youngest or most delayed students, it could consist of objects (such as a cup for a snack, a puzzle piece or marker for the first work task, a roll of toilet paper for the bathroom, a computer disk for time at the computer). The most advanced visual schedules are written lists, similar to the "to do" lists that many neurotypical students and adults use to organize their days (e.g., "math, language arts, gym, Spanish, lunch, science, music, study hall"). For students going to these same classes who need somewhat simpler visual information, a visual schedule might consist of both words and pictures or photographs of objects associated with the class (e.g., calculator, language arts book, basketball, picture of Spanish teacher, lunch tray or lunch menu, science book, piano, backpack). Visual schedules vary both in terms of the degree of concreteness versus abstraction of each item (i.e., the actual object to be used in the activity vs. the written name of the activity) and in terms of the number of items on the schedule (ranging from "what comes next" to a schedule for the entire day).

As students develop additional cognitive and academic skills, the abstraction and scope of their schedules can be increased. Also, once students understand their schedules, it is important to introduce variations into the schedule, so that students do not simply memorize a routine, which would almost inevitably cause distress when the routine is changed because of circumstances such as weather, special assemblies, fire drills, visitors to the school, standardized testing days, and so forth. Another important component to add to schedules is the opportunity for free choice, because making choices strengthens communication skills, increases the student's willingness to cooperate with the schedule, and adds both a sense of control and a source of pleasure to the student's school day.

Work–Activity Systems. Work–activity systems are visually based directions that show the student what to do once the visual schedule has guided him or her to the correct location for the activity. The system provides visual answers to the following questions:

- *What* task or activity am I supposed to do?
- *How much* work (or how many tasks) am I supposed to do? or *How long* will this activity last?
- How can I see that I am *making progress*? and How will I see that the activity is *finished*?
- *What will happen next*?

All work–activity systems should include a way for the student to check off, cross out, remove, or otherwise delete items from the "list" of steps or tasks as each is completed, so that the student sees that progress toward the last item is being made. By allowing students to see that they are making progress, and by making the concept of "finished" concrete and meaningful, work–activity systems reduce the confusion that individuals with ASD often have about whether they are at the beginning, middle, or end of an activity. This in turn helps them experience feelings of satisfaction and closure when a specific activity is completed. In addition, when the person has learned to follow a work–activity system, the system can be transferred to a wide variety of activities in a wide range of settings (e.g., household chores, steps in personal grooming, tasks in occupational therapy or speech–language therapy, community errands like grocery shopping).

Like schedules, work–activity systems are individualized visual systems in a form that the student can understand. A relatively capable person with ASD might have a written system with a list of tasks and directions explained in words. For example,

1. Social studies: Read pp. 23–24, then write the answers to the questions on p. 25.
2. Math: Complete worksheet.

or

9–9:15: Sort these cards by zip code, then alphabetize.

9:15–9:30: Put cards A–M in green envelope; put cards N–Z in red envelope.

The individual would know *what* to do based on the written directions. *How much* work would be seen by the number of items written on the work–activity system or by a written indication of the time the activity session will end. The person would see that *progress* was being made as each of the written tasks was carried out and crossed off; the work is *finished* when all the tasks are crossed off. A written explanation of *what would happen next* would also be part of the written work–activity system (e.g., "Read or computer game until time for Spanish class").

For a less academically advanced student, visual information about the content and amount of the activity can be provided in other ways. A work–activity system for a more concrete learner might use objects, pictures, symbols, numbers, or colors to answer the four questions. For example, a student at this level might have a work–activity system consisting of pictures of different shapes secured on a Velcro strip going from top to bottom on his or her worktable. Each shape would correspond to a shape on a basket containing a task. The student would know *what* task to do by taking a picture from the work–activity system and matching it to the corresponding picture on the basket (which would have a small piece of Velcro on top of the picture, so that the work–activity system piece would remain in place). The student would know *how much* work there was by the number of shapes on the worktable. For example, if there were a circle, a triangle, and a square, that would mean there were three tasks to complete during the work session. *Progress* would be understood by seeing the number of shapes on the table decrease and the baskets moving off the table into the finished area as tasks were completed, and the person would know that the session was *finished* when all of the shapes had been removed from the work–activity system on the worktable, and all the baskets were in the finished area. The activity that *would happen next* after the successful completion of the tasks would be indicated by a picture or object at the bottom of the work–activity system (e.g., a picture of a computer activity, a napkin to take to the snack area, or a cassette box indicating free time to listen to music).

Additional examples of work–activity systems and learning tasks (with photographs) are available in *Visually Structured Tasks: Independent Activities for Students with Autism and Other Visual Learners* (1996) and the Tasks Galore series (Eckenrode, Fennell, & Hearsey, 2003, 2004), available from the Autism Society of North Carolina Bookstore (www.autismsociety-nc.org or 919-743-0204).

Visually Structured Activities. Visually structured activities help make tasks clear, meaningful, and comprehensible through the use of visual instructions, visual organization, and visual clarity.

Visual instructions are particularly important for younger students and more concrete learners, whose understanding of verbal directions is limited. For example, instead of telling the student to "put the blue ones here and the red ones there," we would set up a sorting task with examples of blue and red objects already in clear containers, so that the student could *see* what to do. For other tasks, we might design a "jig," which is a two-dimensional silhouette or a three-dimensional model that shows where items are to be placed (such as silhouettes of a fork, knife, and spoon to be placed on a napkin, then rolled up). Because people with ASD like matching and puzzles, jigs can be a very useful component of visual instructions. As with visual schedules, we have found it important to incorporate flexibility into visual instructions, so that the student does not simply memorize performing a certain task with the materials (e.g., sometimes a set of blocks is used for sorting, sometimes for stacking, sometimes for placing into bags, sometimes for matching to pictures of the same color).

Visual organization refers to keeping learning materials neat, organized, and physically stable. Although some neurotypical students are able to find work materials and complete tasks in the midst of extraneous clutter, materials that fall down or get covered up, or materials that are mixed together, that degree of disorganization can be distracting for students with ASD. We help them to focus on the important information and visual directions by keeping materials physically stabilized and organized, using a variety of means such as separate containers (baskets, colored or labeled file folders, trays, boxes, etc.) and stabilizing materials (two-sided tape, Velcro, paper clips, bookends, etc.).

A related aspect of visually structured activities is simplifying the visual content of activities and highlighting the most important features. It is not unusual for students with ASD to become overwhelmed, distracted, or disorganized when surrounded by written material or equipment that is not part of their learning task. Therefore, students' work spaces should be kept uncluttered, which can mean keeping some items covered or physically removed. Additional, related modifications should be considered and used on an individualized basis, depending on observations of the student at work. For example, some students do better academic work when the relevant portions of books or worksheets are enlarged (using a photocopy machine) to be more visually clear. Conversely, they might also function better when unneeded sections are folded out of sight or covered with blank paper. Further, visual directions might need to be large or colored, marked with a large arrow, or highlighted in some other way.

In summary, Structured Teaching involves the use of visual information to help students with ASD know where to be within the school setting, what work to do, and how to do it. The schedules, work–activity systems, and visual structure of activities set the stage for instruction and learning of educational content.

Range of Educational Settings and Methods

Structured Teaching can be provided in any educational setting. It is not necessary for a student to be in a self-contained or special education setting in order to receive the visual information and organizational supports of Structured Teaching. Described below are examples of both a specialized autism classroom using TEACCH principles, and a general education class in which a student is supported using TEACCH principles. Usually, the students in specialized autism classrooms have significant cognitive or behavioral difficulties associated with ASD, while students in general education classes have adequate cognitive potential to master the curriculum, enough receptive language ability to understand what is being said, and acceptable behavior in typical school settings if they have sufficient Structured Teaching–based supports (Mesibov, Shea, & Adams, 2001).

A Specialized TEACCH-Based Classroom

TEACCH-based classrooms are physically organized in line with the principles of Structured Teaching previously described. We encourage teachers to arrange the room in ways that minimize distractions and maximize the meaningfulness, clarity, and functional efficiency of the space. Examples include having a distractible student's work space face a blank wall; locating the independent play area far from doors and blocked off by sturdy furniture for students who tend to run out of the room; putting the desk of a student with hypersensitivity to noise away from the bathroom, hallway, fan, or intercom; and having locked cabinets for materials that are too enticing for students to ignore.

Another aspect of the physical environment that can be controlled to some extent in a specialized classroom is the sensory stimulation that students experience. It is sometimes possible to provide sound-absorbing panels, dark or enclosed areas where students can go to calm down, work-stations with headphones for listening to music, and so forth.

Schedules. Structured Teaching classrooms use two kinds of schedules simultaneously: the general classroom schedule and individual students' schedules. The general classroom schedule shows the activities for the entire class, such as general work sessions (for one-to-one instruction or independent work), group activities, snack time and lunch, special classes like music or art, and outdoor activities. General classroom schedules are relatively consistent from week to week, except when there are field trips or special events. In addition to the general schedule, each student has an individualized schedule, as discussed previously, with specific activities listed or otherwise communicated in a visual modality that is understandable to the student.

Educational Goals. Students' schedules take them through the planned series of activities of the day, reflecting their individualized educational goals, which are developed based on current skills, the family's priorities, and the ultimate goal of achieving the greatest possible degree of independence as an adult. For elementary school students, goals are typically identified in the areas of communication, cognitive and possibly pre-academic skills, social skills, fine and gross motor development, hygiene and personal care, learning to follow directions (which may include learning to stay in assigned areas, make transitions calmly, and work independently), and independent leisure skills (for students who are not yet able to play safely and independently). Goals in the same areas (presumably at more advanced levels) would usually also be found at the middle-school level, perhaps with increasing emphasis on prevocational skills and functional academics, as opposed to abstract academic skills, if it became clear that a student's degree of mental retardation limited his or her mastery of abstract academic skills. Optimally, at the high school level, there would be a significant emphasis on vocational experiences and training, domestic chores (such as purchasing and cooking food, doing laundry) and community living skills (such as using public transportation, using the telephone).

Instructional Activities. Once goals have been determined, specific activities are designed and instructional methods chosen to meet those goals. Instructional methods almost always include one or more one-to-one teaching sessions daily, independent practice in working with concepts and skills that have been taught, and group activities to work on social and communication goals (groups might be as small as two students or as large as the whole class, possibly with some additional students from regular education classes). We also encourage sessions of physical activity throughout the day, because exercise has been demonstrated to be one of the most effective interventions for reducing stress and behavior problems (Allison, Basile, & MacDonald, 1991; Elliot, Dobbin, Rose, & Soper, 1994; McGimsey & Favell, 1988; Rosenthal-Malek & Mitchell, 1997).

Work–Activity Systems. As described previously, Structured Teaching uses work–activity systems to organize activities and to keep students with ASD engaged in meaningful tasks. The question that arises is How do you teach a student to follow a work–activity system? We usually teach students work–activity systems and new tasks during one-to-one teaching sessions, using an individualized combination of demonstrations, hand-over-hand assistance, visual prompts, simple verbal cues and feedback, social encouragement, and desired activities at the end of the session. Once a student has mastered following a particular task with a work–activity system (which includes getting the materials, doing the task, and putting the materials away in a designated "finished" area), that task is moved to a different place on his or her schedule and to a different location in the classroom (the independent work area), and the student practices working independently and without supervision on the task. Similar work–activity systems continue to be used in one-to-one teaching sessions to learn new tasks, in the independent work area to practice tasks, and in other settings within the classroom and the school.

For example, a work–activity system for a young or concrete learner might involve materials in two containers. The student takes one item from each container, combines them in some way, then puts the finished product into a third container. The task might first be taught using two halves of a toothbrush holder, with two boxes of parts in front of the student. Once the student has learned the system of taking one object from each box and putting them together, the task might be varied using two blocks, a top and bottom from a soap dish or film canister, an index card to put inside an envelope, or an eraser to put on a pencil. In this way, the specific behavior of taking objects from two containers and combining them in some way would be generalized to a variety of objects and a variety of ways of combining them. Later steps might be combining three objects, combining two objects and then doing something else with the product (e.g., putting a card in an envelope and then sorting the envelope according to a symbol on the front), or working for longer periods of time with greater quantities of objects. Eventually, the student might use this kind of work–activity system not just at the work table, but as part of working in the school office (e.g., collating papers or preparing mailings), in the school cafeteria (e.g., filling condiment bottles or emptying the dishwasher) or with the janitorial staff (e.g., sorting recycling).

TEACCH-Based Support in a General Education Classroom

Providing the visual information and organizational support that students with ASD in general education classes need requires time, flexibility, and creativity on the part of the general education teacher or other school personnel who facilitate the inclusion of students with special needs. Many students with ASD have the intellectual skills and academic potential to benefit from general education class placement but have significant difficulty with the social and organizational demands of those placements, and often with the handwriting requirements as well (Klin, Volkmar, & Sparrow, 2000).

Based on more than 3 decades of clinical experience with thousands of individuals with ASD, it is our strong belief that *all* people with ASD, of *all* ages, need support in the form of visual answers to the four questions (what to do, how long to do it, how to know that it is finished, and what will happen next) in situations that they perceive as too complex or too demanding. In school settings, this means that directions, explanations, reminders, rules, warnings, plans, and other information that are typically given verbally should be communicated visually instead or in addition. Students with high-functioning autism or Asperger syndrome (HFA/AS) and students with autism accompanied by mental retardation have equivalent needs for individualized schedules, organized work–activity systems, and visually clear, organized instructions and materials. For higher-functioning students, this information is generally written, rather than pictorial or based on objects, but putting students with HFA/AS into verbally mediated classrooms without individualized visual supports is frequently, often dramatically, unsuccessful.

Examples of the kinds of visual and written supports we typically recommend for students with ASD in general education classes include

- a written schedule of the sequence of classes for the day, located in a place where it can be easily used during transitions;
- a written list of materials needed for each class or activity;
- written reminders about class rules and individual reminders, located on the student's desk or in a notebook (e.g., "Raise your hand and wait for Ms. Jones to call on you," "Do not correct the teacher's mistakes during class," "Keep your shoes on," "It's ok to make a mistake"); and
- for some students, a written list of steps in an activity (i.e., a work–activity system), such as (a) put your name on the paper in the yellow folder; (b) put the date on the paper; (c) write one sentence using each of the words at the bottom of p. 62; (d) write a sentence about what you are going to do this weekend; (e) raise your hand and wait for Ms. Smith to check your work; (f) after your work is checked, you may listen to music or pick out a puzzle.

The overall principle is to provide enough detailed visual and written support for the student to function as independently as other students in the class, without giving more support than the student needs (because it is so labor intensive and because we want to support movement toward independence, rather than encouraging dependence). Some students can even be involved in making their own lists and reminders.

Family Involvement

Eric Schopler, the founder of the TEACCH program, was one of the earliest proponents of the view that parents could be their child's most effective teachers and advocates (Schopler & Reichler, 1971). TEACCH has always been a family-centered program, with strong emphasis on working collaboratively with parents and respecting the skills, perspectives, and resilience of families (Mesibov et al., 2005; Schopler & Mesibov, 1984). In training teachers to use TEACCH's Structured Teaching model, we always include experience with using a daily communication log that goes back and forth with the student between home and school. In our opinion, it is important to work closely with families, transferring information about the student's behaviors, stressors, effective strategies, goals, and triumphs on a regular, frequent basis.

TEACCH centers offer a number of services and supports to families, including

- demonstrations and coaching to teach parents skill-building activities, the use of work–activity systems, and the use of schedules for making transitions between activities;
- videotapes of these demonstrations and written home programs for parents to review at home or share with other family members; arrangements can sometimes be made for home visits to demonstrate these techniques and suggest ways to increase physical structure;
- "make and take" sessions, in which parents and therapists together prepare materials for use at home;
- explanations of the characteristics of autism and how they relate to the youngster's behavior;
- suggested readings and Web sites;
- individual sessions with a parent to provide support and referrals for other needed services;
- family counseling sessions with parents and their adolescent or adult children with HFA/AS;
- workshops for parents, which have included topics such as Structured Teaching and HFA/AS (parents are also welcome at TEACCH training programs for teachers and other professionals);
- facilitation of parent support groups, which have included mothers' groups, fathers' groups, groups for parents of adults with ASD, and groups for parents of youngsters who are participating in social groups at the same time; and
- attendance at school IEP and other agency meetings with parents, as needed and if time permits.

Integration with Typical Peers

In the United States, school-based integration of students with disabilities with typical peers has traditionally taken the form of placement of the students with special needs into general education settings for all or part of the day. This is usually done either for potential educational benefits, for anticipated benefits in terms of social interactions, or both.

Integration for Educational Purposes

The decision about a student's public education placement is made by the IEP team, of which parents are typically members, but TEACCH is generally not involved. Some parents feel strongly that their youngsters with ASD should be educated in general education classes; some prefer smaller special education classes; and other families have no strong opinions about this issue. Some LEAs in the past few years have gone to an "all inclusion" model, in which special education classes have been eliminated (although this trend is gradually reversing). As described above, TEACCH professionals do not believe that any one model of services is appropriate for all students (Mesibov & Shea, 1996).

Integration for Social Purposes

TEACCH supports the potential value for students with ASD (and their families) of learning how to enjoy spending time with typical peers. Possible benefits include language stimulation, increased play skills, increased social skills and self-confidence, and reduced family isolation. However, it has long been established that just having children with ASD and typically developing peers in the same location is not sufficient for social interactions to occur (McHale & Gamble, 1986; Mesibov, 1976; Myles, Simpson, Ormsbee, & Erickson, 1993). Peers who are prepared and interactions that are structured, familiar, and enjoyable for students with ASD are important foundations for building meaningful social connections.

We typically suggest that before a student with ASD is introduced into a new situation to play with a new peer, the activity should be first learned in a one-to-one setting and then practiced in a familiar situation (i.e., with a work–activity system in a familiar location). For example, rather than sending a student into an unfamiliar general education classroom to participate in a new game with a group of youngsters he does not know, it is better to introduce only one element at a time. Consistent with this line of thinking, TEACCH professionals were early supporters of the "reverse mainstreaming" model of having typically developing peers come into specialized autism classes to play with the students with ASD using the materials and routines those students already found familiar and meaningful. Once the youngsters are familiar with each other and with their shared activities, these activities can be successfully moved to new settings, such as a general education classroom or after-school play dates.

A TEACCH staff member has also developed a program called Understanding Friends, which is a way of helping typically developing peers understand the behavior and special needs of students with ASD in their classes or schools. Information on this program is available on the "Educational Approaches" section of the TEACCH Web site (www .teacch.com).

Transitions

The lead agency for early intervention services (birth to 3 years) in North Carolina is the Department of Health and Human Services. The lead agency for preschool special education (3–5 years) and school-age special education (5–21 years) is the Department of Public Instruction. Students with ASD in North Carolina are almost always assigned to grade levels based on their chronological age. As a result, preschool children whose fifth birthday falls before October 15 of a given year enter the public school system classified as kindergartners, regardless of their educational labels or classroom placements. These students move with their chrono-logical-age peers from elementary school to junior high or middle school, and then to high school. Because of limited program resources, TEACCH can be involved with transition planning only on request by individual families in particularly complex situations. We generally encourage families to use both the IEP process and informal communication and planning mechanisms within the school to make transitions smooth. Further, the Autism Society of North Carolina has a statewide parent advocacy program that can assist parents with advocating for the services and supports they want for their child.

Preparation for Adult Years

One of the first books to address the issues of adolescents and adults with ASD was edited by Schopler and Mesibov (1983). Because ASD is a lifelong disorder, we believe that preparation for adulthood should be an element of educational programs beginning in early childhood. Teaching students as young children to communicate, understand organizational systems, and follow visual cues provides the foundation for later learning, whether that learning is abstract and academic or vocational, or concrete and focused on basic self-care.

In 1988, Mesibov, Schopler, Schaffer, and Landrus published the *Adolescent and Adult Psychoeducational Profile* (AAPEP) to assist with the transition from schools to vocational settings. The AAPEP is a criterion-referenced measurement tool that looks at functioning in the areas of independence, communication, leisure, social, vocational skills, and vocational behaviors, and it has been demonstrated to be effective for generating educational objectives. Because of the increasing diversity of the population of individuals with ASD and changes in vocational options, a revised version of the AAPEP (to be called the *TEACCH Transition Assessment Profile*) is in the process of development.

In 1989, TEACCH began an innovative Supported Employment (SE) program for adults, in collaboration with the Autism Society of North Carolina and the North Carolina Vocational Rehabilitation Services. The SE program uses job coaches who apply the principles of individualization, the culture of autism, and Structured Teaching to assist employees with ASD in learning the skills and behaviors needed for their jobs in the competitive job market. The SE program has successfully placed and supported adults with ASD in office and clerical positions and jobs in grocery stores, warehouses, laboratories, food service, janitorial work, landscaping, and libraries (Mesibov et al., 2005). Individuals who learn TEACCH strategies in school have a significant head start in using them in their jobs in the community as adults. However, not all of the individuals in our SE program received TEACCH-based educational services as children, indicating the value of TEACCH strategies and principles even when they are introduced later in life.

Outcomes

Measuring outcomes in autism programs is difficult because of the enormous individual differences among children, the number of treatments each child is exposed to, and the many other methodological factors that enter into measuring and improving learning and behavior. These difficulties are compounded when focusing on outcomes of a specific educational program, because it is hard to isolate the effects of a single factor from the overall program of comprehensive, lifelong services provided by TEACCH. In spite of these problems, we realize how important measuring outcomes is, so we try to accomplish this through multiple strategies. These include specific research studies on the effectiveness of our educational techniques, outcome data, and anecdotal and statistical information about the impact of our educational programs.

As described previously, visual structure and visual organization techniques are primary components of TEACCH interventions. Ozonoff and Cathcart (1998) evaluated the effectiveness of a visually organized TEACCH Structured Teaching intervention program. Following approximately 4 months of training, the participants in this program improved significantly more than control group subjects on imitation, fine motor skills, gross motor skills, and nonverbal conceptual skills. These subjects showed progress three to four times greater than those in a control group classroom receiving an educational program based on discrete trial learning.

The outcome data that most strongly support the effectiveness of Structured Teaching involve school graduates who are successfully involved in Supported Employment activities. More than 200 students in educational programs using TEACCH principles have secured vocational placements working at least 20 hours per week at an average hourly wage (in 2002) of $6.65. The 1-year retention rate for those placed in employment is over 90% (Mesibov et al., 2005).

Informal measures also speak to the effectiveness of the TEACCH educational programs. Over 600 visitors come from virtually every state in the United States and over 20 foreign countries each year to observe TEACCH educational services, and over half of them visit school-age classrooms. Each summer TEACCH offers intensive training workshops to professionals from throughout the United States and all over the world, and over 300 participants attend to learn the strategies described in this chapter to organize and implement the educational programs. An issue of the *International Journal of Mental Health* (Schopler, 2000) described how TEACCH services, especially for elementary-age classrooms, are used on virtually every continent and how they have affected services and promoted the development of more effective educational strategies for students with ASD from all over the world.

In summary, Structured Teaching visual and organizational strategies have received support from the empirical literature in studies done by TEACCH professionals and others. In addition, students participating in these programs have gone on to employment with a higher success rate than has been reported by any other autism program. National and international interest in the TEACCH strategies is very high, and professionals from all over the world come to Chapel Hill to learn these strategies.

Common Myths and Mistakes

TEACCH is a well-known program that has been in existence in North Carolina for a long time, so many parents and professionals across the country have some familiarity with some aspects of the TEACCH approach to educational services. Unfortunately, however, several misconceptions exist as well. Listed below are some of the common myths and mistaken ideas about TEACCH:

• *TEACCH is only for students with mental retardation or only helps very capable students.* TEACCH works with individuals with ASD at all developmental levels, from people with significant mental retardation to people with superior intelligence and academic achievement.

• *TEACCH is only for children.* TEACCH works with individuals with ASD of all ages. For example, our Supported Employment and residential and vocational programs for adults are highly regarded, effective demonstrations of the application of Structured Teaching principles and techniques for adults (Mesibov et al., 2005; Van Bourgondien, Reichle, & Schopler, 2003). We have provided, as needed, individual counseling, marital counseling, and vocational guidance to college students, graduate students, and individuals who have careers and independent lives.

• *TEACCH is only for students in self-contained classes.* Principles and techniques of Structured Teaching can be used to help students understand and meet expectations in all educational settings, including general education classrooms; "specials" such as music, art, PE, and foreign language; and speech–language and occupational therapy sessions, as well as in the cafeteria, on the school bus, and on the playground.

• *The primary TEACCH strategy is using baskets.* Baskets are merely one means of organizing materials, which is one broad principle of Structured Teaching. For students who are working with concrete learning materials, baskets are indeed useful for keeping the materials in one place, instead of rolling around, falling down, or getting mixed up. For students with greater academic skills, however, more typical organizational material would be used, such as folders, notebooks, pencil cases, and backpacks. As described previously, other principles of the TEACCH approach are individualization, understanding and respecting the culture of autism, and using visual information to help students understand and engage in meaningful, productive activities.

• *TEACCH programs don't teach language.* Professionals from TEACCH were innovators in developing methods for teaching and supporting language development in students with ASD (Schopler & Mesibov, 1985; Watson, Lord,

Schaffer, & Schopler, 1989). We consider that meaningful, spontaneous communication is a vital goal for all students with ASD (Mesibov et al., 2004). We do suggest that activities for learning language and social communication should have a visual or physically concrete component, because of the relative strength in visual processing and difficulty with auditory comprehension of students with ASD. Language-only tasks are likely to be unsuccessful. Students' attention is more easily engaged and maintained if there is something to see, hold, or touch.

Many students with ASD are able to learn to communicate using verbal language; for those who do not achieve this level of abstract thinking and expression, we and many others in the field have found that developing receptive and expressive communication using visual methods is often effective (Layton & Watson, 1995; National Research Council, 2001; Schuler, Prizant, & Wetherby, 1997). The use of visual alternate communication devices is not a substitute for teaching language. In fact, TEACCH professionals and others have found that visual supports make language *more* likely to emerge (Frost & Bondy, 1994; Magiati & Howlin, 2003).

- *All directions in TEACCH classrooms are given using pictures.* On the contrary: If all students in a classroom are using the same system for receptive communication, it is almost certain that there is not adequate individualization in the programming.

- *By focusing on independence, TEACCH further isolates already lonely people with ASD.* It is true that Structured Teaching values independence highly and has established it as an important educational priority. However, the development of enjoyable social interactions and meaningful social relationships is also an important priority. Structured Teaching can be an excellent foundation for facilitating social activities that would otherwise be too unpredictable and confusing for students with ASD (Mesibov et al., 2005).

Summary

TEACCH's Structured Teaching principles can be applied flexibly and effectively to the diverse population of school-age students with ASD. With a combination of understanding and respect for the culture of autism, individualization based on unique profiles of scattered skills and family priorities, and visual or written organizational strategies, students with ASD from kindergarten through high school can engage in meaningful learning activities that lead toward the highest possible degree of independence in adulthood.

References

Allison, D. B., Basile, V. C., & MacDonald, R. B. (1991). Brief report: Comparative effects of antecedent exercise and lorazepam on the aggressive behavior of an autistic man. *Journal of Autism and Developmental Disorders, 21,* 89–94.

Eckenrode, L., Fennell, P., & Hearsey, K. (2003). *Tasks galore.* Raleigh, NC: Tasks Galore.

Eckenrode, L., Fennell, P., & Hearsey, K. (2004). *Tasks galore for the real world.* Raleigh, NC: Tasks Galore.

Education for All Handicapped Children Act of 1975, 20 U.S.C. § 1400 *et seq.*

Elliot, R. O., Dobbin, A. R., Rose, G. D., & Soper, H. V. (1994). Vigorous, aerobic exercise versus general motor training activities: Effects on maladaptive and stereotypic behaviors of adults with both autism and mental retardation. *Journal of Autism and Developmental Disorders, 24,* 565–576.

Filipek, P. A., Accardo, P. J., Baranek, G. T., Cook, E. H., Dawson, G., Gordon, B., et al. (1999). The screening and diagnosis of autistic spectrum disorders. *Journal of Autism and Developmental Disorders, 29,* 439–484.

Frith, U. (1989). *Autism: Exploring the enigma.* Malden, MA: Blackwell.

Frost, L. A., & Bondy, A. S. (1994). *The Picture Exchange Communication System training manual.* Cherry Hill, NJ: Pyramid Educational Consultants.

Gray, C. (1998). Social stories and comic strip conversations with students with Asperger syndrome and high-functioning autism. In E. Schopler, G. B. Mesibov, & L. J. Kunce (Eds.), *Asperger syndrome or high-functioning autism?* (pp. 167–198). New York: Plenum Press.

Hodgdon, L. A. (1995). *Visual strategies for improving communication: Practical supports for school and home.* Troy, MI: QuirkRoberts.

Janzen, J. (2003). *Understanding the nature of autism: A guide to the autism spectrum disorders* (2nd ed.). San Antonio, TX: Therapy Skill Builders.

Klin, A., Volkmar, F. R., & Sparrow, S. S. (Eds.). (2000). *Asperger syndrome.* New York: Guilford Press.

Klinger, L. G., & Dawson, G. (1992). Facilitating early social and communicative development in children with autism. In S. W. Warren & J. Reichle (Eds.), *Causes and effects in communication and language intervention* (pp. 157–186). Baltimore: Brookes.

Layton, T., & Watson, L. R. (1995). Enhancing communication in nonverbal children with autism. In K. A. Quill (Ed.), *Teaching children with autism: Strategies to enhance communication and socialization* (pp. 73–103). New York: Delmar.

Lord, C., Rutter, M., DiLavore, P. C., & Risi, S. (2002). *Autism Diagnostic Observation Schedule.* Los Angeles: Western Psychological Services.

Magiati, I., & Howlin, P. (2003). A pilot evaluation study of the Picture Exchange Communication System (PECS) for children with autistic spectrum disorders. *Autism, 7,* 297–320.

McGimsey, J. F., & Favell, J. E. (1988). The effects of increased physical exercise on disruptive behavior in retarded persons. *Journal of Autism and Developmental Disorders, 18,* 167–180.

McHale, S. M., & Gamble, W. C. (1986). Mainstreaming handicapped children in public school settings: Challenges and limitations. In E. Schopler & G. B. Mesibov (Eds.), *Social behavior in autism* (pp. 191–212). New York: Plenum Press.

Mesibov, G. B. (1976). Implications of the normalization principle for psychotic children. *Journal of Autism & Childhood Schizophrenia, 6,* 360–364.

Mesibov, G. B., Browder, D. M., & Kirkland, C. (2002). Using individualized schedules as a component of positive behavioral support for students with developmental disabilities. *Journal of Positive Behavior Interventions, 4,* 73–79.

Mesibov, G. B., Schopler, E., Schaffer, B., & Landrus, R. (1988). *Adolescent and Adult Psychoeducational Profile.* Austin, TX: PRO-ED.

Mesibov, G. B., & Shea, V. (1996). Full inclusion and students with autism. *Journal of Autism and Developmental Disorders, 26,* 337–346.

Mesibov, G. B., Shea, V., & Adams, L. W. (2001). *Understanding Asperger syndrome and high-functioning autism.* New York: Kluwer Academic/Plenum Press.

Mesibov, G. B., Shea, V., & Schopler, E. (with Adams, L., et al.). (2005). *The TEACCH approach to autism spectrum disorders.* New York: Plenum/Kluwer Academic.

Myles, B. S., Simpson, R. L., Ormsbee, C., & Erickson, C. (1993). Integrating preschool children with autism with their normally developing peers: Research findings and best practices recommendations. *Focus on Autistic Behavior, 8,* 1–18.

National Research Council. (2001). *Educating children with autism.* Washington, DC: National Academy Press.

Ozonoff, S., & Cathcart, K. (1998). Effectiveness of a home program intervention for young children with autism. *Journal of Autism and Developmental Disorders, 28,* 25–32.

Quill, K. (1997). Instructional considerations for young children with autism: The rationale for visually cued instructions. *Journal of Autism and Developmental Disorders, 21,* 697–714.

Rosenthal-Malek, A., & Mitchell, S. (1997). The effects of exercise on the self stimulatory behaviors and positive responding of adolescents with autism. *Journal of Autism and Developmental Disabilities, 27,* 193–202.

Schopler, E. (Ed.). (2000). International priorities for developing autism services via the TEACCH model [Special issue]. *International Journal of Mental Health, 29*(1).

Schopler, E., Lansing, M. D., & Marcus, L. M. (in press). *Psychoeducational Profile* (3rd ed.). Austin, TX: PRO-ED.

Schopler, E., & Mesibov, G. B. (Eds.). (1983). *Autism in adolescents and adults.* New York: Plenum Press.

Schopler, E., & Mesibov, G. B. (Eds.). (1984). *The effects of autism on the family.* New York: Plenum Press.

Schopler, E., & Mesibov, G. B. (Eds.). (1985). *Communication problems in autism.* New York: Plenum Press.

Schopler, E., & Reichler, R. J. (1971). Parents as cotherapists in the treatment of psychotic children. *Journal of Autism and Childhood Schizophrenia, 1,* 87–102.

Schopler, E., & Reichler, R. J. (1979). *Individualized assessment and treatment for developmentally disabled children: Vol. 1. Psychoeducational profile.* Baltimore: University Park Press.

Schopler, E., Reichler, R. J., DeVellis, R., & Daly, K. (1980). Toward objective classification of childhood autism: Childhood Autism Rating Scale (CARS). *Journal of Autism and Developmental Disorders, 10,* 91–103.

Schuler, A. L., Prizant, B. M., & Wetherby, A. M. (1997). Enhancing language and communication development: Prelinguistic approaches. In D. J. Cohen & F. R. Volkmar (Eds.), *Handbook of autism and pervasive developmental disorders* (2nd ed., pp. 539–571). New York: Wiley.

Van Bourgondien, M. E., Reichle, N. C., & Schopler, E. (2003). Effects of a model treatment approach on adults with autism. *Journal of Autism and Developmental Disorders, 33,* 131–140.

Visually structured tasks: Independent activities for students with autism and other visual learners. (1996). Chapel Hill, NC: Division TEACCH.

Watson, L. R., Lord, C., Schaffer, B., & Schopler, E. (1989). *Teaching spontaneous communication to autistic and developmentally handicapped children.* Austin, TX: PRO-ED.

The Valley Program

*John McKeon, Kathleen Vuoncino,
Rebecca Brenkert, Karen Dinnell-LoPresti,
Ellen Doyle, Mark Lampert, Michele Madden-Perez,
and Scott Rossig*

In 1994, the superintendents of Region III of Bergen County, New Jersey, asked that a public school program serving preschool through eighth grade be developed to serve the needs of children with autism and related learning difficulties in the Northern Valley area. Neighboring special education regions joined to support the concept of a high-quality program providing research-based interventions together with inclusion opportunities within the community. Region II and Region V became part of the program, to allow more placement opportunities for students living in any of the 36 districts and to share in the overall design and supervision of the program.

A development committee was formed by the program, which included parents, staff, and administration. A consultant from the Douglass Developmental Disabilities Center at Rutgers University was hired to assist in planning the initial phase of the program. After two preschool classes were started, the Eden Family of Services of Princeton, New Jersey, provided ongoing consultation services. PIE (Preschool Instruction for the Exceptional) PLUS, the original name of the program, was changed to the Valley Program in our fourth year. At the same time, Region II joined Region III in providing services. We expanded to work with Region V in our 5th year, with the addition of two more classes. The Valley Program presently offers 16 classes for children 3 to 13 years of age, with inclusion and community resources available at all levels. The plan for the 2004–2005 school year was to house the entire Valley Program under the auspices of Region III to centralize campuses, which will enhance the overall services of students through the coordination of supervision, observation, and evaluation of staff, as well as facilitating access to school and community services.

Students referred to the Valley Program are classified as autistic according to the New Jersey Administrative Code (NJAC 6A:14). According to the code, *autistic* is defined as

> a pervasive developmental disability which significantly impacts verbal and nonverbal communication and social interaction that adversely affects a student's educational performance. Onset is generally evident before age three. Other characteristics often associated with autism are engagement in repetitive activities and stereotyped movements, resistance to environmental change or change in daily routine, unusual responses to sensory experiences and lack of responsiveness to others. The term does not apply if the student's adverse educational performance is due to emotional disturbance…. A child who manifests the characteristics of autism after age three may be classified as autistic if the criteria in this paragraph are met. An assessment by a certified speech–language specialist and an assessment by a physician trained in neurodevelopmental assessment are required. (p. 35)

Diagnosis and Assessment

Students are referred to the Valley Program through the district's child study teams. The teams complete formal assessments and submit their evaluations for review by the Valley Program. The Valley Program staff, consisting of a teacher, speech–language pathologist, and behavior consultant conduct the official intake. The initial screening lasts approximately 30 to 40 minutes and is used to determine some of the child's abilities by means of a checklist of skills. The parents are taken on a tour of the facility by the assistant director and are interviewed to determine the specific needs and current functioning of their child. Once the child is accepted, the teacher and behavior consultant decide on the appropriate placement. When the child is placed in an appropriate class, he or she is probed through a comprehensive skill assessment. This helps determine the student's current level of functioning and guides the teacher in developing appropriate goals and objectives. Speech and language, behavior, and social assessments are also conducted once the child is placed.

After approximately 2 weeks, all challenging behaviors are assessed and a formal behavior plan is developed. A behavior assessment is conducted to determine the cause of the behaviors, and specific interventions are designed if needed. Parents are asked to approve all written behavior plans, which are reviewed and monitored once a month by the behavior consultant and Behavior Management Committee.

Staffing and Administration

The administrative staff of the Valley Program consists of three regional directors, one assistant regional director (who is located on site at the largest facility), and supervisors responsible for staff evaluations. Each region's special education director is responsible for staff observations and evaluations according to the particular board of education requirements. The directors and assistant director meet monthly to discuss program-wide issues, staffing, parent issues, and changes. Staff members are hired through a process of interviews by either the regional director or the assistant director. Individual classrooms are supervised by behavior consultants, but the directors and assistant directors do all formal observations and evaluations of all staff members. Teachers are certified teachers of the handicapped. Teacher assistants, as well as teachers, are trained in applied behavior analysis (ABA) during an extensive 3-day training period using the Valley Program manual. They are also trained in crisis prevention interventions (CPI: Crisis Intervention Institute) by the two certified staff members. New teacher assistants are shadowed by the teacher or lead teacher assistant for approximately 2 weeks in the classroom. A trained teacher assistant first provides ongoing instruction for a 3-day period of shadowing, with a written record of the staff member's strengths and weaknesses. A 60-day probation period is then given to new teacher assistants to ensure skill acquisition. The teachers and behavior consultant also provide a written review of new staff members within 6 weeks. In addition, teachers review all teacher assistants three times per year using a consistent form, and behavior consultants complete a review on the teachers three times a year as well. This provides ongoing feedback to each staff member.

Because the Valley Program is a public school program, its teachers are required to follow the protocol for all teachers in the district that operates the classes. For example, nontenured teachers receive four observations, a midyear evaluation, a clinical observation, and a final observation by the administration. A tenured teacher receives one observation, a clinical observation, and an end-of-the-year evaluation. In addition, these records are reviewed by the superintendent of schools throughout the school year. Teachers of our transition classes in public school settings are also supervised by the building principal.

The Valley staff members are required to attend four scheduled professional development workshops organized by the administration and the behavior consultants. Staff members are also encouraged to attend conferences, such as those sponsored by the New Jersey Center for Outreach Services for the Autism Community (COSAC), the Council for Exceptional Children (CEC), and other related organizations. The staff has also presented at conferences and workshops to child study teams, parents, and teachers; and two behavior consultants are teaching a college-level course on autism. Four Valley staff members are currently board-certified behavior analysts (BCBAs), including an administrator. Several other staff members intend to pursue their BCBA certification when they have completed their required coursework.

The Valley staff includes a full-time nurse, custodians, seven speech–language pathologists, and occupational and physical therapists as needed.

Range of Methods

The Valley Program is an ABA-based program, and many strategies are used to make the student's instruction individually based. The program's primary modes of instruction are discrete trial teaching, small-group instruction, large-group instruction, mainstreaming opportunities (when appropriate), incidental teaching, and community exposure. Each of these strategies is implemented according to the goals and objectives in the child's Individualized Education Program (IEP). Any additional strategies that can enhance a student's performance, such as visual cues, picture schedules, and social stories, are used in teaching, as well. Generalization of new skills and review and maintenance of previously learned skills are also key components in the teaching cycle.

Innovative Curriculum, Instructional Management, and Skill Acquisition

The curriculum for the Valley Program is designed to teach and develop language and communication, appropriate behavior, cognitive development, fine and gross motor development, socialization, daily living, and prevocational skills. These broad areas of instruction are categorized to address the individual needs of the students. Curriculum planning and development are conducted by the teaching team, behavior consultant, speech–language pathologist, adaptive physical education teacher, occupational or physical therapists, if applicable, and the parent. The curriculum developed for each child is reflected in the goals and objectives of the child's IEP. The Valley Program uses *IEP Writer* (developed by Regions II, III, V, Council for Special Education, Bergen County, in 2001) as an instrument to create the IEP document.

The skill development and sequence of the curriculum focuses on establishing learning readiness (e.g., gross motor imitation) and then expands into establishing a balance of language and communication skills, self-care skills, cognitive areas (e.g., reading, mathematics), functional skills, domestic tasks, and socialization, as well as prevocational skills. These skills are also taught and generalized within both school and community settings. Goals are developed for school, as well as community, in order to monitor the progression of skill development in both settings. Community goals may include remaining with an adult, waiting in line at a retail or grocery store, ordering a food item from a menu, reading a grocery list, retrieving an item in a store aisle, and locating a public restroom or vending machine.

The resource for the methods and materials used at the Valley Program is the *Eden Curriculum* (Eden Institute, 2001). The *Eden Curriculum* provides the foundation for the discrete trials programming conducted in the classroom and speech–language sessions. Additional teaching materials include academic reading and math series; discrete trial programs written by faculty, behavior consultants, and speech–language pathologists; manipulatives; workbooks; faculty-developed social storybooks; and therapy equipment. Table 10.1 provides an example of a discrete trial program written by professional staff members (e.g., behavior consultant, speech–language pathologist).

The Valley Program also uses various cognitive and functional curriculum series that have been adapted and translated into discrete trial programming, such as the *Edmark Functional Word Series* (2002), *Edmark Reading Program: Level 1* (1992) and *Level 2* (1993), *Reading Milestones* series (Quigley, McAnally, Rose, & King, 2001), *SRA Multiple Skills Series* (Boning, 1998), and *Touch Math Series* (Innovative Learning Concepts, 2000). Fine motor skills are supplemented with *Handwriting Without Tears* (Olsen, 2001) and computer software such as Type To Learn, Jr. (Sunburst Technology Corp., 2001) and Keys for Kids (Sunburst

Table 10.1

Discrete Trial Program for Taking Turns Using Visual Prompts

Target behavior: When given an object (i.e., in a turn-taking game with game pieces), the student will engage in proper turn sequence.

Prerequisite skills: Program should be taught concurrently with an object manipulation and gross motor imitation program.

Criterion: 90% correct responding for three consecutive sessions for all steps

Measurement: Trial-by-trial data

Procedure

1. Divide game pieces into two piles. Therapist takes turns with student by manipulating object(s). Therapist covers student's game pieces with a piece of paper. Student takes turn when paper is removed.

2. Divide game pieces into two piles. Therapist takes turns with student by manipulating object(s). Therapist covers student's game pieces with a smaller piece of paper or index card. Student takes turn when paper is removed.

3. Divide game pieces into two piles. Therapist takes turns with student by manipulating objects. Therapist covers student's game pieces with a gestural prompt. Student takes turn when the gestural prompt is removed.

4. Divide game pieces into two piles. Therapist takes turns with student by manipulating objects. Student takes turn after therapist.

5. Use the same procedure for all subsequent activities.

6. Generalize the student's responses to various teachers in various settings.

Prompting Techniques

1. Full physical prompt: Manipulate student's hand through the response.

2. Faded physical prompt: Touch student to begin movement.

3. Gestural prompt: Gesture with hands or point to object.

Suggested Activities

1. Playing cards

2. Don't Spill the Beans

3. Don't Break the Ice

4. Connect Four

Author: Ellen Doyle, Valley Program

Communications, 2001), as well as various adaptive and sensory equipment in class and therapy sessions. The speech–language department works collaboratively with the classroom teachers to promote various communication modes such as the Picture Exchange Communication System (PECS; Bondy & Frost, 1994), computerized voice output devices, sign language, and fostering expressive language. Additional speech–language materials include *Boardmaker* (Mayer-Johnson Company, 1998) and Picture This software (Silver Lining Multimedia, 2001).

The progression of skills is monitored and evaluated in several ways. Discrete trial programs are data based. Acquisition as well as generalization of the student's skills is criterion based and monitored by teaching staff and the behavior consultants in the classroom. In addition, quarterly progress reports reflecting all programming and formal behavior treatment plans are received by the student's child study team and parents. Finally, parents are invited to attend clinics four times a year. These clinics provide the opportunity to discuss the overall progress of their child's educational performance, as well as to collaborate with the program staff to continue to promote consistency and meet the needs of their child.

Behavior Management

The Valley Program behavior reduction programs follow a strict protocol in order to create effective and ethical interventions. First, a behavior is assessed to determine whether it (a) is harmful to the individual or others, (b) interferes with the ability to learn, or (c) is socially stigmatizing. Once this has been determined, an operational definition of the behavior must be obtained. This consists of a statement that specifies exactly what behavior to observe. It allows for consistent observation and data collection. Next, a complete assessment of the behavior occurs, beginning with conducting a baseline of the behavior and completing various assessment instruments. Portions of an assessment could include the *Motivation Assessment Scale* (MAS; Durand, 1998), antecedent–behavior–consequence (ABC) data (O'Neill et al., 1997), and anecdotal notations to determine the function of a behavior. When these three components have been completed, a team approach is used to explore possible interventions to treat the behavior. The team consists of the teacher, classroom staff, therapists, behavior consultants, parents, and any additional personnel directly related to the student. When making a selection of interventions, the following considerations are made: their effectiveness, their possible effects on desirable behaviors, the least-to-most list of intrusive treatment hierarchy, the feasibility of the treatment, and what current literature supports the treatment. Alternative teaching strategies must also be developed to support each plan. These strategies are techniques used to increase positive behaviors, such as visual strategies, teaching replacement behaviors, reinforcement systems and schedules, environmental changes, social stories and verbal rehearsals, and sensory activities.

The teacher and behavior consultant collaboratively write the Behavior Reduction Plan (see Figure 10.1) and send all information to the Valley Program Behavior Management Committee for formal approval. The role of the Behavior Management Committee is to ensure that all behavior plans have been properly developed, are clinically appropriate, and are consistent with good clinical practice. The committee includes the director and assistant director of the Valley Program, a Valley Program behavior consultant, a Valley Program teacher representative, a district psychologist, and a speech and occupational therapist. The committee is responsible for the initial approval of a plan, as well as continual supervision and ongoing assessment of its effectiveness. Once a plan has been approved, it is sent home for parental signatures (see Figure 10.2). When the plan has been approved by the parents, the staff is fully trained to implement the procedure, as well as the alternative strategies, and implementation begins.

Integration

It is the philosophy of the Valley Program and the belief of all staff members that our primary goal is to integrate our students into the school community. As a public school program, we understand the importance of inclusion in the community to the fullest and most appropriate extent possible for all students. This push for integration begins when a student attends one of our classrooms for the first time. Integration may be in the form of gaining access to a less restrictive special education classroom within our program or the child's home district; mainstreaming and inclusion into general education classes; participation in a Valley "transition" class; or experiences in our local community.

In preschool, we begin by developing a well-rounded educational program for each child. By implementing teaching programs to foster learning readiness, communication, academic, self-help, vocational, and social and play skills, we aim to increase opportunities for successful integration

VALLEY PROGRAM
BEHAVIOR REDUCTION PLAN
PROCEDURAL REQUIREMENTS

Student Name: Student's first and last name.

Baseline Rate and Date: Average of the baseline rate, date of the baseline.

Current Rate and Date: Average of the current rate once the procedure begins.

Operational Definition of the Target Behavior: A complete definition of the behavior.

Functional Assessment: Results of the assessments used to determine the function of the behavior.

Rationale for Intervention: Reasons for the need of a behavior plan (harmful to self and others, stigmatizing in the community, interfering with work, etc.).

Alternative Teaching Plan: The activities being done in conjunction with the behavior plan (schedules, language programs, teaching the use of the augmentative device, visuals, etc.).

Operational Definition of the Treatment: Definition of the procedure, including the Discriminative Stimulus and explanation of the steps of the procedure.

Negative Ancillary Effects: Any possible negative effects to behavior plan.

Method of Data Collection: How data is being collected (e.g., frequency, duration, during certain times of the day).

Literature Review: Current references for the behavior plan.

Treatment History: Any other procedures that were implemented for this behavior (e.g., a token loss procedure was implemented to reduce John's spitting behavior 2/00–6/00; this is the second formal plan for spitting).

Signature _____   Signature _____
                Classroom Teacher   Behavior Consultant

Figure 10.1. Sample Behavior Reduction Plan.

VALLEY PROGRAM
BEHAVIOR REDUCTION
PLAN ASSENT FORM

Student Name: Student's first and last name.

Date: Date the plan was written.

I have read and approve the treatment of the following behavior defined as:

The definition of the behavior from page one.

_____

Parent Initial

Initial

I have read and approve the implementation of the following treatment for my child:

The explanation of the treatment from page one.

_____

Parent initial

Initial

I understand that the following negative ancillary effects may occur as a result of the implementation of the treatment program:

The negative ancillary effects from page one.

_____

Parent initial

Initial

*Please help us in monitoring the effects of this program so that we can make modifications as necessary.

*I understand that no Behavior Reduction Plan will be implemented without my consent.

*This program will be reviewed for effectiveness by the program staff and the Behavior Management Committee.

Parent's signature _____ Date of signature _____

Figure 10.2. Sample Behavior Reduction Plan Assent Form.

in the future. There is an emphasis on fostering independent play skills, increasing time on task, developing leisure skills to assist students in learning at an early age, and structuring their "down time." A staff of five provides early intensive instruction to a class of six children. Individual attention can help a child acquire the skills needed for independence quickly, while the introduction of small- and large-group work provides opportunity for young children to experience communal learning.

As our students move to the primary-age classes (ages 5–8 years) and then on to the upper elementary classes (ages 9–13 years), the ratio in the classrooms shifts to 1 adult per 2 children. The development of independent skills is fostered through the ongoing emphasis on having children learn to remain with a task for extended periods of time, and by continuing to find appropriate activities that promote leisure and enjoyment. Small- and large-group instruction becomes more prevalent as the children grow older. It is at the primary level that the Valley Program begins its Community Experience program for all of the children.

Valley Community Experience

As a core part of our program, our community experiences include meaningful trips into the local communities of the children we serve. For example, at the primary level, we begin by visiting community settings once every 2 weeks for 2 hours at a time. When students reach the upper elementary classes, their community visits take place each week. Our trips occur in the towns in which our students live, so that each of them may "experience" their own community. We visit places that children may see with their own families such as local merchants, supermarkets, dining establishments, malls, department stores, and recreational facilities. Settings are selected based on the individual needs of the children. For example, when visiting a local strip mall, some students may eat in a fast-food establishment, while others may enjoy a more leisurely lunch in a more formal environment. Goals are developed for each student, focusing on the necessary skills needed for success in the community, such as waiting in line, ordering and paying for food, walking at an acceptable pace through the mall, greeting community members, waiting appropriately while shopping, locating items in a store, and shopping for oneself when given a list of items. The experiences in the community afford the students the opportunities they need to generalize many of the skills they acquire within the classroom.

Valley Transition Classes

Providing opportunities to spend increased amounts of classroom time with typically developing peers is beneficial to many of our students. As a public school program, we are afforded the opportunity to interact with typical children on a daily basis, very often right next door to our Valley class. The Valley Transition Program maintains classes in local elementary schools within our region of the northern Valley. Although, in most cases, the Valley Program groups children heterogeneously in classes, children in our transition classes are grouped according to common interests and abilities. These transition classes are designed based on specific criteria (see Figure 10.3) and provide students with opportunities to work more frequently in small and large groups and to spend increasing amounts of time in age-appropriate general education classes. The Valley transition classes are slightly larger in number of students, as part of our goal to prepare students for participation in significantly larger general education classes. Valley also maintains a transition class at each age level within our program. Preschool students have opportunities for mainstreaming into the region's PIE classes, where the classes are slightly

---

**VALLEY PROGRAM
TRANSITION CLASS PLAN LIST**

Students should have mastered or are currently learning the following skills.

Social:
- Taking turns
- Following classroom procedures and transitions from one activity to the next independently
- Following the classroom routine with some level of independence
- Waiting
- Peer awareness
- Imitating peers
- Parallel play skills
- Isolated toy play
- Awareness of environmental and social cues
- Beginning to organize his or her own materials

(continues)

Figure 10.3. Sample Transition Class Plan List. *Note.* Adapted from *Valley Teacher Manual,* Valley Program, 2003. Adapted with permission.

Language:
- Understanding functional language
- Following varied forms of directions
- Following multiple directions
- Spontaneous language past basic wants and needs
- Beginning basic conversation and reciprocal skills
- Auditory comprehension skills, answers basic questions
- Working productively in small speech group

Daily living:
- Basic bathroom skills, has begun using a public bathroom
- Independence with daily self-help skills

Groups:
- Imitating a group leader in a group of four or more children
- Following directions in a group of four or more with only one leader
- Following along in a group with occasional prompting from a shadow
- Beginning independent work skills
- Imitating and following directions in a large group with some prompting
- Learning through typical teaching techniques, moving away from discrete trial instruction
- Following a visual model in a group setting
- Beginning to use problem-solving skills in a group without being given a direction to follow
- Learning skills in a less restrictive environment with a shadow

Attending:
- Working seated across the table from the teacher
- Working in a discrete trial teaching environment with two other students
- Attending to task for extended periods of time without a break
- Attending independently in various settings

Behavior:
- Behaviors can be managed appropriately in a public school setting with minimal intervention
- Shows awareness and responds to less restrictive discipline techniques

Academics:
Close to mastery of the Eden academic and speech curriculum

Figure 10.3. *Continued.*

larger. PIE is a preschool program for students with developmental disabilities. Though the students are classified, their social skills and play skills are typically more appropriate, and they can act as "models" for our students with autism. This provides students with increased opportunities for socialization, as well as language and play skill development. Additionally, our preschoolers can participate in outside general education preschool programs. The staff in the transition classrooms have the ever important roles of "preteaching" skills needed for successful integration into general education, as well as shadowing the students while they spend time in classrooms with their typical peers. We recognize collaboration as being the key to success, as without the adults bridging the gaps between general and special education, our students would find it difficult to achieve in the general education setting. Teachers, teacher assistants, parents, behavior consultants, and administration are in constant communication to ensure the appropriate level of inclusion and educational programming for each child.

Data collection is key in the Valley transition program. Goals are set for group learning within the Valley class and also within the inclusive setting. These goals are monitored closely and adjusted accordingly. Social skills training is also an integral component. Students are taught specific social skills in a group setting, one time per week, and it is the responsibility of all staff in the room to follow through and generalize the skills learned in both the Valley class and the inclusive setting. The importance of modeling social behavior is emphasized consistently in the classroom. Staff is monitored and evaluated throughout the year on their ability to facilitate group instruction and shadow students in inclusive settings. Staff effectiveness is also monitored systemically (see Figure 10.4).

Integration of school-age children with autism spectrum disorders (ASD) into the least restrictive environments is key to improving rates of success in the community. It provides an opportunity for the true generalization of all skills that are taught within the confines of the self-contained special education classroom. Whether it is a visit to local merchants, placement in a Valley transition class, or participation in an inclusive school setting, the Valley program believes integration to be part of the important continuum of educating students with ASD and assisting them in assimilating to the community.

Family Involvement

The Valley Program is committed to fostering a strong connection between the home and school environments. Parent involvement is essential in providing a comprehensive educational program for each student. This partnership between home and school is critical for the generalization

VALLEY PROGRAM
TRANSITION CHECKLIST
FOR TEACHER ASSISTANTS

Assistant name: _____ Date: _____

Teacher/consultant: _____

Shadowing

_____ Arranges the environment conducive to the group learning situation

_____ Redirects attending

_____ Uses appropriate physical prompts

_____ Uses appropriate gestural prompts

_____ Uses appropriate verbal prompts

_____ Prompts student to keep the pace of the group

_____ Consistently implements formal behavior plans

_____ Appropriately addresses informal behavior plans

_____ Responds to cues from the teacher of the group

_____ Leaves appropriate distance from the student

_____ Moves around the group, prompting all students

| ✓ Satisfactory |
| ✓ – Needs Improvement |

Comments:

Figure 10.4. Sample Transition Checklist for Teacher Assistants. *Note.* Adapted from Valley Transition Staff Evaluation Form for shadowing a student in inclusive settings. Adapted with permission.

and maintenance of skills, as well as for the development of effective approaches for increasing and reducing challenging behaviors in both settings. To meet these goals, parents are encouraged to participate in the educational process on a variety of levels, beginning with a training program for parents of new Valley students.

Upon entering the program, new parents attend a series of training workshops covering a range of topics, including discrete trial teaching, general principles of applied behavior analysis, language acquisition, self-care skills, behavior management, and activity schedules. Workshops are offered for both evening and afternoon sessions to accommodate the varied schedules and needs of the parents. A second component of the training allows the parents to come into the classroom and work directly with their child under the guidance of the classroom teacher. These sessions may address specific self-care issues, such as feeding and toileting, or they may be designed to assist the parent in establishing general instructional control. A third component of parent training involves a series of visits to work on specific skills in the home setting. These visits are not tutoring sessions but are instead designed to work directly with the parent to develop effective teaching skills, behavioral strategies, and daily routines for family living. A behavior consultant meets with the parent to select appropriate goals and outcomes, and then designs an appropriate program to meet the specific needs of the individual family. After the initial consultation and home visit with the behavior consultant, an ABA therapist (which may be a teacher or teacher assistant) will conduct follow-up visits to the home to assist the parent in implementing those strategies. This combination of workshops, classroom visitation, and home visits is designed to provide a comprehensive approach to parent training, as well as to ensure consistency between the home and school environment.

The philosophy of collaboration is continued with parents who have already completed parent training. Home visits are offered to all students in the Valley Program throughout the school year, to monitor progress and to address new concerns as they arise. At times these visits are conducted in the community setting where a specific skill is being targeted, such as the dentist, grocery store, or barber. Classroom observations are also offered to all parents on a monthly basis. In addition, parent conferences or clinics are offered a minimum of four times per year and are often held more frequently, based on individual needs. At the clinics, the teacher, parent, speech–language pathologist, and behavior consultant review the student's progress on all goals in the school setting and discuss progress on goals for the home setting. A member of the child study team is invited to attend these meetings, as is anyone involved with the child at home, such as a private therapist or other family members. Formal IEP meetings are held in addition to the clinics.

The Valley Program also offers family support through a Parent Support Group and a Sibling Support Group. The Parent Support Group meets bimonthly to provide an opportunity for parents to share resources, information, and concerns with one another. The group is facilitated by a school psychologist from the Valley Program. Guest speakers on a variety of topics are also arranged. The Sibling Support Group meets monthly to provide an opportunity for children to interact with other peers who have a sibling with special needs. Meetings are designed to facilitate communication and foster supportive relationships in an effort to decrease feelings of isolation. The meetings are held in the early evening, and a pizza dinner is served to help foster a social atmosphere where the children can express themselves through play, art, and discussion.

Transitions

The Valley Program moves students from level to level with a great deal of caution, collaboration, and planning. The program considers the student's skill acquisition, as well as the process of moving a student, and informs the family during the process throughout the years of schooling. Staff who work with the Valley students at any level continue to plan and develop educational programming throughout the student's educational experience.

Students who are recommended for transition to the next level of programming are at 5, 9, and 13 years of age. The levels are based on ensuring appropriate age levels within the same classroom. Our program consists of three levels: preschool (ages 3–5), primary (ages 5–8), and upper elementary (ages 9–13). The process of transition begins with discussions between the current behavioral consultant, therapists, and teacher and the receiving staff members. The students are observed in their current classroom, therapy sessions, and other educational settings, such as inclusion. Topics such as behavioral plans, current or past communication systems, future programming ideas, and parent and family involvement are discussed. Records are reviewed, and the current teacher shares past experiences and learning styles of the particular student. In

September, the new teacher is given a completed Valley Program transition form, which presents the summer observation and reviews the input from the previous staff. Observations and consultation with the previous staff members continue as needed into the new school year. In individual cases, a staff member from the previous year accompanies the student for a certain amount of time to ensure a smoother transition. Additional training is also provided to the receiving staff on any topics or procedures that require more guidance.

Consistency is a goal of programming. For example, the records are carefully reviewed by the current staff to ensure that programming is documented and will be understood by the receiving staff members. Current and receiving teachers meet frequently, and all data and materials are passed from the previous classroom to the next, in order to continue the current programming. IEP documents and current evaluations, as well as the medical, psychological, learning, and social histories, are reviewed by the future teacher.

The transition plan is discussed with the parents during a special meeting or at the IEP meeting in the winter prior to the change in setting. The teaching staff and the child study team discuss the changes being proposed for the following year. The parent is introduced to the transition process and is given all available information. IEP changes are made, and if necessary, a consultant or a teacher from the receiving staff team will attend the meeting to assist with any issues or to receive any useful information. A student visitation will be scheduled with parental consent, and a tour of the future classroom or an example of that level of classroom or a similar level of classroom is offered to the parent.

The teaching staff at the Valley Program follow a systematic curriculum and sequence of skills, to which the students will be exposed at each classroom level. Acquired skills become the foundation for unlearned abilities, and functional teaching is emphasized for each student. A goal for the students is to acquire a fluency of skills in the areas of attending, small group learning, functional academics, socializing, independence, self-care, and communication on each level. The teachers are thoroughly trained on exit goals for each student at the level they are teaching. Part of their training also includes exposure to the previous level and the following level of the curriculum.

The preschool teachers focus on skills to get their students ready for primary school-age programming. Learning readiness skills, such as appropriate sitting behavior, eye contact, imitation, waiting, and following one-step directions, are initially taught in order to expand to higher-level skills. For example, compliance is a skill taught to young students to enable them to follow directions from a variety of people both at school and at home. The preschool student is also taught basic dressing skills, and a successful toileting schedule is established. On a pre-academic track, the students are taught matching skills. Speech–language pathologists also work with the children to establish an effective means of communication. In addition, the preschool trains the students to work in small groups (three to six students) and in dyadic discrete trial sessions.

Primary-level students entering the upper elementary level at age 9 years (middle-school age) have a greater ability to follow directions. The teachers continue to teach the students in dyadic discrete trial and small-group settings, and the students can work independently for about 10-minute intervals (e.g., they will have mastered sorting and simple activities without prompting to remain on the task). These students have also learned dressing and eating skills, independent toilet use, and simple grooming skills. The speech department continues to improve the student's established communication system.

For students entering the secondary level at age 13 years, teachers build upon the skills learned in the upper elementary level. Prevocational tasks such as object assembly and expanded sorting skills are taught. The students also continue to learn functional academic programs, sight words, money skills, and number concepts. In addition, basic domestic skills such as table setting, laundry sorting, and simple lunch preparation are introduced into the programming. Self-care skills are taught to a fluency level. Word or picture activity schedules are used to teach the students to engage in leisure and prevocational tasks for a longer period of time, and students are taught to work independently for over 15 minutes on a single task. In the community, students are taught to follow the directions with the group and to perform generalized skills taught in school. Community skills such as choosing a meal from a menu, carrying money, and waiting appropriately in lines continue to be addressed.

Preparation for the Adult Years

The Valley Program currently serves children from the ages of 3 to 13 years. In September 2003, the program entered into a cooperative venture with the local county school district to design a specialized autism program to meet the needs of students in the high school years. The goal is to bring together the resources and expertise of the two programs to create a quality specialized high school.

The new program will remain grounded in the philosophy of applied behavior analysis. Emphasis will focus on preparing students for the adult years through a balanced curriculum of academics, language, self-care, domestics, vocational skills, and behavior management. A new building is designed to meet all of these goals, with structured classrooms for individualized instruction, a personal care suite for teaching daily living and self-care skills, vocational rooms to teach specific job skills, kitchen facilities for meal preparation, and laundry facilities for domestic skills. Community involvement and employment experiences are also integral components. The students access community settings, including grocery stores, shopping malls, libraries, bowling alleys, and restaurants, on a weekly basis. Employment opportunities are arranged with local businesses and facilities and are coordinated with the assistance of a job coach.

Many of the goals for the high school students have been targeted at an introductory level throughout their education at the Valley Program. Preparation for adulthood cannot begin in the teen years. Developing appropriate self-care skills, increasing time on task, developing leisure skills, and fostering independence are core goals for students at all levels. The high school program expands upon ongoing goals with a practical and functional approach to prepare students for adult living.

Outcome

The Valley Program is dedicated to providing students with an appropriate education within the least restrictive environment. Once students have shown proficiency in a general education classroom, they are considered potential graduation candidates. Once the decision has been made for a student to graduate from the Valley Program, a pretransition plan is developed to provide a smooth inclusion process. Pretransition planning is a collaborative effort, involving the Valley behavior consultant and teacher, the graduating students' case manager, the parents, and the new teacher. The transition process assists in preparing students for their new school environment by providing them with several pretransition visits. Valley staff members remain active participants throughout the transition process. To assist receiving schools in providing effective educational and behavioral interventions, training is offered to classroom aides of the receiving school at the request of the district.

Following the student's transition into the new school environment, the Valley Program continues to provide support by offering six follow-up visits by a Valley behavior consultant. Typically, visits follow a schedule of three visits in September through October, one visit in November, one visit in January, and one visit in March. Additional support is provided through workshops presented by the Valley staff that focus on classroom issues often faced by teachers involved in the transition process. Home visits and school consultation on behavioral issues are also provided as needed. Finally, the Valley Program provides continual assistance to parents by offering guidance and resources such as invitations to parent support groups and training and access to our parent resource guide and availability of home consultation visits.

Summary

The Valley Program is a public school program, derived from three special education regions in Bergen County, designed to meet the needs of students with autism. Valley serves children ages 3 to 14 years with an ABA-based program and many strategies used to make the student's instruction individually based. Discrete trial teaching, small-group instruction, large-group instruction, mainstreaming opportunities (when appropriate), incidental teaching, and community exposure are the program's primary modes of instruction. Behavior management is clearly a priority, and the program's behavior consultants create effective and ethical interventions. The Valley Program's primary goal is to integrate our students into the school community, and it provides transition classes and inclusion opportunities when appropriate. Community experiences include meaningful trips into the local communities of the children we serve. The Valley Program is committed to fostering a strong connection between home and school environments, so parents are encouraged to participate in the educational process on a variety of levels, beginning with a training program. This program also offers a Parent Support Group and Sibling Support Group. For students who transition out of the Valley Program, support is provided by one of the behavior consultants into the new school environment.

References

Bondy, A., & Frost, L. (1994). *Picture exchange communication systems.* Newark, DE: Pyramid Educational Consultants.

Durand, V. M. (1988). The Motivation Assessment Scale. In M. Hersen & A. S. Bellack (Eds.), *Dictionary of behavioral assessment techniques* (Appendix). New York: Pergamon Press.

Eden Institute. (2001). *Eden Institute and Valley Program Curriculum.* Princeton, NJ: Author.

Edmark reading program: Level 1. (2001). Austin, TX: PRO-ED.

Edmark reading program: Level 2. (2002). Austin, TX: PRO-ED.

Fouse, B., & Wheeler, M. (1997). *A treasure chest of behavioral strategies for individuals with autism.* Dallas, TX: Future Horizons.

Gotthilf, T. J., Lanpert, R. E., McKeon, J. W., Wagner, S. L., & Varvassi, V. J. (2001). *IEP Writer.* Hazelton, PA: Leader Services.

Handwriting without tears. (2001). Cabin John, MD: Olsen.

Maurice, C. (1996). *Behavioral intervention for young children with autism.* Austin, TX: PRO-ED.

Mayer-Johnson Company. (1998). *Boardmaker.* Solana Beach, CA: Author.

National Research Council. (2001). *Educating children with autism.* Washington, DC: National Academy Press.

New Jersey Administrative Code. (2003). NJAC 6A:14.

O'Neill, R. E., Horner, R. H., Albin, W. W., Sprague, J. R., Storey, K., & Newton, J. S. (1997). *Functional assessment and program development for problem behavior.* Pacific Grove, CA: Brooks/Cole.

Picture This [Computer software]. (2001). Petersborough, NH: Silver Lining Multimedia.

Quigley, S. P., McAnally, P. L., Rose, S., & King, C. M. (2001). *Reading milestones.* Austin, TX: PRO-ED.

SRA multiple skills series. (1998). Columbus, OH: McGraw-Hill.

Sundberg, M. L., & Partington, J. W. (1998). *Teaching language to children with autism or other developmental disabilities.* Pleasant Hill, CA: Behavior Analysts.

Touch math series. (2000). Colorado Springs, CO: Innovative Learning Concepts.

Type to learn, Jr. (2001). Pleasantville, NY: Sunburst Technology Corp.

Graduating from Preschool

11

Mary Jane Weiss

· ·

G raduation from preschool is an enormous milestone for all children and their parents. It signifies entry into the world of school and is associated with major leaps in independence and in expectations. Even for children in preschool, the home is usually the center of the world. As children enter school, that center shifts. Over the next several years, primary involvement is in school-related activities. Friends may replace siblings as closest playmates. The family enters a world that is oriented toward the community at large, not just the family at home.

For the family of a child with an autism spectrum disorder (ASD), the change is even more monumental. Often, families of children with ASD will be leaving the familiarity and support of a specialized program where the child received expert and individualized services. They may wonder whether they have made the right choice in leaving a program where expertise in autism is substantial. They are often taking a leap of faith into a system with limited expertise in educating students with ASD. They may also have children who struggle with transitions, and whose parents fear they will regress under the stress of a change. Other families may continue to receive specialized supports for their child. While a specialized placement affords the best access to intensive and individualized instruction, it also usually entails a transition. There may be a shift in the instructional ratio, in the skills emphasized, or in other aspects of the child's education.

The nature of graduation from preschool for children with ASD is by no means a singular one. There are myriad options to meet the needs of different children. The nature of autism and the outcomes associated with early intensive behavioral intervention are variable. While some students will make substantial progress (to the point of being indistinguishable

269

from typical peers, in some cases), others will require ongoing, specialized supports of many types.

There is considerable ambiguity for parents during the preschool years. Over the course of preschool, some of the questions begin to resolve, but it can still be confusing for parents to determine what kind of next school placement is most appropriate. For example, one family might have concerns about the extent of contact with peers who can provide modeling of appropriate behavior, and the parents of another child might question whether their child's gains will slow down if less intensive direct instruction is available.

Readiness for School

Readiness skills are a topic that gets a lot of attention during the preschool years. Teachers may speak of a child's readiness skills for socialization experiences, for small-group instruction, for more naturalistic teaching, and for group learning. When graduation is approached, all of these readiness skills become more salient and more ridden with anxiety for the family.

Of course, even among typical learners, there is considerable variability in the skills of children entering kindergarten. Some children do not recognize all of their letters; others identify some words or even show early reading skills. Some children still exhibit an immature pencil grasp, others struggle to trace letters, and still others write their names and other words with ease. Some students can barely stay within the lines when coloring a picture; others can color well, and some can even draw freehand clearly.

The nature of the kindergarten class is a heterogeneous mix of abilities. Development happens in an uneven way and at different rates for all children. Parents and educators worry more about lags in development, however, when students have a developmental delay or disability. For such students, readiness has more salience, as we know they may struggle more with skill acquisition and with socialization.

For the student entering a specialized program, the concerns may be different. Instruction will be highly individualized, so lags in development are not a central concern. Nevertheless, parents may have concerns about peers and whether there will be children of similar abilities and interests in the classroom. Such similarities help to build social connections. Parents might also be concerned about behavior problems and about how to best reduce the extent to which such behaviors interfere with learning.

And they may also be very concerned with building their children's independence and helping them adapt to receiving less help than they may have been accustomed to in preschool.

Bridging from Preschool

How do we bridge from preschool to elementary school? What skills matter the most for success in the school environment? How do we equip students with those skills so that they can navigate the requirements of a new and complex environment with maximal success? These are some of the important questions that parents and professionals might ask.

For any child, entering kindergarten can be a daunting experience. For children with ASD, it can be especially challenging because of their communication difficulties. Will this child be able to express himself or herself? Will this child be understood? Will he or she be able to follow directions? Will he or she be able to attend long enough to meaningfully participate in group lessons? Will the child understand more complex questions?

What about self-care? Is he or she relatively independent at using the toilet, washing hands, and dressing? The extent to which the child is discrepant from age peers will have implications for whether more supports are needed in the classroom (to ensure adequate assistance). Furthermore, it will have implications for which classrooms might be the most appropriate choices.

What about social skills? How does the child respond to other children? Does he or she reciprocate greetings? Answer a peer's questions? What about play skills? Sharing? Can he or she express feelings of anger or negotiate conflicts with peers without resorting to aggression?

In the preschool environment, the issue of independence may not have been as relevant as it will be in kindergarten, first grade, and beyond. In preschool classes, there is often a need for considerable support in many tasks throughout the day. If the preschool class was a mixed-age class, the variability in level of independence may have been even more pronounced. There may well have been students in diapers, students learning to use the potty, and fully trained children in the same classroom. At lunchtime, there may have been students who were independently managing all the tasks of lunch sitting next to children who required help to open their juice boxes and pudding containers.

In kindergarten and beyond, however, independence in such activities is the norm. The expectation for students is independence with these tasks. Children who require a great deal of assistance will begin to look quite discrepant from their classmates, and severe lags may even be stigmatizing. Parents and teachers preparing preschoolers for transition need to examine not just the demonstration of skills, but the independence level associated with the skill.

Whether for a typical kindergarten class or a special education setting, the degree to which the child demonstrates readiness skills will directly affect the success of the transition. For those students entering a more specialized setting, there are still many advantages. Specialized settings are much more able to provide intensive teaching. For students who learn most effectively through intensive or individualized instructional approaches, there is no substitute for the expertise and precision found in specialized settings. Furthermore, for children who have very challenging behaviors, specialized settings are maximally able to alter the environment to reduce the likelihood of behavioral escalations, to provide rewards at frequent intervals for appropriate behavior, and to provide many practice opportunities to teach appropriate replacement skills. Therefore, it is often the case that a specialized setting will provide the most appropriate instructional environment for building skills. Nevertheless, there are also concerns for students in this circumstance. Parents may wonder how to best address socialization needs and how to ensure that their child is sufficiently challenged.

Continuum of Options: How to Choose the Appropriate Environment

The good news is that there are many possible placements for students with ASD leaving preschool, and the bad news is that there are many possible placements for students with ASD leaving preschool. It can be overwhelming to contemplate the options available. The task of identifying an appropriate setting is basically one of matching a student's strengths, needs, and characteristics to the best environment available.

A Fully Inclusive Education

In the early months after diagnosis, and throughout a child's preschool years, virtually all parents of children with ASD hope for eventual placement in a fully inclusive environment. In fact, in many discussions by professionals about the outcome of preschoolers, this placement is equated with success and is even termed *best outcome* (e.g., Lovass, 1987; McEachin, Smith, & Lovaas, 1993).

The advantages of this placement are obvious. First, children who are able to be fully included can be educated in their neighborhood school. Their school peers and friends will be the same children they see on their block, at their local parks, at the pool in the summer. There is a level of normalcy in this option that is irreplaceable. The value of such immersion in the community is something we may take for granted, but it is a priceless gift to a child with ASD.

Furthermore, there is evidence that children with ASD benefit from placement with their typically developing peers (e.g., Harris & Handleman, 1997). They are exposed to appropriate role models from whom they can learn. They may make substantial gains in language and in play skills from their exposure to typical peers, but the greatest area of gain is likely to be in the realm of social skills (e.g., Buysee & Bailey, 1993; Harris & Handleman, 1997).

Some students with ASD can indeed be fully included. Students who are the best candidates for this experience are those whose cognitive, language, and other skills are at or beyond age level when leaving preschool. In addition, they are usually children who can learn quite naturalistically, just as their typically developing peers learn. They do not need elaborate teaching procedures, undue repetition, or specialized procedures to acquire new knowledge. Students such as Sammy, in the following case scenario, who can communicate their needs well, including the need for help, are good candidates for such an environment.

 CASE STUDY 1

When Sammy was ready for kindergarten, he was well beyond his peers in reading and in math. He could read simple books, he could add up to 20, he could copy whole sentences, and he could cut and color well. His language deficits had abated; he was close to age level in language skills, though his spontaneous speech was not equivalent to his peers'. However, he could answer questions, ask questions, and request help. Socially, he was quiet and a bit solitary. But he could answer his friends, he joined when asked to participate in games, and he did not ignore his classmates. Sometimes his interests were a little bit unusual. Whereas some kids were interested in astronauts, he was interested in the mechanics of telescopes and rocket ships. It was clear that Sammy was able to be included academically. With the help of the teaching staff, some peers with similar interests (and high intelligence) were paired with him for certain activities. This helped to solidify some social connections and foster the beginning of friendships.

Full Inclusion with Supports

Sometimes even though the fully inclusive environment is the best option, the child needs specific supports to be successful. It may be that the student is at or near age level in many areas and can learn new material in a variety of natural ways but still requires help to attend or to complete work effectively. In such a case, you may want to have the child in the inclusive setting for all of the reasons previously cited. You may be reluctant to move the student to a special education placement when he or she could succeed in the general education classroom. It is clearly in the interests of the child to be in as least restrictive an environment as possible. It may simply be a matter of adding a level of support to facilitate functioning in the inclusive environment.

Often, in this circumstance, a shadow—an individual (not a second teacher) who uses systematic prompting (i.e., assistance to facilitate correct responding; Cooper, Heron, & Heward, 1987) and reinforcement (i.e., rewards contingent on appropriate behavior; Cooper et al., 1987) to support a student's participation in a more inclusive, less restrictive environment—may be designated to help the student in ways that will facilitate responding to the classroom teacher and participating meaningfully in the classroom environment. In the following case scenario, the complex role of the shadow is described.

 CASE STUDY 2

Ellen did very well in an intensive home-based applied behavior analysis (ABA) program for 2 years. She then spent a year attending preschool with a shadow 2 days per week, while still doing an ABA program at home. She will now enter kindergarten. While she has much academic strength, she has a lot of difficulty staying on task, especially in large groups. She also has trouble with transitions. It is hard for her to follow multistep directions. With peers, she watches activities but is reluctant to join even if asked. She requires frequent feedback and support, especially for math and reading, and her stamina for work is lower than that of her peers. A shadow will help ensure that she receives prompts and reinforcement to maximize her participation.

The terms *shadow, instructional aide,* and *teaching assistant* are sometimes used interchangeably to describe additive support in the classroom for a student with ASD. It may be helpful, however, to conceptualize shadowing as distinct from instructional assistance. Some students with ASD are in need of specialized help to make the transition to regular education but do not require continuous or permanent assistance. Some students with ASD do need continuous assistance from a designated aide throughout the day. This aide may provide instruction in completely different ways from the classroom teacher and may even teach activities that are unrelated to those going on in the classroom. Alternately, a shadow supports the student with ASD to participate in and respond to the natural demands in the environment. A shadow assists the learner in responding to the classroom teacher. A shadow does not provide the same level of assistance as an instructional aide. There are a number of dimensions on which there are different approaches and different goals. These are summarized in Table 11.1.

Many different kinds of people can serve as shadows. People from a variety of backgrounds and experiences can be successful in this role. The background and experience of the shadow significantly affects the facility of the individual within the role and the role definition within the educational team. Sometimes the shadow will have previously shadowed the student in question or another, similar student. At other times, the shadow may have had a role in assisting other students with disabilities. Occasionally, a certified teacher serves a shadowing role.

When an individual who has taught the student in a home-based program is available to shadow the student, a unique option arises that has both advantages and disadvantages. A shadow who has worked with the student previously may have developed a good rapport with the student, and the student may, therefore, be more responsive than he or she would

Table 11.1
Differences Between an Instructional Aide and a Shadow

The 1:1 Aide	The Shadow
Devotes full attention and time to one student	Mixes offering assistance and fostering independence
May provide special lesson or adaptations	Usually supports student in typical classroom activities
Often sits in front of or adjacent to student	Often sits or stands behind student
Offers intrusive assistance	Offers least intrusive assistance
Offers very direct reinforcement	Uses subtle forms of reinforcement whenever possible
Uses continuous or very frequent reinforcement	Uses an intermittent reinforcement schedule and seeks to thin schedule
Emphasizes skill acquisition	Emphasizes incidental learning and generalization across settings
May provide modeling of desired responses	Directs student's attention to peer models
Gives student instruction	Student takes instruction from the teacher
Collects data on skill acquisition	Typically collects data on the maintenance and generalization of skills, the spontaneous use of language, social interaction, and so forth

otherwise be in a novel environment with many new challenges. The shadow would also know the student's skills and abilities, which could assist in targeting ways for the student to participate in group activities. Furthermore, the shadow may know what kinds of social, tangible, and edible stimuli have served as effective reinforcers over time, thus streamlining the process of identifying reinforcers. The shadow may also know about various treatment approaches and which strategies have proved best for the student. For example, he or she may know that physical prompts are not preferred, that picture cues work well, or that social stories have successfully addressed several social skill deficits. A shadow who has worked with the student at home may also have achieved a level of comfort and familiarity with the family and may be able to suggest ways to convey or share information that would be agreeable to the family.

There are some disadvantages to a previous relationship, however. Specifically, the student may rely too heavily on the shadow. The familiarity may actually impede generalization to new instructors and foster dependency on the familiar instructor. The shadow's previous relationship with the family can also present challenges in terms of misdirected communication or reduced parent–teacher contact. Parents may naturally go to the shadow, whom they already know, rather than to a teacher with whom they have yet to form a relationship. Shadows in this context sometimes also inadvertently undermine the teacher's authority or breach confidentiality. It is a complex role in the best of circumstances, and a preexisting relationship only heightens the nuances and complexities of the role. Finally, the role of a shadow is vastly different from that of an instructor in a home-based ABA program. The skills required are different. While the principles of ABA are still evident, they are employed in a much more subtle fashion. For some instructors, this transition is a difficult one, and they may require supervision and support as they interact differently with the student than they do during direct instruction.

Perhaps the most critical responsibility of the shadow is to be a good observer. This is especially important in the first few months of shadowing, during the transition to the classroom environment. Another important dimension of the role is the need to recognize the boundaries of the job responsibilities and respect the authority of the classroom teacher. Shadows assisting students on the autism spectrum must attend to a wide variety of behaviors and skills, and must employ a variety of strategies to help the learner succeed in the educational setting (e.g., Doyle, 1997; Twatchman-Cullen, 2000).

In their interactions with the student, shadows try to

- provide guidance and feedback in as least intrusive a manner as possible;
- provide feedback in a manner that minimizes prompt dependency;
- promote the transfer of skills to the classroom environment;
- promote the learning of new skills within the classroom environment;
- constantly assess and evaluate the effectiveness of potential reinforcers;

- enhance the student's socialization with classroom peers during both group work and social activities;
- facilitate learning from peers;
- promote transitions across activities with minimal disruptive behaviors;
- promote appropriate independent activities; and
- minimize and prevent challenging behaviors.

Role definition is critically important. Shadows and teachers need to agree on who is responsible for the multiple tasks that must be accomplished daily. For example, teachers and shadows need to agree on who will write the daily note home, who will graph the data, who will provide regular progress updates to the parent. Although the teacher will be responsible for all of the instruction to the child, she or he may wish for the shadow, with his or her intimate knowledge of the details of the day, to assume several of those responsibilities.

Shadows are designed to be faded out. A child who requires ongoing support over many years is in need of an instructional assistant or aide. A child who needs support to participate, but who can learn in the regular education environment, is in need of a shadow. The need for shadows often declines over time, because the child may need the most support in the first few years of school. Some children need such support only for the first part of a new school year. Other children can share the support from the shadow with other students until they no longer require a designated shadow or assistant.

Shadowing requires training in a variety of domains. Shadows (and all of the educational professionals working with a particular student) need to know about ASD and about the learning characteristics of students with these disorders. They also need to know about the application of effective prompting and reinforcement procedures. Ideally, a shadow should learn theoretical and comprehensive information about the principles and techniques of ABA. They will also need to be trained as astute observers and as reliable data gatherers. Finally, they need to understand their role definition and be coached in how to work effectively and productively with all members of the educational team (see, e.g., Cavallaro & Haney, 1999). Perhaps most important, they need to get to know this particular learner and which methods have historically been effective with this learner. It is not enough to teach these principles and procedures didactically; it is essential that individuals be trained to implement them. Such training should include extensive modeling; comprehensive, repetitive, and ongoing feedback; and competency-based assessment of skill possession.

Training shadows is a tall order, especially when many school districts will not even identify the individuals who will serve as shadows before the school year begins. Of course, the classroom teacher needs to know shadowing skills as well, or at least be familiar with their importance. In some cases, all members of a team might be provided with specialized training on ASD. In addition, some districts may be able to arrange for training for this all-important shadow role. Finally, there needs to be some guidance for the shadow and teacher once the student arrives. A behavior analyst, school psychologist, or other knowledgeable team member may be able to provide assistance, modeling, and feedback during the early days of instruction—which are critically important—and shadows and teachers should be provided with maximal support to make a successful start. In some cases, parents may be able to assist in that process or may be willing to send help from a home-based program. Although these arrangements are complex in terms of role definitions, among other things, they may be an expeditious way to create continuity and clarity for a student undergoing a major transition. (See Appendix 11.A for resources on the use of paraprofessionals.)

Other Supports in an Inclusive Setting

Other supports may be given to a student in a fully inclusive situation besides the shadow. For example, the student may still require speech therapy. Even when there are no longer language delays (in reference to age norms), there may be issues in the use of language. Perhaps the student cannot make his or her needs known on a consistent basis, takes too long to answer questions, can't find words to communicate when upset, or has difficulty processing abstract questions or conveying complex information. Speech therapy may help to address these targeted deficits, which have real implications for social and academic success.

Most students with ASD benefit from the substantial involvement of a special educator. In some districts, special educators and general classroom educators will co-teach in an inclusive classroom. In that way, the expertise of the special educator is made available, but the student does not lose access to the general education environment.

The student who has difficulty with social skills may benefit from targeted training in this area (e.g., Baker, 2002, 2003; Wagner, 1999). In some cases, a school may have several students in need of that specific level of support and may decide to form a social skills group to help address those skills. Among the topics that such a group might address are taking conversational turns, following up in conversation, learning not to interrupt, asking for a desired toy that another student has, and using words to express anger.

Part-Time Inclusion

Some students can benefit from an inclusive environment but require more specialized instruction to learn new skills. For such students, a part-time inclusive environment may be the best option. Students can be placed in the general education environment for the subjects in which they have strengths but receive more specialized instruction in their areas of weakness. This placement has the advantage of continuing to provide the learner with the opportunity to receive individualized instruction in a highly systematic manner. It also affords the student, such as Joseph in the following case scenario, with the opportunity to interact with typical peers during activities that are reinforcing and fun.

 CASE STUDY 3

Joseph is a 6-year-old with autistic disorder. He has made substantial progress with intensive ABA instruction; nevertheless, he requires planning and repetition to learn any new skills, and his transfer of those skills depends on careful instruction. He is good at puzzles and with other visual activities. He has an extensive sight word vocabulary. He loves music. He is also exceptionally agile, and he enjoys sports. He engages in a great deal of hand flapping, especially when excited. When he is frustrated, he generally falls out of his seat and curls into a ball. He is very proficient at using the *Picture Exchange Communication System* (PECS; Frost & Bondy, 2002) to communicate and vocalizes often, as well. He is included for reading, gym, and music classes.

This particular placement requires attention in staffing. A staff member must be trained in intensive teaching methods, such as discrete trial instruction, incidental teaching, and natural environment training. Furthermore, a staff member (perhaps the same individual) will need to learn effective reinforcement and prompting procedures for use in the inclusive activities. The paraprofessional will need guidance, and coordination between the intensive teaching and the inclusive activities is necessary for maximal success. It is therefore essential to assign a key staff member to serve this supervisory and coordination function. It will also be necessary to have frequent meetings to ensure that all relevant staff members have current information about the student.

A Specialized Placement

There are also students who are served best outside of the mainstream educational environment. Students who are highly distractible, who struggle tremendously to acquire new skills, who respond best to highly repetitive instruction, who require specialized rewards to be effectively motivated, and who present very challenging or dangerous behaviors are often best served in a specialized placement. In such a setting, they will have access to instructors with expertise on how to best teach students with such characteristics. They will also have access to a much higher degree of consistency, more precise data collection and analysis to guide program planning on a daily basis, and state-of-the-art instructional techniques designed specifically for this population of learners. These settings usually also offer services to coordinate efforts between home and school, which is essential for learners with complex needs such as Oliver's, in the following case scenario.

 CASE STUDY 4

Oliver is a 6-year-old boy with autistic disorder. He is also severely apraxic. He has a history of self-injurious behavior and biting, and both of these behaviors still occur daily. He has made excellent progress on basic skills through discrete trial instruction, but he requires a frequent maintenance schedule to ensure his retention of skills. He has made substantial progress in communicating via PECS. He also understands a pictorial daily schedule. He is very easily distracted, and he is bothered by excessive noise, crowding, and novel environments. Oliver is best served in a specialized placement, where his skills and behavior can be addressed in a highly systematic manner, and where every accommodation can be made to reduce his stress and frustration.

Some students who attend specialized placements will need to do so for only a few years, while others will require such comprehensive and expert services for much of their lives. For those students who can be moved to a less restrictive setting, it is a careful and slow process. Within the specialized program, efforts can be made to approximate the next educational setting in variables such as availability and types of reinforcement, teaching techniques, and instructional supports. Once transition occurs, extra supports put in place to ensure success can be gradually reduced as the learner adapts to the new setting.

Planning for Successful Inclusion

The special instructional needs of the child with autism will not be intuitively clear to most teaching staff members. As a result, training is essential to success and must include student characteristics, instructional approaches, behavior management strategies, individualized goal development, and team building (Webber, 1997).

Understanding the Learning Characteristics of Students with ASD

What is important to know about students with ASD? The teacher and the instructional team need to know about the learning characteristics of individuals with ASD. Of course, students with ASD are all different, and each manifests particular strengths and challenges. Nevertheless, there are common attentional, learning, and communication difficulties of which one should be aware.

Difficulties with Attending. It is hard for children with ASD to attend to instruction. For some students, the move to a class with a larger number of students will present major challenges. They may have received a great deal of individual instruction, but their experiences with group instruction may be limited, and their capacity to attend to instruction from a distance may be limited. Furthermore, some children with ASD find it difficult to attend to the most salient or important aspects of an instructional context. They may experience stimulus overselectivity, in which they attend to only one (and perhaps not the most important) aspect of an instruction or prompt (e.g., Rosenblatt, Bloom, & Koegel, 1995).

Students with ASD may also have difficulty following multistep directions. They may attend only to short segments of instruction or respond only to the first part of a series of instructions. This makes it difficult for them to manage in a classroom environment in which many different instructions are given simultaneously. The extent to which directions are given verbally might also affect this ability. Many students with ASD can engage in multistep tasks with some supports, such as textual instructions.

Difficulties with Learning. Many individuals with ASD have great difficulty learning new skills and may require much repetition to master new concepts. It may be helpful for instructors to use little variation in the way a skill is presented in the early stages of instruction. These needs are sometimes totally discrepant from what is offered to their peers, because typically developing students thrive on variation and novelty. Creative classroom teachers modify how they present concepts and how they ask students to demonstrate knowledge on a moment-to-moment basis.

It is important for the instructional team to assess how much standardization in instruction is required for the individual student to learn most effectively. It will also help to plan with the student's parents how best to provide the appropriate amount of repetition and exposure to new material to ensure that the student with ASD can benefit from the group instruction.

Difficulties with Language. Language proficiency varies widely among children with ASD. There are issues in the modality of communication (vocal, sign, PECS); in the complexity of communication (affecting both the breadth of things that can be communicated and the comprehensibility of such communication); and in the independence of communication (varying from independent to prompted, which may include subtle suggestions as well as fully prompted sentences). Even students with ASD who have well-developed language skills often struggle to communicate effectively in school.

One major deficit is in the realm of requesting. Many students with autism do not spontaneously request items that they want or need. In part, this deficit is a function of the instruction students with ASD may have received. Much of the emphasis in teaching children with autism focuses on teaching responsivity to instructions, as opposed to initiating communication. Students may become proficient at labeling and at answering questions but not necessarily at navigating their environments. In recent years, there has been much more emphasis on teaching requesting skills (Sundberg & Partington, 1998, 1999). Such skills can be taught via vocalization, via sign, or through a picture-based system such as PECS.

In addition, some children with autism are unable to use their language skills at all times. For example, they may fail to use language when they are anxious or angry; they may engage in disruptive behavior instead. Often, students with ASD need extra supports to help them communicate effectively when they are agitated. Many students respond well to using cards (e.g., to request a break).

Difficulties with Socialization. Students with ASD usually have difficulty developing peer relationships. They tend to have trouble establishing emotional reciprocity, or the reciprocal connections that characterize most relationships. Many students with ASD do not seek to include others in or draw the attention of others to their ongoing activities. Even responding to the social bids of others is highly variable. While some students are more adept at this kind of give and take, they may struggle when circumstances become more abstract or emotionally charged, or when interaction is required for longer durations. It is also difficult for students with ASD to read and understand the nonverbal communication of others, and their own use of nonverbal communication strategies is usually limited. This often makes it difficult for them to understand or function effectively in social situations, and they may hit roadblocks with their peers even when they are interested in them.

Difficulties in Behavior. Many students with ASD are preoccupied with stereotypic interests that may make them unresponsive to other kinds of instruction. They may also have rigid or inflexible routines or rituals that can be difficult to interrupt. They may engage in repetitive motor mannerisms. All of these characteristics predispose the learner with ASD to behavioral challenges. Furthermore, communicative difficulties make it difficult and sometimes impossible for learners with ASD to make their needs, desires, and frustrations known. They may resort to aberrant behavior in the absence of a functional communication system.

Careful assessment of the maintaining factors associated with challenging behaviors is critical to comprehensive intervention. Much can be done to prevent behavioral difficulties by creating a supportive environment through a variety of appropriate and tailored accommodations. Furthermore, students can be taught a variety of communicative and other skills to more efficiently get their needs met.

Preparing Staff for Their Roles

It is critically important that the entire instructional team decide who will coordinate the inclusion effort. Teachers, administrators, and child study team members can all serve successfully in the role. The important issue is that someone must be designated. The other critical task is to define roles and responsibilities for all professionals involved. Inclusion is a complex undertaking, and the collaboration of many professionals is key to success (Snell & Janney, 2000). Furthermore, all team members involved should meet and discuss their expectations and concerns, and should ask for assistance with the elements of their role definitions that seem most daunting. It is generally recommended that teachers learn inclusion strategies and behavior management strategies prior to the entry of the student into the classroom (e.g., Demchak & Drinkwater, 1992; Harris & Handleman, 1997).

Of course, such training and planning are not restricted to inclusive options and are not one-time events. There must be opportunities for ongoing problem solving and evaluation of progress in every educational team. Regular opportunities to review areas of success and areas of concern can prevent the need for crisis-oriented meetings, and can reduce the isolation felt by individual team members in their instructional efforts.

Creating Educational Goals

It is important for the entire educational team to identify what the student is to gain from the placement (e.g., Snell & Janney, 2000; Webber, 1997).

Is the time in this setting designed to build academic skills, specific social skills, group instruction skills, attentional skills, self-monitoring skills, language skills, pragmatic skills, self-help skills? For every goal identified, a teaching plan and measurement system must be in place.

It is imperative to do a thorough assessment of the student's abilities. Several commercially available resources and curricula exist (e.g., Leaf & McEachin, 1999; Maurice, Green, & Luce, 1996). The *Assessment of Basic Language and Learning Skills* (Partington & Sundberg, 1998) is an excellent tool that has several advantages. First, it assesses for the extent and breadth of the skill in question and focuses on the contextual use of the skill demonstration. These are important to the generalization of the skill and to the spontaneous use of the skill, both elements of functional skill mastery.

In choosing goals, functionality is of central importance (Snell & Brown, 2000). Skills taught should be those that are necessary in the current and future environments. Furthermore, skills selected should be ones that will be practiced and reinforced in the natural environment.

All goals developed should be evaluated frequently, and direct observational data should be collected for each instructional objective. It is possible to collect such data on a sampling or probe basis, to reduce the demand on instructional staff, but it remains essential to collect objective data regularly. Review of progress should be ongoing, and adjustments should be made immediately in response to learner difficulty.

Assessing the Need for Supports

What kinds of supports are needed to help this learner succeed? Areas to consider include staffing, communication needs, and space. In terms of staffing, it is important to consider direct instruction, coordination of teaching efforts, behavioral consultation needs, home–school coordination, speech therapy, occupational therapy, and adaptive physical education. There are also indirect staffing demands for tasks such as creating materials and analyzing data. Communication system needs may include procuring and arranging an augmentative system, as well as the ongoing upkeep and development of such a system. It may also be necessary to consider whether space must be allocated for specialized reasons, such as individual instruction, a break area, or a reward area.

Preparing the Environment

It is important to prepare the classroom as much as possible to help the student with ASD transition effectively into it and function comfortably within it. The process of preparing the environment is an extension of the process of getting to know the characteristics of the learner. For example, is the child highly distractible? Consider the possible sources of distraction in the target classroom, including such items as doors, windows, and boards. Also consider the placement of the student's desk. Will it be near the teacher to facilitate attending? Is the child responsive to the presence of visual cues? Consider a posted daily schedule, labels for cubbies and desks, well-marked areas for centers, and mats or rugs for sitting in a circle. Plan the types of minischedules that will be used to keep the student on task during independent work activities. Consider the use of reminder cards to cue the student to get back on track when attention is diverted. Consider how to present material more visually during instruction, or across multiple senses to facilitate comprehension.

There are other characteristics of the learner to consider. Does the child respond well to visual incentive systems? Consider creating individual- and group-oriented motivational charts for target activities (e.g., cleaning up, listening to the teacher). Also, does the child have difficulty with transitions? Consider what types of class-wide signals will be given for transitions. Decide on whether and how timers might be useful to cue transitions.

Preparing the Student

Transition planning begins early in a student's educational career. Even when a student is in the early stages of learning, steps can be taken to prepare him or her for the next educational placement. For example, goals such as helping students perform tasks in visually and auditorially distracting environments or with novel language present in the command help to prepare them for the settings in which they will eventually need to function. It is helpful to consider the ultimate goals even in the earliest stages of instruction, so that children are taught as naturalistically as possible.

Transitioning a student with ASD takes planning at every educational stage, and the need to plan for transitioning increases as the child ages.

Careful planning is needed when it is finally time to help the student adjust to a new educational environment. Ideally, a student will benefit from visits to the new classroom environment before he or she is a full-time member of the classroom. This can easily be achieved when a student is transitioning into a classroom environment from a more segregated setting. Students may even attend each setting part time.

When students will be attending a new classroom, it is helpful for them to experience the environment prior to the beginning of the school year. Visits to the classroom help orient students to the environment. They also provide opportunities to meet classroom teaching staff with fewer distractions. At times, a student may meet the new teaching staff outside of the classroom environment. It may be feasible for teachers to meet the student at home or in another part of the school (especially if the classroom is in disarray for the summer). Any kind of initial meeting will increase the familiarity of the staff.

Preparing the Parent

Many parents of students with ASD have a long history of intense involvement in their child's educational program. This level of involvement has helped their child to succeed, to master skills, to make progress. In fact, the learning characteristics of children with ASD mandate this level of involvement. Parental involvement ensures consistency in instruction to foster rapid acquisition of skills, assists in the generalization of skills from one setting to another, and contributes to timely adjustments in the methods of instruction to facilitate learning and reduce frustration.

The learning history of parents of children with ASD may also contain experiences that have made them disinclined to reduce their level of involvement. For example, their child may have regressed in skills or experienced behavioral difficulties when their involvement was reduced. Also, parents are the undisputed experts about their children and have a vast amount of useful knowledge that will help the educational team be effective and efficient with the student.

Many parents of students with special needs have a great deal of anxiety about an inclusive experience (Snell & Janney, 2000). However, most report that their children have more friends, better play skills, more social interaction, and higher self-esteem as a result of the inclusive experience (Green & Shinn, 1994; Guralnick, Connor, & Hammond, 1995; Reichert et al., 1989). Ambivalence toward inclusion among parents of children with autism stems largely from fears that their child's needs might not be adequately met within an included environment (Kasari, Freeman, Bauminger, & Alkin, 1999; Palmer, Fuller, Arora, & Nelson, 2001). Parents are drawn to the social benefits of the setting but are also concerned with ensuring appropriate services.

It is important to recognize that, as in any collaboration, there will be differences of opinion and awkward moments. Parents and educators may not agree about the best direction to take. This is especially likely to occur with ASD, because the students are so different in different settings. It is important to use such circumstances as opportunities to gather more information about the learner and to work toward mutual and collaborative solutions.

Involving the Parent

There are many ways for parents of students with ASD to continue to be involved in their child's educational program. Since many students with ASD are more interested in material that is somewhat familiar, teachers can share information about books that will be read to the class in upcoming weeks. They can also provide a list of themes, with sample activities to be done. If parents are providing extra instruction at home, such information is extremely useful to link the home-based and school-based instructional agendas.

Evaluating Success

There are many dimensions to the evaluation of a student's educational experience. It is obvious that progress on educational goals and challenging behaviors must be examined. It may also be useful to examine consumer satisfaction, with consumers broadly defined to include the student, staff, parents, peers, and the parents of peers. Furthermore, it is helpful to look at the social realm and examine integration with peers.

When there are difficulties in any area of instruction, it is helpful to be as specific as possible in identifying the area of concern. It is also helpful to engage in treatment integrity checks—that is, to check whether proposed treatments or educational teaching protocols are being implemented as planned and designed. Educators have a tendency to drift from the original goals outlined. Inconsistencies between instructors can create major challenges for a learner. Sometimes difficulties can be addressed by checking each staff member's adherence to instructional protocols. It is also helpful to evaluate whether the provision of additional cues or more motivating rewards would alter performance, or whether tasks could be modified to reduce frustration.

Preparing Peers

There is wide variability in what peer students can or should be told about a student with ASD, partly because of the diversity of students with ASD and of settings. Furthermore, parents of the child with ASD may have strong opinions about what information about their child they would like to have shared. They are key players in the decision about whether and how to prepare peers. In some cases, a parent of a child with ASD may volunteer to tell the group about their child or about autism.

Whether or not a diagnosis is shared, and regardless of who shares the information with students, students can be helped with sensitivity training. The scope of this training can be much broader than autism, and certainly much broader than the target child. The focus should be on ways people are different. Some schools report success in using the Kids on the Block puppet show (www.kotb.com), which describes many disabilities, including autism. (See Appendix 11.A for some resources on explaining autism to children.)

Sometimes, there is so much emphasis on the differences between children with autism and their peers that we may forget to emphasize the commonalities among them. It is helpful to share information on how a child with ASD also has a pet, for example, or likes to skateboard or play with trains. At times, a parent may wish to come in to share some of these everyday facts and interests of the student and their family. Such mundane information helps peers to perceive the student as a person, and not just as a person with special needs.

It is also important for peers to recognize that a child with ASD has strengths as well as challenges. Many students with ASD are better in one or more areas than their age peers, but that is often not what peers know or are exposed to about them. They may see the child with ASD as a student who cannot speak well or who gets upset easily. It may help peers to develop a more comprehensive view of their classmate to also know what he or she is good at. Teachers can look for opportunities to showcase the strong abilities of students with ASD. Students with ASD may be asked to read the class a book, to solve some math problems at the board, or to bring in a puzzle they can do for show and tell.

It may be necessary to prepare peers for how to be successful in interactions with the student with ASD. Perhaps they need to learn how to get the student's attention before greeting him or her or asking a question. In fact, this has been shown to be an effective strategy for siblings of children with autism (Celiberti & Harris, 1993). Peer training models have been highly successful (e.g., Odom & Strain, 1986; Strain, 1983; Strain, Kerr, & Ragland, 1979). Pivotal skills for peers include establishing attention, providing prompts and feedback, and persisting in efforts to interact (e.g., Carr & Darcy, 1990; McGee, Almeida, Sulzer-Azaroff, & Feldman, 1992). It might also be helpful to teach peers to interact in ways that are less demanding of the child with ASD, such as by offering comments rather than posing a question (e.g., Goldstein, Kaczmarek, Pennington, & Shafer, 1992). Depending on the characteristics of the learner with ASD, it may be helpful to equip peers with several of these skills. It will make the peers more successful, and it will decrease the likelihood that they will become discouraged in their attempts to interact. It is also usually the case that assistance to peers from adults can and should be substantially faded over time (e.g., McGee et al., 1992; Odom, Chandler, Ostrosky, McConnell, & Reaney, 1992; Odom & Watts, 1991).

Helpful Methods To Use for Success

The use of a variety of teaching methods powerfully affects the success of learners with ASD. One of the most fundamental strategies is reinforcement, which entails the provision of rewards, contingent upon appropriate behavior, to increase the future likelihood of the desirable behavior (e.g., Cooper et al., 1987). Reinforcement is usually given frequently to children in the early stages of learning (e.g., Leaf & McEachin, 1999). As skills become more established, reinforcement is thinned and provided less frequently. It is important for students in inclusive settings to be able to tolerate delays in reinforcement. A dependence on immediate and frequent reinforcement can be disruptive to the classroom. It also significantly distinguishes the student with ASD from his or her peers and can impede the student's ability to be integrated successfully. Students may see the child in need of frequent reinforcement as less able. They may also resent the increased access to rewards.

Reinforcement Systems. Reinforcement and motivation are powerful aspects of behavioral teaching, and their use cannot be underestimated. Many students with ASD have a good understanding of reinforcement and a positive history of the application of rewards. These students will do well in an environment that offers rewards for appropriate behavior and high-quality work (e.g., Maurice, Green, & Luce, 1996; Snell & Brown, 2000).

Often students with ASD in inclusive settings are no longer in need of immediate rewards. Preparing students with ASD to tolerate more delayed contingencies of reinforcement will facilitate their adjustment to and participation in the environment.

Delayed Reinforcement Systems. The simplest way to bridge to a more delayed delivery of rewards is to use a token system (e.g., Cooper et al., 1987). Token systems offer small concrete rewards such as a penny or a poker chip that lead to a reinforcer. After students have earned a certain number of pennies or chips, they can exchange them for the reward (e.g., an opportunity to play with a preferred toy or go on a walk). Token systems are very versatile, and they can be adjusted based on a child's changing needs and abilities.

The disadvantages of token systems stem largely from their intrusiveness. It may be difficult to be subtle about the provision or exchange of tokens. Other students may question the use of a token system or the access to the rewards that it offers the student with ASD. Many shadows are good at being subtle in their token delivery. For example, they may keep the token board in their possession and simply flash the child a penny to indicate earning. Other shadows fade from tokens to a point system and simply tally the points. In this way, a shadow can show the student the tally count or whisper to them how many points they have.

Contingency contracts avoid the intrusiveness of tokens (e.g., Cooper et al., 1987). A contingency contract is an agreement between the student and the teaching staff that specifies both expected behavior and anticipated rewards. The document is signed by both parties, and adherence to the contract is reviewed. Rewards are earned for adhering to the terms of the contract. Like token systems, contingency contracts are very versatile and can be adjusted to an individual child's needs and abilities. They are considerably less intrusive than token systems, which makes them helpful in inclusive settings.

Self-monitoring involves the student with ASD in the evaluation of his or her own behavior (e.g., Cooper et al., 1987). A student who is learning self-monitoring can be involved in evaluating whether he earned his contingency contract. At times, teachers may assign bonus points for accurate reporting of behavior. Self-monitoring is an important extension of externally delivered reward systems, as it builds independence and self-control.

Individual and Group Contingencies. Most of the contingencies implemented are individual contingencies. However, there are also opportunities for group-oriented contingencies. In fact, group-oriented contingencies provide a great opportunity to build prosocial skills in all students (e.g., Cooper et al., 1987). Targeted skills for a student with ASD are often skills that all students can improve upon, and teachers can make the intervention class-wide instead of individual. In this way, there is less stigma for the student with ASD, and every student receives instruction and reinforcement for increasing positive behaviors.

Sometimes a teacher can target a skill such as listening or sharing. All students in the class can earn a reward for listening, sharing, or another important school-relevant skill. For example, students might earn listening or sharing stars throughout the day or at the conclusion of each activity. (Alternatively, every student could begin the day with a certain number of stars and lose them contingent on maladaptive behavior.) Generally, there is a reward for each individual that is linked to his or her performance in the system. For example, in the Small Wonders integrated preschool classroom at the Douglass Developmental Disabilities Center (see Harris, Handleman, Arnold, & Gordon, 2001, for a full description of the preschool model and classroom), students can get two treats at the end of the day if they kept both of their "listening faces." If they have only one left, they receive one treat.

At times, teachers might add a layer of incentive for helping one's peers achieve success within the group contingency. In the Small Wonders classroom at the DDDC, for example, a special cheer is done if all the students keep their listening faces. In this way, the group gets an extra reward on days when everyone has followed the rules. This provides an opportunity for the whole group to celebrate their communal success.

Special Incentives for Hard Skills. For skills that are especially difficult, it may be necessary to reward extra effort. It is important to match rewards to the difficulty of the task. A student who has great difficulty in math, for example, might work for computer time following math. Special incentives can also be implemented in a group fashion. For example, a teacher might reward every student for certain behaviors such as talking nicely to a friend or cleaning up after playtime.

Special Topic: Delivering Reinforcement in Noninvasive Ways. Delivering rewards in the context of a typical classroom poses several challenges. It is potentially disruptive to the ongoing activities of the classroom. It may also stigmatize the student with ASD. Furthermore, it may create jealousy on the part of other learners, who seek to receive the same rewards. For all of these reasons, it is quite advantageous to deliver such feedback and rewards in as noninvasive a manner as possible. Some shadows, for example, find it helpful to deliver their feedback through hand signals from across the room (e.g., a thumbs-up sign or a checkmark in the air). When shadows do need to provide verbal feedback, it is best done in a whisper and from behind or to the side of the student.

Learning Social Skills

Social skills, which are central to the success of the student, are among the most elusive targets to teach. There is often little intrinsic interest on the part of learners with ASD, and it is often difficult to conceptualize how to teach such skills. Several strategies can be useful in this regard.

Weiss and Harris (2001) provided a thorough description of several strategies for teaching social skills to young children on the autism spectrum. A few strategies are briefly reviewed in this section. Many of these strategies have limited empirical support to date or have been empirically validated with other populations. Nevertheless, they may be useful in the clinical context of teaching social skills. They should be used in combination with other procedures. Several commercially available social skills chapters and curricula have well-formulated and clear lessons for a variety of social skill instructional targets (e.g., Baker, 2002, 2003; McGinness & Goldstein, 1997; Richardson, 1996; Taylor, 2001; Taylor & Jasper, 2001; Walker et al., 1988; see Appendix 11.A for a list of curricular resources).

Social Stories. Social stories, a concept developed by Carol Gray (Gray, 1993, 1994), provide information about social situations and the behavior that is expected in those situations. Gray has suggested that one directive statement be given for every three to five informational statements, to ensure that the story is largely a vehicle for conveying information about a complex or hard-to-define circumstance.

Social stories can be written with pictures to accompany the text and can be adapted for an individual (including using the names of those they know and using the first person). Social stories can be used to convey information and expectations for multi-element tasks (such as cleaning up or waiting in line). They can also be used as part of a package of interventions to address challenging behaviors, offering functional alternatives to the target behavior, such as asking for help instead of throwing materials. There is encouraging preliminary empirical support for the efficacy of social stories in increasing social communication skills (e.g., Thiemann & Goldstein, 2001).

Role Playing. Role playing is another avenue for providing an opportunity to rehearse desired behaviors (e.g., Snell & Janney, 2000; Weiss & Harris, 2001). Students with ASD often need multiple opportunities to learn and practice desired skills. Role playing can create such additional opportunities to supplement too few naturally occurring events. Role playing can be used to target aspects of interaction that are central to success, including orientation to the speaker, maintaining eye contact, and answering questions appropriately. Role playing can also be done with characters and puppets, and with people (including the target student). The student can take on different roles, demonstrating the initial skill or the response. Role playing is always used in combination with feedback on performance.

Rule Cards. Rule cards assist students in following the social rules associated with particular activities (e.g., Weiss & Harris, 2001). A rule card clearly states the behavioral expectations for an activity. Rule cards can be reviewed prior to a particular activity and can be used in combination with other procedures (such as behavior rehearsal). Rule cards are helpful for targeting skills such as sharing toys, taking turns, asking peers for desired items, and accepting a peer's answer. They can also be used for explaining expected behavior in a particular environment or activity, such as the media center and school assemblies.

Scripts. Some students with autism have a difficult time engaging in to-and-fro conversational exchange and creative play. If their social skill deficits were addressed, they might engage in much more such interactions.

One way to address this issue is to provide scripts for prolonged conversations or creative play. Scripts can be in the form of sentences, words, or pictures, and they can be used in a variety of circumstances (e.g., Snell & Janney, 2000). Scripts can also be developed for specific games and activities. Through scripts, the learner can be helped to engage in social interactions longer and stay on topic.

Roteness of response can be a concern, so it is important to program in and reinforce variability. For a learner to speak about a topic in only one way would not be functional. Furthermore, because we cannot predict how people will interact with or question one another, we need to prepare learners for the wide variety of circumstances they are likely to encounter in their interactions.

Video Modeling. Video modeling has received attention as an effective vehicle for building a variety of skills, including functional academic skills, community relevant skills, conversational exchanges, and play skills (e.g., Snell & Brown, 2000; Taylor, 2001; Weiss & Harris, 2001). Many students with ASD are strong visual learners, and many enjoy watching videos. They may attend better to a model presented in a video clip than they would to a live model demonstrating a skill. Video modeling with an adult demonstrating a skill is often done first. With an adult model, it is easier to ensure that the salient aspects of the target behavior will be highlighted. Alternatively, older peer tutors or mature peers can be used as models, the advantage of which is their similarity to the target student.

While there is some variability in how video modeling is implemented to build play skills, it usually involves having the learners observe a video clip of play and then enact it themselves. At times, there may first be concurrent imitation of what is being watched (doing the actions along with the model on the tape), followed by delayed imitation of what was observed (watching the clip and then engaging in the play). As in scripting, roteness of response can be a concern, so it is important to program in variability. Eventually, the learner can be rewarded for expanding upon the script.

Another extension of video teaching is to use videotape as a source of feedback to the learners on their performance during play activities. Reinforcement and corrective feedback can be provided, and better strategies for targeted areas of weakness can be modeled and rehearsed (e.g., Taylor, 2001). This may be especially useful for circumstances in which a learner has demonstrated difficulty comprehending social nuances, such as staying on topic in a conversation.

Problem Solving. Solving problems is an important part of success in school. Children with ASD often have difficulties with the ambiguity of presenting problems and with evaluating options for a course of action. They may be impulsive or fail to see the range of options. Problem solving training (e.g., Shure, 2000, 2001) can help students with ASD identify problems, generate alternative solutions, evaluate the effectiveness of different potential courses of action, and choose the best option. This can be done as a class-wide intervention, perhaps at a learning center. The group of students can listen together to a dilemma and follow the steps of problem solving to address the issue.

Specialized Educational Settings

Autism spectrum disorders are highly variable in their presentation, and learners present with very different needs. For some learners, a more specialized placement will be the best choice in the short term for teaching fundamental skills. Such a specialized option can also be the best educational option for meeting educational needs on a longer term basis. Many of the skills and strategies discussed within this chapter are relevant for learners in both integrated and segregated settings. Even when learners require high levels of prompting and reinforcement, efforts can be made to reduce dependence on adults and to maximize independence. Social bridges can be built with adults and with disabled peers, as they can be with typically developing peers. Parents and educators alike need to be open to the complexity and variability of learners, and ensure that their needs are adequately addressed within the educational setting.

Summary

More children with ASD are included in general education settings than ever before. The options for students with ASD have been increasing as more public schools are working hard to ensure that adequate supports exist for students with ASD. The variability of ASD, however, requires that there be many different options. Full inclusion, full inclusion with supports, part-time inclusion, and specialized placements are all feasible and appropriate options for different learners on the autism spectrum.

Any inclusive experience will require the preparation of all participants. Regardless of the setting, role definition is critically important in helping every team member to function as effectively as possible. One particular support requiring careful training and role definition is the shadow. Shadows work to facilitate a student's functioning within the regular education environment and support the student in that goal. In addition, a wide variety of instructional supports and techniques can maximize the learner's success. These include the wide range of reinforcement systems as well as specific instructional approaches, such as social stories, problem solving, and video modeling.

Appendix 11.A
Resources List

Paraprofessionals and Shadowing

Cavallaro, C. C., & Haney, M. *Preschool Inclusion* (Baltimore: Brookes, 1999). This book provides information on many aspects of preschool inclusion, including the use of positive behavior supports and strategies for facilitating transitions. Case studies illustrate the use of many strategies.

Doyle, M. B. *The Paraprofessional's Guide to the Inclusive Classroom* (Baltimore: Brookes, 1997). This book provides simple descriptions of prompting techniques, guidelines on how to use an IEP, and suggestions for maximizing performance in daily routines.

Twatchman-Cullen, D. *How To Be a Para Pro: A Comprehensive Training Manual for Paraprofessionals* (Higganum, CT: Starfish Specialty Press, 2000). This book reviews a number of strategies for building compliance, social skills, and academic performance. Guidelines for paraprofessionals are clear and thorough.

Wagner, S. *Inclusive Programming for Elementary Students with Autism* (Arlington, TX: Future Horizons, 1999). This book provides recommendations for the assessment of the student, environment, and personnel involved in inclusion. It also contains creative ideas for building social skills and improving behavior.

Explaining Autism to Peers

Kids on the Block, 800-368-5437, www.kotb.com. Provides disability-oriented puppet shows to school-age children. Autism is one of the disabilities specifically addressed, and there are many others. Puppets are used in scenarios to explain aspects of the disability and to foster understanding.

Lears, L. *Ian's Walk: A Story About Autism* (New York: Albert Whitman, 1998).

Thompson, M. *Andy and His Yellow Frisbee* (Bethesda, MD: Woodbine House, 1996).

Curricular Assistance, Goal Development, and Activities

Baker, J. E. *Social Skills Picture Books* (Arlington, TX: Future Horizons, 2002) and *Social Skills Training* (Shawnee Mission, KS: Autism Asperger Publishing, 2003). These are excellent resources for teaching a variety of social skills to students with ASD. Skills targeted include conversation, friendship building, and empathy.

Gray, C. *The Original Social Story Book* (Arlington, TX: Future Horizons, 1993) and *The New Social Story Book* (Arlington, TX: Future Horizons, 1994). These are *the* sources for sample social stories and for instructions on their appropriate use.

Gray, C. *Comic Strip Conversations* (Arlington, TX: Future Horizons, 1994). This provides a nice visual strategy for building and understanding conversational speech.

McGinnis, E., & Goldstein, A. P. *Skillstreaming in Early Childhood: New Strategies and Perspectives for Teaching Prosocial Skills* (Champaign, IL: Research Press, 1997). This series provides excellent suggestions for addressing important skills such as waiting, sharing, and being polite.

Meiners, C. J. *Be Polite and Kind* and *Join In and Play* (Minneapolis, MN: Free Spirit Press, 2004); *Listen and Learn, Share and Take Turns, Understand and Care,* and *When I Feel Afraid* (Minneapolis, MN: Free Spirit Press, 2003). These books are an excellent resource for teaching a variety of social skills. Suggestions for activities and extensions of the books are included.

Partington, J. W., & Sundberg, M. L. *The Assessment of Basic Language and Learning Skills* (Pleasant Hill, CA: Behavior Analysts, 1998). This is a comprehensive assessment and curricular planning tool. Areas include skills that are ordinarily significant deficits for learners with autism, such as group instruction, requesting, and conversational speech. Emphasis is on the assessment of skill use in natural contexts.

Richardson, R. *Connecting with Others: Lessons for Teaching Social and Emotional Competence* (Champaign, IL: Research Press, 1996). There are two volumes in this series (K–2 and Grades 3–5), emphasizing sharing, empathy, communication, and problem solving.

Shure, M. *I Can Problem Solve* (Champaign, IL: Research Press, 2001). This book provides methodical and clear information on teaching problem-solving skills to children.

Shure, M. *Raising a Thinking Child Workbook: Teaching Young Children How To Resolve Everyday Conflicts and Get Along with Others* (Champaign, IL: Research Press, 2000). This book provides suggestions on teaching children how to solve people problems, how to anticipate the consequences of various courses of action, and how to evaluate choices.

Walker, H. M., McConnell, S., Holmes, D., Todis, B., Walker, J., & Golden, N. *The Accepts Program* (Austin, TX: PRO-ED, 1988). This curriculum contains a variety of instructional sequences for building social skills. Classroom-relevant skills are emphasized.

Visual Timer. Developed by Jan Rogers, available from Generaction, 877/771-TIME.

References

Baker, J. E. (2002). *Social skills picture book: Teaching play, emotion, and communication to children with autism.* Arlington, TX: Future Horizons.

Baker, J. E. (2003). *Social skills training.* Shawnee Mission, KS: Autism Asperger Publishing.

Buysee, V., & Bailey, D. B. (1993). Behavioral and developmental outcomes in young children with disabilities in integrated and segregated settings: A review of comparative studies. *The Journal of Special Education, 26,* 434–461.

Carr, E. G., & Darcy, M. (1990). Setting generality of peer modeling in children with autism. *Journal of Autism and Developmental Disorders, 20,* 45–59.

Cavallaro, C. C., & Haney, M. (1999). *Preschool inclusion.* Baltimore: Brookes.

Celiberti, D. A., & Harris, S. L. (1993). The effects of a play skills intervention for siblings of children with autism. *Behavior Therapy, 24,* 573–599.

Cooper, J. O., Heron, T. E., & Heward, W. L. (1987). *Applied behavior analysis.* Upper Saddle River, NJ: Prentice Hall.

Demchak, M., & Drinkwater, S. (1992). Preschoolers with severe disabilities: The case against segregation. *Topics in Early Childhood Education, 11,* 70–83.

Doyle, M. B. (1997). *The paraprofessional's guide to the inclusive classroom.* Baltimore: Brookes.

Frost, L., & Bondy, A. (2002). *The Picture Exchange Communication System training manual.* Newark, DE: Pyramid Educational Products.

Goldstein, H., Kaczmarek, L., Pennington, R., & Shafer, K. (1992). Peer-mediated intervention: Attending to, commenting on, and acknowledging the behavior of preschoolers with autism. *Journal of Applied Behavior Analysis, 25,* 289–305.

Gray, C. (1993). *The original social story book.* Arlington, TX: Future Horizons.

Gray, C. (1994). *The new social story book.* Arlington, TX: Future Horizons.

Green, S. K., & Shinn, M. R. (1994). Parent attitudes about special education and reintegration: What is the role of student outcomes? *Exceptional Children, 61,* 269–281.

Guralnick, M. J., Connor, R. T., & Hammond, M. (1995). Parent perspectives of peer relationships and friendships in integrated and specialized programs. *American Journal of Mental Retardation, 99,* 457–476.

Harris, S. L., & Handleman, J. S. (1997). Helping children with autism enter the mainstream. In D. J. Cohen & F. R. Volkmar (Eds.), *Handbook of autism and pervasive developmental disorders* (2nd ed.). New York: Wiley.

Harris, S. L., Handleman, J. S., Arnold, M. S., & Gordon, R. F. (2001). The Douglass Developmental Disabilities Center: Two models of service delivery. In J. S. Handleman & S. L. Harris (Eds.), *Preschool education programs for children with autism* (2nd ed.). Austin, TX: PRO-ED.

Kasari, C., Freeman, S. F. N., Bauminger, N., & Alkin, M. C. (1999). Parental perspective in inclusion: Effects of autism and Down syndrome. *Journal of Autism and Developmental Disorders, 29,* 297–305.

Leaf, R., & McEachin, J. (1999). *A work in progress.* New York: Autism Partnership.

Lovaas, O. I. (1987). Behavioral treatment and normal educational and intellectual functioning in young autistic children. *Journal of Consulting and Clinical Psychology, 55,* 3–9.

Maurice, C., Green, G., & Luce, S. (1996). *Behavioral intervention for young children with autism: A manual for parents and professionals.* Austin, TX: PRO-ED.

McEachin, J. J., Smith, T., & Lovaas, O. I. (1993). Long-term outcome for children with autism who received early intensive behavioral treatment. *American Journal of Mental Retardation, 97,* 359–372.

McGee, G. G., Almeida, M. C., Sulzer-Azaroff, B., & Feldman, R. S. (1992). Prompting reciprocal interactions via peer incidental teaching. *Journal of Applied Behavior Analysis, 25,* 117–126.

McGinnis, E., & Goldstein, A. P. (1997). *Skillstreaming in early childhood: New strategies and perspectives for teaching prosocial skills.* Champaign, IL: Research Press.

Odom, S. L., Chandler, L. K., Ostrosky, M., McConnell, S. R., & Reaney S. (1992). Fading teacher prompts from peer-initiation interventions for young children with disabilities. *Journal of Applied Behavior Analysis, 25,* 307–317.

Odom, S. L., & Strain, P. S. (1986). A comparison of peer-initiation and teacher-antecedent intervention for promoting reciprocal social interactions of autistic preschoolers. *Journal of Applied Behavior Analysis, 19,* 59–71.

Odom, S. L., & Watts, E. (1991). Reducing teacher prompts in peer-mediated interventions for young children with autism. *The Journal of Special Education, 25,* 26–43.

Palmer, D. S., Fuller, K., Arora, T., & Nelson, M. (2001). Taking sides: Parent views on inclusion for their children with severe disabilities. *Exceptional Children, 67,* 467–484.

Partington, J. W., & Sundberg, M. L. (1998). *The Assessment of Basic Language and Learning Skills.* Pleasant Hill, CA: Behavior Analysts.

Reichert, D. C., Lynch, E. C., Anderson, B. C., Svobodny, L. A., DiCola, J. M., & Mercury, M. G. (1989). Parental perspectives on integrated preschool opportunities for children with handicaps and children without handicaps. *Journal of Early Intervention, 13,* 6–13.

Richardson, R. (1996). *Connecting with others: Lessons for teaching social and emotional competence.* Champaign, IL: Research Press.

Rosenblatt, J., Bloom, P., & Koegel, R. L. (1995). Overselective responding: Description, implications, and intervention. In R. L. Koegel & L. K. Koegel (Eds.), *Teaching children with autism: Strategies for initiating positive interactions and improving learning opportunities.* Baltimore: Brookes.

Shure, M. (2000). *Raising a thinking child workbook: Teaching young children how to resolve everyday conflicts and get along with others.* Champaign, IL: Research Press.

Shure, M. (2001). *I can problem solve.* Champaign, IL: Research Press.

Snell, M. E., & Brown, F. (2000). *Instruction of students with severe handicaps.* Upper Saddle River, NJ: Prentice Hall.

Snell, M. E., & Janney, R. (2000). *Social relationships and peer support*. Baltimore: Brookes.

Strain, P. S. (1983). Generalization of autistic children's social behavior change: Effects of developmentally integrated and segregated settings. *Analysis and Intervention in Developmental Disabilities, 3*, 23–34.

Strain, P. S., Kerr, M. M., & Ragland, E. U. (1979). Effects of peer-mediated social initiations and prompting/reinforcement procedures on the social behavior of autistic children. *Journal of Autism and Developmental Disorders, 9*, 41–54.

Sundberg, M. L., & Partington, J. W. (1998). *Teaching language to children with autism or other developmental disabilities*. Pleasant Hill, CA: Behavior Analysts.

Sundberg, M. L., & Partington, J. W. (1999). In P. M. Ghezzi, W. L. Williams, & J. E. Carr (Eds.), *Autism: Behavior analytic perspectives*. Reno, NV: Context Press.

Taylor, B. A. (2001). Teaching peer social skills to children with autism. In C. Maurice, G. Green, & R. Foxx (Eds.), *Making a difference: Behavioral intervention for autism*. Austin, TX: PRO-ED.

Taylor, B. A., & Jasper, S. (2001). Teaching programs to increase peer interaction. In C. Maurice, G. Green, & R. Foxx (Eds.), *Making a difference: Behavioral intervention for autism*. Austin, TX: PRO-ED.

Thiemann, K. S., & Goldstein, H. (2001). Social stories, written text cues, and video feedback: Effects on social communication in children with autism. *Journal of Applied Behavior Analysis, 34*, 425–446.

Twatchman-Cullen, D. (2000). *How to be a para pro: A comprehensive training manual for paraprofessionals*. Higganum, CT: Starfish Specialty Press.

Wagner, S. (1999). *Inclusive programming for elementary students with autism*. Arlington, TX: Future Horizons.

Walker, H. M., McConnell, S., Holmes, D., Todis, B., Walker, J., & Golden, N. (1988). *The ACCEPTS program*. Austin, TX: PRO-ED.

Webber, J. (1997). Responsible inclusion: Key components for success. In P. Zionts (Ed.), *Inclusion strategies for students with learning and behavior problems*. Austin, TX: PRO-ED.

Weiss, M. J., & Harris, S. L. (2001). *Reaching out, joining in: Teaching social skills to young children with autism*. Bethesda, MD: Woodbine House.

Negotiating the School Years and Preparing for Adulthood

12

Marlene Cohen

· ·

O ne of the major transitions facing every adolescent with autism and his or her family is getting ready to move into the adult years. Graduating from school and embarking on one's adulthood is a major event in anyone's life, and this is even truer for people with autism. The support structure created by the school system evaporates when a child graduates from high school, and the replacements that are provided vary greatly from state to state and community to community. The more independently a young person can function in terms of both daily living and vocational activities, the easier it will be to find an appropriate niche for him or for her as adulthood arrives.

Helping a student prepare for that level of independence requires planning from early adolescence through the time of graduation. Precisely how independently a person will be able to function as an adult is determined by a variety of factors, including one's intellectual skills, social awareness, repertoire of adaptive behaviors, and so forth. It also hinges on the ability of the family and school to identify the individual's strengths and areas of need, and work toward using strengths to compensate for areas of greater need in selecting appropriate vocational goals.

Students along the autistic spectrum have varying needs. For example, suitable goals for a person profoundly affected by autism and with significant mental retardation will clearly be different from those for a person with Asperger syndrome who has average or better intelligence. The first may need a very supportive work environment with close supervision; the second may be college bound with some special support. In choosing an educational setting for one's adolescent who has a disorder on the autism spectrum, it is important to identify a school that will be able to target his or her specific needs. This is a time to be realistic about the extent to which a young person needs traditional academic instruction, as opposed to more vocationally oriented schooling. The goal is to ensure that the child's remaining school years focus on building those skills that are most suitable for the future.

There have been many changes in the education of students with disabilities since the enactment of the Education for All Handicapped Children Act of 1975 and the entitlement to a free and appropriate education. The changes in the way we educate very young children reflect the stark contrast between our initial efforts 30 years ago and the very elegant methods of contemporary applied behavior analysis (ABA). Those changes are as important to the adolescent with autism as they are to very young children who receive intensive early intervention. What we teach is obviously very different across the age spectrum, but the underlying principles of ABA remain at the heart of the educational enterprise.

Negotiating the School Years

Continuing to monitor and fine-tune educational programming after a student with autism leaves a preschool program can be quite complex. For example, choosing a school setting and a classroom within that setting is complicated by the number of options that are available. In some rural or isolated communities, there may be only a single class, and one is then confronted with how to make that class work for a specific student. In more urban settings, there may be a range of classroom environments designed for the broad range of students on the autism spectrum. One is then faced with having to select the class that works best for a given student. Curricular planning also becomes more intricate when teachers and parents are faced with the balancing of traditional and functional academics. How much of the standard academic curriculum can a student master and use effectively? How much focus should there be on life skills and prevocational training? Those are decisions that must be made for each student, and there is no simple formula upon which to base one's decision. These are also ongoing decisions as the ratio of traditional to functional academics may shift as a child grows up. The transitions that the student encounters through the elementary, middle, and high school years must be well planned in order to promote success in adulthood.

The very good news is that placement options for school-age students with autism are growing. The small handful of specialized programs that served these youngsters 30 years ago has been joined by numerous private schools and most recently by many public school programs. This growth has resulted in a range of settings, especially in urban areas, in which educational services can be delivered:

- *Full inclusion.* In this placement option, students are enrolled in general education classes and receive the same services as the typical child. Some related services, such as speech therapy, may be provided, as well as some accommodations (e.g., untimed tests).
- *Inclusion with supports.* Students who are included in regular classes with supports attend school full-time and receive some form of individual assistance. This help can take the form of a dedicated "shadow instructor" or sharing a classroom assistant with other students. Sometimes these students are "pulled out" of the regular classroom to receive supplemental or remedial instruction.
- *Partial inclusion.* Students in this placement option attend regular classes on a part-time basis (e.g., one subject or half a day), usually with the support of an assistant. The remainder of the day is spent either in a resource setting or a self-contained class for children with autism or varied disabilities.
- *Self-contained class with social inclusion.* Students in this placement option are enrolled in a special class full time and are provided with social experiences with their typically developing peers. Some opportunities for inclusion include playing on the playground, eating lunch, and participating in an after-school activity.
- *Specialized school.* Some students will require the supports of a specialized program. Depending on the needs of the student, the school may be exclusively for children with autism, or could be for children with various disabilities. In a specialized program, curriculum, methods, and staffing can all be systematically arranged to meet the highly individual needs of the student. For most students, this placement option can be a springboard for the range of inclusion experiences, as well.

As students with autism grow older, curricular planning becomes more challenging. When younger, often very specialized curricula are used to teach basic skills, as well as social and communication skills (e.g., *Individual Goal Setting Curriculum;* Romanczyk & Lockshin, 1982). When the student approaches adolescence, however, it becomes important to ensure that goals are functional and promote the acquisition of life skills and prevocational abilities.

Often, educational experiences for the middle school or high school student take place outside of the classroom. Visits to the community provide opportunities to learn and practice important life skills. Trips to the theater or shopping center allow students to enjoy leisure and social experiences. Programming in the home can help to introduce life skills, and combined with visits to the community can facilitate the generalization of learning. Being able to generalize one's skills beyond home and classroom should be a goal for every student.

In the final years of schooling, the student with an autism spectrum disorder will benefit from prevocational programming that first allows the student to sample a variety of tasks, then focuses on developing more skills in preferred activities. Student-centered planning can facilitate finding a job that is best suited for a particular student. These part-time work opportunities are effective ways to increase success and prepare the student for postsecondary placements.

Ensuring the Quality of the Program

Programs for children with autism spectrum disorders are either developmental or behavioral in orientation. Within the range of options, ensuring the effectiveness of a particular program is a complicated task. In order to provide a framework to evaluate the quality of an educational program for students with autism, the National Research Council of the National Academy of Science (2001) proposed the following program quality indicators:

- specific curricula
- highly supportive instructional environments
- maintenance and generalization strategies
- predictable routines
- functional behavior management procedures
- systematic transitional planning
- collaborative family involvement
- family supports
- low student-to-staff ratios
- highly trained staff
- comprehensive professional resources
- staff supervision and program review mechanisms

The influence of the National Research Council's recommendations is recognized in a growing number of programs now using evidenced-based methods and state departments of education adopting similar quality indicators (e.g., New Jersey Department of Education, 2004).

The most widely used scientifically validated approach for educating children with autism is ABA. Three decades of experience and hundreds of research investigations support its efficacy for students with autism. The ABA approach uses specific techniques to help the student acquire or change behaviors; and reflects each of the National Research Council's quality indicators. ABA is effective for students across the life span and is equally implemented in early intervention, elementary, secondary, and adult programs. The TEACCH model is also widely used and is discussed by Shea and Mesibov in Chapter 9.

A key component of a program that can ensure quality services is input from experienced professionals and consultants who can guide and monitor educational decision making. To promote an effective and positive school–consultant relationship, sufficient time should be scheduled to enable this specialist, as a member of the instructional team, to (a) offer input into the Individualized Educational Program (IEP), (b) train staff, (c) conduct functional behavioral assessments when needed, (d) design and monitor educational programming and behavior intervention plans, and (e) consult to the family. The need for specialized consultation will depend on the resources that a particular program has available. For example, a specialized ABA program for students with autism will probably require limited outside consultation, while a single classroom located in a public school setting may require more outside support.

In order to successfully negotiate the school years and prepare for adulthood, systematic transition planning is vital. Prior to a change in educational program or experiences, school staff and the family should initiate a transition plan. The goal of approximating the new setting within the old or through visits should be established, in order to avoid rapid changes and possible behavioral regression. This goal can be typically accomplished with a number of steps: (a) assessing the proposed setting, in order to approximate a student–placement match considering variables such as teachers, students, curriculum, and teaching strategies; (b) assessing the student for compatibility with the proposed placement in areas of school life, classroom life, and curriculum; and (c) conducting previsits to the proposed setting to confirm the choice of placement. The transition plan that results should occur over a 9- to 12-month period, target skill deficiencies, provide for gradual systematic inclusion, and be data driven and monitored. Through the collaborative efforts of the family and professionals, the student with autism can be provided with the necessary services and supports to successfully traverse the school years and enter adulthood.

Preparing for Adulthood

While some people with autism may no longer require extensive special services once they become adults, many others continue to require the kind of attention that has been placed on the younger student. Increasingly, learners with autism are being prepared for productive, fulfilling lives as adults. The variables for successful outcomes as adults are many, and this chapter touches on those issues that are important to consider in the education of adolescents with autism.

A Rich Learning Environment

The first standard to seek in selecting an appropriate placement for an adolescent with autism is a rich learning environment. Whether you are a parent of a child with autism or a professional learning more about educational options, there are a number of indicators that you can look for in identifying such an environment. For example, what about the instructional ratio? Are there enough staff to provide the level of support required by your adolescent? Are the staff members attentive to the students in the program, and do they keep them engaged in learning, in work, and in recreational activities? On a very basic level, it is probably possible to tell within the first few minutes of visiting a program whether good things are happening; often you can feel it the moment you walk in the door. Look at people's faces and listen to what is being said. For example, do the students appear safe and relaxed, and are the staff members respectful of the students? Do the interactions between the students and the staff members seem positive? Do you see smiles and hear laughter? Are adults reinforcing appropriate behavior and dealing with behavior challenges in an appropriate way?

Administrative and Financial Support

The administrative and financial support available in a school program can have an impact on outcomes. The federal legislation in the Individuals with Disabilities Education Act (IDEA) calls for an appropriate education for students with special needs. The word "appropriate," however, means that parents might have to accept placements that are less than the best options available. In order to meet the very complex needs of the older learner with autism and ensure that each learner has access to necessary services and equipment, school programs are likely to encounter costs that less experienced administrators might not anticipate. The resources that students need when younger will change as they grow into adolescence and adulthood. Some of these changes may include additional staff training, continued education for staff in teaching methods that suit the older student or adult, materials that address the skills necessary to function well as an adult, and professionals who can address ongoing issues related to the older student. For example, when a student using a picture communication system expands his or her vocabulary to the extent that a computerized augmentative communication system is indicated, resources must be identified so as not to limit the language growth of the student. Another example might include the need to certify staff in crisis intervention and prevention to diffuse challenging behavior. A temper tantrum on the part of a 5-year-old can be safely handled by a caring adult; a tantrum by a 19-year-old who is 6 feet tall is quite another matter and requires a great deal of staff training so that he can be managed safely.

Many public school systems have only recently started to include students with autism in their general education classes or in their community-based school buildings. Some administrators may not fully understand that the needs of students with autism can differ significantly from the needs of students with other disabilities, and that additional supports may be required through adolescence. Richard Lavoie (1990), a professional who works with students with learning disabilities, talks in this regard about the concept of fairness in his video *F.A.T. City*. He says that in the classroom, what is equitable is not necessarily fair. Students may require less or more than the "average" in order to receive the same educational benefit.

Funding should be available to ensure a safe and effective educational environment. When a lack of resources places staff members in a situation where they are not able to achieve their goals on an ongoing basis, there can be a negative impact on their performance and on the performance of their students. This is the kind of situation where staff goals may shift from educational growth to survival. It is the responsibility of the community and the school board to ensure that funds are available to meet the needs of these students. In addition, a creative administrator or teacher may also wish to go beyond the basics and develop special resources for a student. Finding sufficient resources means thinking in flexible and creative ways. When financial resources for special projects are unavailable in the regular school budget, there are other options to consider, such as the school's PTA, a grant from a foundation, or a donation from a community group such as the Kiwanis. While these sources can be helpful for special projects one wishes to introduce, it is also essential that the school administration, the school board, and the community be made aware of the needs of people with autism so that appropriate funding can be built into the school's budget.

Evaluating Outcomes

There has been no other approach to autism outside of the field of ABA that can match its demonstrated effectiveness. Although ABA is often equated with discrete trial teaching (DTI) and perhaps with punishment procedures, the methodology is actually very broad and includes a range of teaching methods that, while grounded in research, appear quite natural to the learner and to the outside observer (Behavior Analyst Certification Board Task List, 1997). Other methods may be highly structured, but ABA reflects careful thought about the creation of supportive environmental systems, such as an incentive system to make activities attractive to students. This powerful technology enables us to have a significant impact on students of any age. Not only has ABA made a major difference in the lives of very young children who have had the benefits of early intensive intervention, it has also had an impact on adolescents and adults, who, through the support of a good ABA program, learn the daily living and vocational skills that enable them to lead good lives in their communities.

Parents of preschool-age children hope that their child with autism will eventually be fully integrated in the general educational system. That does happen for some students, but for many others it does not. The long-term outcome for a child who continues to require considerable educational support will be different than for the child who learns to function well in an elementary school setting. The teachers and parents of adolescents and adults with autism will have different goals than the parents of very young children with autism.

An example of how one defines a positive outcome for an older student with autism is reflected in the progress of one of our clients at the Adult Program of the Douglass Developmental Disabilities Center of Rutgers University. George demonstrated some fairly obvious characteristics of autism. Although he had language, he didn't communicate frequently or expansively, he made noises that drew the attention of outsiders, and he made many repetitive statements in an effort to be assured that he was doing the right thing. George was employed at a local store in a position that was a good job match, and he performed his responsibilities so well that he received a customer service award. Corporate headquarters was so impressed by his productivity that they revised their standards for all employees performing the same job. This outcome was not popular among staff members who might have been less diligent, but the important point is that George performed the job better than anyone else. Success is measured by how we define it, and this learner with autism is a success by the standards of many.

Measuring the outcomes of an educational program requires a universal language. Anecdotes and stories are interesting, but only when you have clear and objective measures of progress. When you bring a child to a pediatrician to find out if he or she is demonstrating a healthy growth pattern, you ask for the actual measures and examine the growth chart. When you want to lose weight and are checking your progress, you look at the scale or measure inches lost. These scenarios exemplify quantified measures of day-to-day experiences. Lilienfeld, Lynn, and Lohr (2003) express this well in the following statement: "The field of clinical psychology must focus on identifying not only empirically supported treatment, but also treatments that are clearly devoid of empirical support" (p. 462). It is important for consumers to remain critical about unsupported claims and to hold programs to high standards in terms of their being able to demonstrate that their teaching methods are empirically supported and that the progress of individual students can be documented.

The Competence of the Support Staff

Basing one's educational program on sound research is a good start, but a successful program requires more. Having enough staff and ensuring that they are trained to a high level of competence in the empirically supported treatment methods are critical. There are a variety of standards that are used to assess staff competency. For example, teachers and speech–language pathologists are usually certified; clinical and school psychologists are typically licensed by the state in which they work; and paraprofessional staff may have some specialized training. In the field of ABA, a national board reviews training credentials and administers a nationwide examination that one must pass to become a board-certified behavior analyst. High-quality programs using ABA should have at least one board-certified person on staff or available as a consultant. It is also important that the program provide continuous education to staff members, including ongoing supervision, as well as introducing new effective teaching methods.

Teaching is a dynamic process, and there is always something new to learn. Truly competent professionals ask questions, struggle to gain deeper understanding of principles, and keep abreast of changes in their field. The field of ABA continues to evolve and now includes a fuller range of methods than it did even 5 or 10 years ago. Professionals need to be aware of new research and integrate it into their teaching.

Technical knowledge is critical to good teaching, but so too is one's respect for students and enthusiasm for one's work. This was demonstrated to us by a 17-year-old who expressed interest in working in the Douglass Adult Program. In the past, our staff members have all been at least a few years older, so this was an unusual request, but the program supervisor agreed to employ him on a trial basis. After a few weeks, staff members were delighted to find that he performed his job responsibilities with some skill and with a maturity that went beyond his years. Good training and motivation on the part of this new staff member provided a strong foundation for his continued professional development.

Family Support for Older Learners with Autism

Any discussion of services for learners with autism must include the need for family support. Often, it is not the amount of support provided, but how the services are perceived by the family. Parents can achieve better results if they feel supported in their efforts. Some professionals may equate family support with teaching parents how to apply the same behavioral methods that are used in the school. Although the mastery of such skills is vital, it is not the same thing as family support; and such support must be carefully dovetailed with teaching of technical skills. An example of an unsuccessful approach to the needs of the family was illustrated by a young assistant teacher who went into the home of a young child with a timer, a clipboard, and a data sheet. The visit consisted of teaching the parents to set the timer for 10 minutes and then take their son to the toilet every time the timer rang. The assistant reviewed how data should be collected, performed a trial of instruction, left a selection of food reinforcers, and scheduled a return visit for a month later. This well-intentioned person was unaware that she might have been setting the parents up for failure by being unaware of what they perceived as support. Important questions to have asked before doing the training would have included "Does this family have the necessary resources to be successful?" and "How can I adapt my plans to the needs of this specific family?"

As students get older, the needs of the family change. Adolescence can be a trying time for parents of typical kids, and when you take into account the additional impact of having a child with autism, planning for the future can be daunting. Professionals need to know that there are times when it is best to just listen and to try to understand how to be supportive. For example, a father of a student with Asperger syndrome had developed a habit of engaging in angry conversations with the professional staff whenever he was having difficulty with his daughter. He had a number of other problems at home that resulted in his having to carry essentially the full burden of caring for his daughter. In this case, support from the staff consisted of allowing him to relieve his frustrations by providing him with a sympathetic ear. When he knew that he had access to the staff, the stress level of the entire family decreased. More was accomplished by providing this support than would have been accomplished by placing additional demands on an already taxed family unit. Support for the parents of older learners can include a variety of options, such as a support group, support for siblings, identifying resources for medical needs, recreational activities, respite, summer camps, and in-home assistance.

Collaboration of the Instructional Team

A comprehensive educational program requires coordinated efforts. Collaboration can be accomplished with scheduled meetings, logbooks, phone calls, or e-mails. The exact mechanisms for collaboration are not as critical as creation of a plan for it to take place. Unless everyone working with a student is informed about what is going on in all environments, confusion on the part of the learner can occur. Even when there are many competent people available to serve a student, if these individuals do not coordinate their efforts, the best interests of the adolescent may not be met. A program can appear comprehensive by the number of services available but fail the student because of missed opportunities to collaborate. The successful program schedules time for collaboration.

Addressing Problematic Behavior

Long-term success in addressing problematic behaviors such as self-injury, aggression, and tantrums depends on an intervention that is structured to teach the individual to manage his own behavior. Although this process takes time, a well-trained behavior analyst can usually develop an effective behavior intervention by analyzing the environment and the conditions under which the behavior occurs, evaluating the consequences that are maintaining the behavior, and determining what skills the learner needs in order to gain control over the environment in a socially acceptable way. The challenges involved in completing a comprehensive functional analysis and developing a successful intervention lie in the fact that it takes time, and the passage of time can feel uncomfortable in the midst of the day-to-day responsibilities of the staff. They urgently want their students to be safe, and they want to feel safe themselves so they can be effective teachers. Unfortunately, achieving that level of comfort often takes considerable work. If a program invests the time to address the challenge correctly, the results can include prevention of the behavior based on environmental changes, development of skills that require a low response effort and address the function of the behavior, and a learner whose quality of life has improved because he can manage his own behavior and get his needs met in ways that are reinforced by the general community.

In selecting a program for an older adolescent or adult who has significant behavior problems, look for a setting that does a comprehensive functional analysis and that understands the value of associating the learning environment and instructional staff with positive reinforcement. Teaching adaptive alternative responses, coupling reinforcement with an engaging instructional environment, and working toward greater self-control on the part of the student all increase the likelihood that challenging behavior will decrease and cease to be problematic for the student, his family, and the school.

Visual Supports: A Bridge to Independence

Considering the challenges students with autism spectrum disorders have with language, it is easy to lose sight of the fact that intelligence can be reflected by performance in areas other than spoken language. Many new staff members are surprised that a learner with limited verbal expression can be more capable than some learners with more expansive verbal language. Temple Grandin, an accomplished adult with autism, highlights this challenge for people with autism when she writes about the importance of visual images to her understanding of her world. She writes about her own need to translate a language concept into a visual form in order for it to have meaning (Grandin, 1996).

We all use visual supports (e.g., calendars or PDAs, stickies, lists, highlighted text), and by providing those supports to students with autism, you can enhance learning by using a relatively stronger modality. For example, Roger, an adolescent with autism, had a history of severe aggression, and when he entered the Douglass Adult Program, we initially created a richly reinforcing environment for him while making few demands on him for work. Once his rates of aggression decreased in this very appealing context, the staff initiated a contingent reinforcement system where some small demands were imposed. Initial attempts included asking Roger to select a reinforcer and telling him that he could earn it for "keeping his hands quiet" (i.e., no occurrences of aggression). Unexpectedly, during the introduction of this procedure, Roger engaged in aggression during the time when he was waiting for a reinforcer. When the intervention was assessed more carefully, it became evident that Roger didn't understand the need to wait with quiet hands. By adding the visual support of pictures that were cut up into three pieces and pairing this with a timer, positive results were achieved. Roger quickly learned that when he earned all three pictures and the picture was whole, he would receive reinforcement.

Data we collected when Roger first came to the center reflected 87 aggressions for the baseline month, 6 of which were severe. A rating of severe meant a staff member required treatment at the medical center and was probably out of work for a day or two. Data taken when the treatment program was underway indicated a total of 11 aggressions for the first month of treatment, none of which was more severe than a slap or scratch. Although Roger engaged in aggression, no one was getting hurt.

A few months after the intervention began, the data indicated 2 aggressions for the month, neither of which was severe. Both of those incidents were managed by a single staff person.

Roger's success with using a visual strategy positively affected the quality of his life. He used to come to school with an anxious look on his face, and most staff would avoid interacting with him. Now he interacts freely with all of the staff (and sometimes his peers) and demonstrates an interest in learning. He travels to a local gym weekly for a fitness routine and is preparing to begin part-time employment cleaning a local restaurant prior to opening.

Teaching Fluency Skills

In educating students with autism it is important to consider the response effort required to perform skills. A response that is slow and difficult for a student to perform may be resisted and may also fall short of being adequate for a work setting. While it is typical to base mastery criteria on accurate performance, when a student gets older, accurate performance alone may not result in desired outcomes. Fluency-based instruction (Binder, 1996) offers a different way to assess performance.

Many adult learners with autism are dysfluent in the performance of one or more fine motor skills. This means that their rate (speed) of performance is slow compared to that of competent performers. Fine motor skills are important for many of the tasks that adults with autism might do on the job, and lack of speed undercuts their job potential. For example, if a person cannot easily pick up an item from a box and set it carefully on a shelf, he will not do well at stacking shelves in a grocery store. Learning the fine motor skills of grasping and releasing to a high level of fluency may contribute to his vocational success. In addition, being fluent in those tasks may serve to reduce problematic behavior when the adolescent or adult is asked to perform a complex task based on these more basic skills.

The effectiveness of fluency-based instruction can be seen in the case of Harry, a 16-year-old student with autism who engaged in high rates of aggression and self-injury during vocational training tasks. As Harry grew more fluent at using a machine to trifold paper, his rates of aggression and self-injury declined. His rate of trifolding increased from 8.4 per minute to an average of 13 per minute, and his rate of aggression and self-injury decreased from 8 per minute to an average of .2 per minute over the course of 20 weeks. We then taught him a new skill of envelope stuffing, and, again, as he grew fluent in that skill, his aggression and self-injury were reduced to zero.

The effect of fluency-based instruction of fine motor skills (e.g., grasp and release and squeeze), as related to performance of activities of daily living, was also demonstrated by Sally. Sally is an adult with autism who had a stroke in infancy that resulted in her requiring consistent prompting to use her right hand to perform skills. This significantly reduced her level of independence. Sally's performance on 21 activities of daily living was baselined, and fluency-based instruction of fine motor skills was introduced over the course of 11 months. Following fluency-based instruction in basic motor skills, Sally was able to perform 11 more daily living skills than at original baseline. This had a significant impact on her level of independence, as well as a positive impact on her quality of life.

How Progress Transfers to the Natural Community

Learning to use skills in the classroom is not sufficient to promote productive living. To be meaningful, skills must transfer from the classroom to the home, to the community, and to the workplace. When working with adolescents and adults with autism, participation in the community and on the job is considered a measure of long-term effectiveness.

If we are to facilitate the transfer of skills to many settings, it is important to consider the differences between the training environment and the natural environment and to examine variables that may influence performance, such as reinforcement schedules, reinforcement options, and the variety of responses required. For example, artificial systems of support that are common in school settings such as token cards, predictable schedules of reinforcement, and consistent verbal cues do not exist in the natural community. As a result, we need to help students learn to respond to more naturally occurring systems of reinforcement, including those they administer to themselves or receive after a prolonged period of delay.

Not only does the student need to learn the specific vocational skills necessary to complete a job, in almost every kind of meaningful work, he or she must also be able to handle basic social interactions. It is important to teach social skills within the context of the social environment in which the student will live and work. Social skill instruction should take place during informal interactions, allowing the learner to become adept at interacting with other people in a variety of natural ways. Simple conversations and humor can ensure rich social interactions that cannot be achieved in a simulated setting.

Taking learners into the community and evaluating their responses to people in the natural environment can provide a good measure of social success. We have found that many of our students with autism can progress from engaging in little social interaction to seeking out interaction on a regular basis as a result of ongoing social skills training. This has tremendous relevance when evaluating employment options for people with autism. Graduating from school with numerous academic skills but minimal social skills often results in an unsuccessful integration into the community and the lack of opportunity to receive ongoing reinforcement. Most people with autism can enjoy being around other people if given the skills to do so.

Transition from Student
to Adult Life: The Research

People working in the field of autism have long recognized the challenges their students face in dealing with transitions. Critical to any transition is the development of a plan that includes assessment of the current placement, the new setting, and the student (Handleman, 1979). In addition, providing educational experiences in as normalized a setting as possible can increase the probability of generalization.

In an early study, Benz, Yavanoff, and Doren (1977) found that work-based learning opportunities for learners with autism are critical to future success. These opportunities include community service, job shadowing, school-based enterprises, apprenticeships, and paid work experiences. Benz and his colleagues also found that participation in two or more work experiences during the last 2 years of school, performance of a job search, and social skills training are all strong predictors of competitive employment. The research also indicated that it is important to provide continuing education.

Current data from the National Center on Secondary Education and Transition (2004) state that while students with disabilities graduate with a standard diploma (56%) more than ever; only 30% of those with no post-secondary education are employed, and just 45% of students with some postsecondary education are employed. The Council for Exceptional Children has seen the emergence of some innovative programs that allow for real-life skill development and job experience in addition to the academic curriculum (2004). These programs have been established in response to the need for more extensive transition experiences for some students (e.g., LifeLink PSU; Pennsylvania State University, 2002).

The Office of Special Education of the Oregon Department of Education (2002) has stated that successful outcomes for students with autism involve comprehensive, appropriate educational programs, collaboration and trust among everyone involved in the transition process, truly individualized programs, early diagnosis and intensive intervention, transition to adult life and continuation of available services, and funding according to need. Temple Grandin (2002) recommends gradual transitions to work that begin in school, supportive employers and mentors, education of employers and employees, and the use of portfolios.

Transition planning should cover the following areas:

- community participation
- daily living
- employment
- financial and income management
- health
- independent living
- leisure and recreation
- postsecondary education
- relationships and social skills
- transportation and mobility
- vocational training
- self-determination

Assessment of those areas is necessary to determine any discrepancy between where the learner is and where he or she needs to be by the end of the school program. Assessment should be ongoing and varied; it should be coordinated with 3-year reevaluations of the IEP process. It should be efficient and is best done with a person designated as the transition coordinator. Assessment strategies include situational assessment (i.e., observation in a specific setting), curriculum-based assessment, environmental assessment (i.e., observation in the school and home environments), assessment of self-determination skills and adaptive behavior, interviews with relevant persons, and a physical exam to determine present and future medical needs.

The New Jersey Division of Developmental Disabilities (2002) uses a three-part assessment profile. The assessment looks at student skills (e.g., vocational skills, worker traits, and work restrictions); conducts a preference assessment (e.g., work environment, work endurance, and task type); and assesses skills that are required for a particular job. Once the process is completed, a comparison of all three assessments is made in order to develop goals and to select a good match between the student and the employment options available.

Formal assessments are also available for the transition process. These are normed assessments and can be used to determine areas of strength and weakness, which can be helpful in transition planning; for example, *Social and Prevocational Information Battery–Revised* (Halpern, Irvin, & Munkres, 1986), *Tests for Every Day Living* (Halpern, Irvin, & Landman, 1979), *LCCE Knowledge Battery* (Brolin, 1992), and the *Transition Planning Inventory* (Clark & Patton, 1997). Some of these assessments, like the *Transition Behavior Scale* (McCarney & Anderson, 2000), include an accompanying guide that lists possible transition goals that coincide with areas of strength and weakness.

Both types of assessments will be useful in determining the possible postsecondary options that should be considered for the learner with autism. Depending on the ability and the preference of the learner, these options include postsecondary school (e.g., college, technical school, specialized transitional programs), as well as a variety of employment options (e.g., competitive employment, supported employment, shelter workshop). All of the skills necessary to succeed in the targeted postsecondary setting should be carefully considered and addressed in the transition plan. It is easy to focus on completing academic requirements prior to graduation, but social skills, language skills, self-determination, and ability to access the community are areas that can often be overlooked. Skills such as completing a job application, attending a job interview, banking, and using an ATM card need to be considered, as well. Even if a student will most likely require supervision as an adult, the educational staff should focus on involving the student in each aspect of his or her life to the maximum extent possible.

Perspectives of Employers
of Adults with Disabilities

In today's working environment, employers are often faced with employees who are undermotivated, unreliable, and unproductive. While many of the characteristics of learners on the autism spectrum present challenges, some characteristics, such as interest in performing repetitive tasks, reduced tendency to allow social interactions to interfere with performance, and greater appreciation of the opportunity to work can make them attractive potential employees. Professionals who assist adults on the autism spectrum to find and maintain employment can emphasize the qualities of the worker that will appeal to employers. Employers who have had negative past experiences with hiring people with disabilities and those employers who have not done so at all may need to be educated about the strengths, as well as the challenges, of people with autism.

The U.S. Department of Education, in conjunction with the U.S. Chamber of Commerce, has developed a useful publication entitled *Disability Employment 101* (2003), which can be downloaded from the Web site www.ed.gov by searching for "Disability Employment 101" or by writing to ED Publishers, Education Publications Center, U.S. Department of Education, PO Box 1398, Jessup, Maryland, 20794-1398. It includes topics for potential employers such as finding qualified workers with disabilities, disability-friendly strategies in the workplace, and tax credits for hiring people with disabilities. The information in this guide is also useful for professionals who are searching for employment for their clients.

A group of employers was surveyed by the author with regard to their experiences with employees with disabilities. Some of the comments included: "He is a productive member of our team," "They are more anxious to work than I am," and "I have never had a negative experience with the employees." In a world where employers often complain about the caliber of their employees, people with autism, if well matched to their job, can excel.

Summary

For years parents and professionals have witnessed the successes of young children with autism, but only recently have we begun to recognize the substantial progress that older students with autism are capable of making. Variables such as effective programs, science-based methods, staff competency, family supports, and transitional planning have contributed to very positive outcomes for many young people on the autism spectrum. The range of vocational and community living options for the adolescent with autism as he grows into adulthood has increased. Now, more than ever, the adult with autism who is in a specialized adult program or a supported employment program can be as proud of his or her personal successes as those who are independently employed.

References

Behavior Analyst Certification Board. (1997). *Task List* (available at www.bacb.com/tasklist).

Benz, M. R., Yavanoff, P., & Doren, B. (1997). School-to-work components that predict post-school success for students with and without disabilities. *Exceptional Children, 63,* 151–165.

Binder, C. (1996). Behavior fluency: Evolution of a new paradigm. *Behavior Analyst, 19*(2), 163–197.

Brolin, D. E. (1992). *Life centered career education.* Arlington, VA: The Council for Exceptional Children.

Clark, G., & Patton, J. (1997). *Transition Planning Inventory.* Austin, TX: PRO-ED.

Education of All Handicapped Children Act of 1975, 20 U.S.C. § 1400 *et seq.*

Grandin, T. (1996). *Thinking in pictures.* New York: Vintage Books.

Grandin, T. (2002). Making the transition from the world of school into the world of work. Salem, OR: Center for the Study of Autism (available at www.autism.org/temple/transition.html).

Halpern, A. S., Irvin, L. K., & Landman, J. (1979). *Tests for Everyday Living.* Monterey, CA: CTB/McGraw-Hill.

Halpern, A. S., Irvin, L. K., & Munkres, A. W. (1986). *Social and prevocational information battery–Revised.* Monterey, CA: CTB/McGraw-Hill.

Handleman, J. S. (1979). Program transition for autistic-type children. *Journal for Special Educators, 15,* 273–279.

Individuals with Disabilities Education Act of 1990, 20 U.S.C. § 1400 *et seq.*

Lavoie, R. (1990). *How Difficult Can This Be? The F.A.T. City Workshop.* Alexandria, VA: Greater Washington Educational Telecommunications Association.

Lilienfeld, S. O., Lynn, S. J., & Lohr, J. M. (2003). *Science and Pseudoscience in Clinical Psychology.* New York: Guilford Press.

McCarney, S. B., & Anderson, P. D. (2000). *Transition Behavior Scale*. Columbia, MO: Hawthorne.

National Center on Secondary Education and Transition. (2004). Current challenges facing the future of secondary education and transition services for youth (available at www.ncset.org/publications/discussionpaper/default.asp).

National Research Council. (2001). *Educating children with autism*. Washington, DC: National Academy Press.

New Jersey Department of Education. (2004). Autism program quality indicators: A self-review and quality improvement guide for programs serving young students with autism spectrum disorders. Trenton, NJ: Author.

New Jersey Division of Developmental Disabilities. (2002). *Supported employment and day program manual*. Trenton, NJ: Author.

Oregon Department of Education. (2002). *Outcomes for children with autism* (available at www.ode.state.or.us/groups/supportstaff/specializedservices/autism/appendixa/aspx).

Pennsylvania State University. (2002). *LifeLink PSU helps special education students experience university life* (available at www.psu.edu/ur/archives/intercom_2002/Oct10/lifelink.htm).

Romanczyk, R., & Lockshin, S. (1982). *The Individual Goal Setting Curriculum*. Vestal, NY: Clinical Behavior Therapy Associates.

U.S. Department of Education. (2003). *Disability employment 101*. Jessup, MD: ED Publishers.

About the Editors

Jan S. Handleman, EdD, earned his doctoral degree in special education from Rutgers, The State University of New Jersey. He is currently director of the Douglass Developmental Disabilities Center of Rutgers and professor of psychology for the Graduate School of Applied and Professional Psychology. He has celebrated more than 30 years with the center. Dr. Handleman is the author of a number of books, book chapters, and articles and has widely presented at national and international conferences. He serves on numerous editorial boards and boards of agencies serving individuals with autism. He has consulted to many programs for individuals with autism and has provided expert testimony for legal decisions regarding their educational rights. He has devoted his career to serving individuals with autism, their families, and the professionals who serve them.

Sandra L. Harris, PhD, is a professor of clinical psychology and executive director of the Douglass Developmental Disabilities Center of Rutgers, The State University of New Jersey. Her research and clinical interests focus on children with autism and their families. She has written extensively in this area, including several books and dozens of journal articles and book chapters. She consults nationally to schools and organizations that serve people with autism and has served as an expert witness in legal cases concerning the rights of people with developmental disabilities. She is an associate editor of the *Journal of Autism and Developmental Disorders,* a fellow in the APA divisions of Clinical Psychology and Child and Youth Services, and a fellow in the American Psychological Society. Dr. Harris is a licensed psychologist in New Jersey. Her book *Siblings of Children with Autism* received the 1995 Autism Society of America Award for Literary Achievement. She was also named a Distinguished Service Professor by the board of governors of Rutgers University in 2002.